S0-BIW-493

THE COLLECTED ESSAYS OF SIR LEWIS NAMIER

*Volume I*

# VANISHED SUPREMACIES

*By the same Author*

THE STRUCTURE OF POLITICS AT THE ACCESSION OF GEORGE III

ENGLAND IN THE AGE OF THE AMERICAN REVOLUTION VOL. I

SKYSCRAPERS

ADDITIONS AND CORRECTIONS TO SIR JOHN FORTESCUE'S EDITION OF THE CORRESPONDENCE OF KING GEORGE III

IN THE MARGIN OF HISTORY

CONFLICTS

1848: THE REVOLUTION OF THE INTELLECTUALS

FACING EAST

DIPLOMATIC PRELUDE, 1938–9

EUROPE IN DECAY, 1936–1940

AVENUES OF HISTORY

IN THE NAZI ERA

PERSONALITIES AND POWERS

SIR LEWIS NAMIER

# Vanished Supremacies

*ESSAYS ON EUROPEAN HISTORY*
1812–1918

BOOKS FOR LIBRARIES PRESS
Freeport, New York

*First published in Great Britain,* 1958
*by Hamish Hamilton Ltd*
90 *Great Russell Street, London, W.C.*1


REPRINTED IN THIS EDITION FOR
BOOKS FOR LIBRARIES PRESS 1970

Standard Book Number 8369-5195-6
Library of Congress Catalog Number 73-119603

PRINTED IN GREAT BRITAIN

# INTRODUCTION

For forty years I have wanted to write a history of Europe 1812–1918, and I studied various aspects of it in days when Europe was still supreme in the world. But circumstances were against the scheme, and the best years I had for historical research were taken up by work on British Parliamentary history and on pre-1939 diplomacy; and now, at the age of nearly seventy, I see the rest of my working life under a heavy mortgage to the *History of Parliament*, and to further work on materials which I have been collecting for it most of my life. With the darkness of old age rapidly advancing, I can hardly hope to return to my other pet scheme. But my main ideas on the subject I have developed in various essays, almost all of them out of print; these are now gathered in the first volume of my Collected Essays.

Work on the eighteenth century Parliament I started before 1914, on European history during the First World War. The essays in this volume are arranged chronologically, but the earliest is that on 'The Downfall of the Habsburg Monarchy', the fruit of war-work in Intelligence Departments, first under, and next in, the Foreign Office: it is remarkable how much perception is sharpened when the work serves a practical purpose of absorbing interest. I recommend a reading of the essay to those who regret the destruction of the Habsburg Monarchy, and imagine that a federation of free and equal nations could have been established within a framework of which national supremacies were the sense and justification.

While a lecturer at Balliol, 1919–21, I took up the study of 1848; and I resumed the work towards the end of the Second World War; my Raleigh Lecture at the British Academy in 1944 was on '1848: the Revolution of the Intellectuals'. Expanded into a book, more than twice the length of 'The Downfall of the Habsburg Monarchy', and reprinted several times, it is omitted from this collection; which includes, however, the paper reviewing the story of 1848 from the angle of 'Nationality and Liberty', presented to the Tenth 'Volta' Conference of the Accademia Nationale dei Lincei in 1948. Lastly, the Creighton Lecture in History, delivered at London University in 1952, 'Basic Factors in Nineteenth-Century European History', reviews and sums up the theme of the book. Taken as a whole, this collection is the nearest substitute I can offer for the continuous narrative which was originally intended.

L. B. NAMIER

60 The Grampians,
London, W.6.
21 October 1957

# ACKNOWLEDGEMENTS

ACKNOWLEDGEMENTS are due to Messrs. Macmillan and Co. for permission to reprint essays I, II, and the first three essays here grouped together as IX, from *In the Margin of History* (1939) and III from *Skyscrapers* (1931); and to the Oxford University Press and Messrs. Hodder & Stoughton for permission to reprint X from *A History of the Peace Conference of Paris*, edited by Professor Harold Temperley (1921). Of the remaining essays in this book, IV, V, VI, VIII, IX (4), and XII come from *Avenues of History* (1952), VII from *Facing East* (1947) and XI from *Personalities and Powers* (1955).

# CONTENTS

# I

# THE END OF NAPOLEON

## 1. 'MY HEALTH IS GOOD, MY AFFAIRS ARE GOING WELL' (1812–1813)

THE first long absence of Napoleon from Marie Louise occurred during the Russian campaign of 1812; some ninety of his letters to her[1] cover its six months—that is, there are about fifteen to a month—most of them impersonal, empty letters, from a self-centred man absorbed in his work. He cares for the woman who has her place in his world scheme, the daughter of emperors, the mother of 'the little King' (thus Napoleon almost invariably refers to his son, aged one). Where advice has to be given it is attentive, clear, and detailed, like his army orders or decrees, but there is never any intimate talk between the two. The disparity is probably too great, the personal element in him seems lost; in the immensity of action he has forfeited his human existence. Words of endearment, significantly, appear as a rule in the language of his early youth: 'mio dolce amore,' 'mio bene.' Many a letter reads as if the writer was at a loss how to fill the sheet of paper; so little has he to tell her about himself that even short letters are often padded with speculations about her—where she is, what she is doing, what she has experienced. Besides, there are weather reports to fall back upon: dust, excessive heat, rain, a beautiful autumn, and in the end the cold, the intolerable cold. These bulletins, trite and awkward in themselves, become gruesome as they pipe the man and his army to their doom. And there enters into that unconscious dirge a stereotyped phrase, which appears first in a letter from Kovno, on 26 June 1812: 'My health is good, my affairs are going well.' Indifferent to begin with and devoid of contents, it becomes fixed while the campaign is moving towards its crisis—a painted smile, a mask, which in its incongruity

[1] *The Letters of Napoleon to Marie Louise*, ed. Charles de la Roncière.

gives an ironic, lugubrious, and finally a frantic turn to the scene. On 3 September Napoleon writes from Gat:

> I am leaving tonight to advance in the direction of Moscow. We are in autumn here.... The granaries are full, the earth is covered with vegetables; consequently the troops are well, which is a great point. My affairs are going well. My health is good....

He has repeated the phrase for the thirtieth time. On 14 September Napoleon reaches Moscow, and on the 16th the city and his plans vanish in a sea of flames. The phrase is forgotten; it recurs in two letters of 20 September, but fades out again during the fatal weeks of hesitation at Moscow. 'My health is good' (and nothing about his affairs) this is the formula used in seven letters between 21 September and 4 October. And then, in one of the last letters from Moscow:

> Write to your father frequently. Send him special couriers; advise him to reinforce Schwarzenberg's Corps, so that it may be a credit to him.

Napoleon begins to talk business to his big doll in Paris, and seeks to secure help through her; the thing is unpleasant, almost painful. The retreat has started, and the formula about his health and affairs reappears, but only four times, last on 3 November. On 26 October Napoleon writes, 'I share your desire to see the end of all this'; and on 20 November, 'I am in good health and drawing nearer to you'. Now he has reached the Beresina.

> 24 November: The weather is cold.... My health is very good.
> 26 November: My health is very good, the cold is very great.
> 28 November: My health is perfect, the weather very bad and very cold.
> 1 December: The weather is very cold, my health is very good.

And in the last letter from Russia, dated 5 December:

> You will have seen in the Army Orders that things have [not?] gone as well as I would have wished, yet affairs are not going badly just now.... Live in hope and do not worry.

What does the omission of the 'not' signify? Usually mistakes of this kind disclose the truth which the writer meant to hide. Napoleon for once intended to tell the truth and finished with a lie.

Another six months, from April to November 1813—Napoleon's last campaign in Germany—more than a hundred letters. The old formula reappears and is repeated twenty-two times in five months, up to the Battle of Leipzig. But Marie Louise is constantly urged to write to 'Papa François', to inform him, to plead with him. Austria holds the key to the European position.

> 2 May: Write and tell Papa François not to allow himself to be led away by the hatred his wife bears us, that it would be fatal to himself and the source of many calamities. . . .
>
> 5 May: Papa François is not behaving very well. . . .
>
> 14 May: People are trying to mislead Papa François. Metternich is a mere intriguer.
>
> 27 June: I want peace, but it must be an honourable one.
>
> 7 July: If they attempt to impose shameful terms upon me, I will make war upon them. Austria will pay for it all.
>
> 17 August: Deceived by Metternich, your father has sided with my enemies.
>
> 18 August: Do not worry too much about your father's conduct.

In this second stage, while Napoleon is trying to work through Marie Louise, the correspondence gains in contents and acquires something of a human touch.

And next: 1814. The Empire has disappeared, France is invaded, the faith and awe which surrounded Napoleon's person are gone—a dead scene with a cold aftermath. A fortnight before the final catastrophe, on 17 March 1814, Napoleon writes from Rheims to Marie Louise:

> MA BONNE LOUISE.—I have received your letter. I hope the weather in Paris is as fine as it is in Rheims. It will be very convenient for your outings and will do good for your health. Give a kiss to the King and never doubt the love I bear you.
>
> Ton
>
> NAP.

When the end has come he appeals to the woman, his wife, the mother of his son, to join him. The doll hesitates for a moment, and then there is no reply.

## 2. 'LA DÉGRINGOLADE' (1814)

THE story of March and April 1814, of Napoleon's defeat and abdication, can be summed up in the word 'la dégringolade', which in colloquial English means 'how everything went to pieces'. It is a depressing story in which no one is at his best; the narrative meanders in an atmosphere of supreme malaise; nothing is great or impressive, not even the so-called betrayal and desertion of Napoleon by his Marshals and Ministers. Tired men fumble and slither about on ground on which they cannot stand or walk. In the closing stages of history's greatest epic they have but one wish: that it were all over. Selfishness, cowardice, and resentments had their share, but they were not the determining factor. Napoleon claimed that had he not been betrayed and abandoned he could yet have won; but could any enlightened Frenchman wish him to win? The only result would have been further wars and a prolonged agony which some time, somewhere, was bound to find its disastrous term. There are circumstances in which even defeatism has its excuse.

By 1814 France, no less than the rest of Europe, had realized that a durable peace was not possible with and under Napoleon; further, that he was neither invincible nor infallible. He had started blundering even in matters of strategy, and blunders, like crimes, produce offspring at the rate of insects. Something had gone wrong; something had slipped from him; strike a wrong key and you get out of touch with your machine; he had lost the grip of things. The man who in the past was able to gauge others, forestall them, lead them, or force them into his own ways, and who, above all men, knew the value of time, now began to lag behind events rather than meet and master them. At Prague, at Frankfort, and at Chatillon he had a chance of securing a respite. He knew that he needed it; otherwise he would not have entered into negotiations while the tide was running against him and his opponents could stake out their claims in terms of an anticipated future. But no sooner did he perceive, or think he perceived, a glimmer of hope than he would go back on the instructions and powers which he had given to his plenipotentiaries. Even when the time had come for unconditional abdication, he still tried to prevaricate, forgetting that ambiguity, like moral indignation and rudeness, is the privilege of the stronger. Napoleon only recovered his intellectual greatness when he abandoned hope; till then he was self-conscious and preoccupied, given over to self-deception and to accusing others. What he said at that time about the French was true of himself: 'They are unhappy, and the unhappy are unjust.' But when at last he gave up the game for lost, before his attempted suicide and after, he once more came to view men and matters with impersonal objectivity; and the talks which he had in those days with Caulaincourt form the most interesting chapter in vol. II of his *Memoirs*.[2]

[2] *Memoirs of General de Caulaincourt, Duke of Vicenza*, vol. ii, 1814, ed. Jean Hanoteau.

Accurate evaluation correlated to a purpose was Napoleon's normal approach to human beings. He assessed but did not value them; was lavish in rewards and chary of praise; disparaging, but not prone to blame and still less to punish. He was a hard taskmaster, exhausting and discouraging; altogether inhuman. And, in turn, men with whom he was in closer contact had little human feeling for him. So long as he was victorious, they followed him in mute admiration. He thought, spoke, and acted for all. Only when he began to totter France regained voice and action; and the long-suppressed protest, fanned by patriotic fears, broke out in betrayal and desertion. Marshal Ney, Prince de la Moskowa, who a year later was to rejoin Napoleon and suffer execution for it, when sent by him to the headquarters of the Allies in Paris, in the presence of the Tsar indulged in indiscreet and injudicious criticisms of Napoleon; but then it was new to him to be able to speak his mind.

At the very end Caulaincourt remained correctly loyal and consciously correct. But there is something strained about his attitude, a degree of self-congratulation on having 'pulled it off', which, combined with an almost envious condemnation of the others, shows how much it must have cost him not to follow their example. Even he did not love Napoleon, and Napoleon knew it; nor could he have contemplated new Napoleonic victories without apprehension. He merely wished the Emperor to secure a reasonable existence within reasonable frontiers; which, seeing the nature and antecedents of the man, was not a reasonable wish. It might even be asked whether Caulaincourt's more enduring attachment to Napoleon was not perhaps, at least subconsciously, connected with the part, mistakenly but widely, ascribed to Caulaincourt in the capture and execution of the Duc d'Enghien.

## 3. A ST. HELENA JOURNAL

GENIUS is capacity for great constructive achievement, but it does not exempt from blunders or weakness. How else could Napoleon have let General Gourgaud be one of the few companions allowed to him at St. Helena?[3] It is enough to look at the man's picture, his garrulous, wide-open eyes, at his blabbing, argumentative mouth, at his forehead of a half-wit, at the excitable stupidity of his face, to

[3] *The St. Helena Journal of General Baron Gourgaud, 1815–1818,* trans. Sydney Gillard and ed. Norman Edwards.

see what Napoleon let himself in for; it 'portrays a man who would have tried the patience of Job'. But then Napoleon had not chosen him. 'I have often heard the Emperor say to the Empress Josephine', writes Gourgaud, 'that he yields to one thing only—importunity.' Gourgaud was at Rochefort; when he heard that he was to be left behind he made a violent scene. Napoleon gave in; and Gourgaud continued making scenes.

He was jealous, touchy, egotistical, and always on his dignity—or his 'honour', as he called it. 'Honour' had bid him accompany Napoleon into exile (or rather force his company on the Emperor); and after that he claimed to have made a sacrifice of his life, and thought he should be treated accordingly. At every opportunity he recounted what he had done for Napoleon; there was especially one incident he could not forget (nor accurately remember): how once with a pistol-shot he had saved the Emperor's life when an enemy rushed at him; sometimes it was a hussar with a sword, and sometimes a Cossack with a lance. When the wife of one of the other companions of Napoleon expected a child and a room was added for them, Gourgaud wrote: 'I couldn't bear to see building being done for the Montholons if something similar was not done for me.' Whether he was properly placed in a picture of the party at Longwood, or how he was mentioned in a letter by Napoleon, was of course of supreme importance to him.

> How do you wish me to speak of you? (asked the Emperor.) You are always afraid of compromising yourself. I should have to consult you on every occasion to know whether what I say pleases you or not. That's not my custom, and it doesn't suit me.

'I am too richly endowed with affection' is Gourgaud's own diagnosis of his case.

What is the value of the memoirs of such a man? In certain ways small, in other ways considerable. Comparatively little appears in this Journal of Napoleon's personality, but as Gourgaud was too egotistical and too stupid to fall in with the drama which Napoleon staged at St. Helena, the braying of the jackass often breaks in on it in a manner valuable to those who want to get at the real facts. Moreover, the degradation of that life in a cage was fully within the range of Gourgaud's powers to experience and describe. A Boswell might have overlooked it, entranced by the Emperor's mind and engrossed in recording his sayings; or it might have escaped the observation of a truly devoted companion trying to make things more tolerable for the Emperor. But if anyone wants a pitiful, hopeless, ludicrous picture of the great captive, grappling, for instance, with the problem of a cow, and getting angry when things went wrong, here he can find it.

> The Emperor is in a very bad humour, and full of the cow incident. At dinner, the Emperor asks Archambault: 'Did you let the cow get away? If it is lost, you'll pay for it, you blackguard!' Archambault assures his Majesty that he caught the cow again at the other end of the park; that she twice broke her rope, and that she gives no milk. I hold my tongue throughout the meal. His Majesty, in a very bad humour, retires at 10.30, muttering: 'Moscow! Half a million men!'

And lastly, that picture of unspeakable boredom: 'I am oppressed with boredom,' writes Gourgaud. 'Boredom. . . . Great boredom. . . . Terrible boredom.'

'What's the time?' inquired the Emperor. 'Ten o'clock, sire.' 'Let's go to bed, then.'

## 4. NAPOLEON II

THE Emperor died with his eyes fixed in silence on the portraits and bust of his son. What was the personality of that boy on whom the title of 'King of Rome' was bestowed in his cradle, to whom a World Empire was to have descended as inheritance, and who, in turn, by his birth had seemed to add to the stability and duration of that Empire? Chateaubriand said about the son of the Corsican and the Austrian archduchess that 'his mother gave him the past, his father the future'; but 'the future' was dead before the boy could understand its meaning, and 'the past' became for him a golden cage.[4] 'My birth and my death—that is my whole story,' said Napoleon's son on his death-bed.

In 1814 he was separated from his father, who adored him, and soon after deserted by his mother; he was brought up by his grandfather, the Emperor Francis I of Austria, who loved him in a human way but left the making, or rather the unmaking, of his life to Metternich. And in that child Metternich still waged war on the shadow and memory of the man whom he had feared, loathed, cajoled, fought, and vanquished in the great battle of his life. The boy was deprived of his royal title, even of his name; he was no longer King of Rome, nor Napoleon, nor a Frenchman, but

[4] *Napoleon II, the King of Rome*, by Octave Aubry.

'Francis', a Habsburg, an Austrian prince, Duke of Reichstadt. The name and memory of the father, which with ever-growing force resounded throughout the world in posthumous conquest, were to be extinguished from the consciousness of his son. None the less, as he grew up the legend reached him, and the tragedy of his life began, to be cut short by death from consumption at the age of twenty-one.

Metternich now wrote to the Austrian Ambassador in Paris asking him to call Louis-Philippe's attention 'to the person who will succeed the Duke'.

> I use the word 'succeed', for in the Bonapartist hierarchy there is a succession openly avowed and respected by the party. Young Louis Bonaparte is deeply involved in intrigues of faction; he was never placed, like the Duke of Reichstadt, under the safeguard of the Emperor's principles.

And the Emperor Francis, according to M. Aubry,

> mourned the innocent child, the delightful youth who had been his favourite. But he could not help regarding his death as a deliverance. He was beyond suffering, and he had ceased to be a political embarrassment. The grandfather . . . had been neither willing nor able to achieve the boy's happiness. He was glad to shoulder off the responsibility upon God.

# II

# TALLEYRAND

TALLEYRAND was born in 1754, fifteen years before Napoleon, and died on 17 May 1838, surviving him by another seventeen years. He collaborated with Mirabeau and Sieyès in 1789, and with Guizot and Thiers under the July Monarchy. Of high aristocracy, he entered the Church because lameness, due to an accident in childhood, precluded army service. As Bishop of Autun he was returned by the clergy to the States-General, had a share in drafting the Declaration of the Rights of Man, and played a leading part in the Constituent Assembly. In October 1789 he moved the appropriation of the Church property by the State, and on 14 July 1790, at the feast on the Champ de Mars commemorating the Bastille, in the presence of Louis XVI, he celebrated Mass ('Pray, don't make me laugh,' he whispered to Lafayette). Early in 1791 he discarded the vestments which had never meant anything to him. When six years later his appointment to the Foreign Office was discussed in the Directory, Carnot objected: he would sell them all. 'Whom has he sold' replied La Revellière. 'First, his God.' 'He was never a believer.' '. . . Next, his order.' 'A mark of philosophy.' 'Rather of ambition. Lastly, his King.' 'It is hardly for us to reproach him with that.'

Talleyrand had no moral principles or scruples, few illusions or dreams. He was the least romantic of men. Metternich was a romantic with regard to his doctrines; Talleyrand had no doctrines. He had a strong sense of reality and clear judgment. He appreciated spiritual values, but in a curiously detached manner. He was lazy, and boasted of it. Neglected by his parents in early childhood and brought up by dependents, he was a *grand seigneur* towards men of other classes but had no love for his own and contributed with cold indifference to its downfall. He had few deeper human contacts and knew neither gratitude nor personal loyalty. He had self-love but little self-respect, no love or respect for others. The world of the *ancien régime* had its standards of honour, its conventions and barriers (though few sincere prejudices); these aids to morality, or substitutes for it, had been swept away. Talleyrand, emotionally detached and spiritually free, worked in a moral and social void. He loved women and money; he cared for France. There was hardly a limit to which he would not demean himself for the sake of money; he took colossal bribes for treaties and frontiers—the jackal of Napoleon's campaigns. This craving was pathological and in a way pathetic; to him money stood for concrete security in a world full of dangers and unreality. Foremost, he meant to live.

Survival, free of the stigma of emigration, was his aim under the Terror. 'I placed myself at the disposal of events, and, provided I remained a Frenchman, I would put up with anything.' After 10 August 1792, he wrote an exculpating diplomatic circular, but for himself secured a passport from Danton: 'Laissez passer, &c. Maurice Talleyrand, allant à Londres par nos ordres.' He remained in this country till expelled in 1794. He then proceeded to the United States, where he tried his hand at land speculation (he was even scheming to make Hindu gentlemen invest in American real estate). He was allowed to return to France in 1796. In July 1797 he was given the Foreign Office—a subordinate post, as policy was made by the Directory. On his way to thank Barras he muttered rapturously that now he would amass 'une fortune immense, une immense fortune, une immense fortune, une fortune immense'. The Americans were shocked when, to obtain justice from one they had so lately befriended, they had to bribe him with £50,000. By 1799 he had 3,000,000 francs on deposit with Hamburg and London banks; in 1805 his fortune was valued at 40,000,000.

M. Lacour-Gayet in his great work on Talleyrand paints his first meeting with Bonaparte. Tall, with his hair powdered as under the *ancien régime*, high cheek-bones, round chin, his eyes fixed, his pointed nose insolently raised, his lips curved in irony and disdain, a very high stock round his neck, stiff and immobile to disguise his limp, he bore an air of fatigue and supreme indifference which made him look older than forty-three. The other man, small and thin, with quick, nervous movements, olive skin, long black hair, severe countenance, sharp nose, tight lips, protruding chin, already conveyed an impression of irresistible force; he had conquered Italy, was about to attack England, wore the uniform of commander-in-chief, and was twenty-eight. 'Il y a là de l'avenir' was Talleyrand's comment on Bonaparte. In November 1792 Talleyrand had argued the uselessness of conquests, 'France should remain within her own frontiers'—she owes this to herself and to others. In July 1798: 'The Republic inspires respect rather than confidence; through confidence alone is it possible to gain true and useful allies.' In 1800 he foresaw that further conquests would prove 'a career without term.' He preached moderation; he was to serve Napoleon. 'He signed events but did not make them.'

Talleyrand now professed unbounded admiration for Napoleon. Napoleon appreciated Talleyrand: 'He has great advantages as a negotiator . . . he knows the foreign courts, has finesse . . . an utterly impassive face, and a great name. To the Revolution he belongs only by his misconduct. . . .' Yet it was not an easy partnership between the cultured and lazy aristocrat and the man who worked like no one else and was *inamusable*. The Napoleonic Empire was fast becoming a danger to France, and after Eylau Talleyrand said to Prince Dalberg that had Napoleon been killed they would have made Joseph his successor, but proclaimed 'an immediate and absolute withdrawal of France to her Rhine frontier'.

Gradually his misgivings thickened, and he resigned the Foreign Office in August 1807. Still he remained at Court, and in 1808, a secret enemy, accompanied Napoleon to the famous interview with Tsar Alexander at Erfurt. 'The French people is civilized, but not its sovereign,' he said to Alexander; 'Russia's sovereign is civilized, but not its people; the Russian sovereign should therefore be the ally of the French people.' And again: 'The Rhine, the Alps, and the Pyrenees are the conquests of France; the rest, of the Emperor; they mean nothing to France.' An entente was established between the two against Napoleon.

When news about Talleyrand's activities and Austria's intrigues reached Napoleon, he suddenly returned to his capital, and on 28 January 1809, received Talleyrand in the presence of several Court officials and Ministers. For half an hour he poured out a torrent of the most violent abuse against Talleyrand, concluding with a coarse reference to his wife. When leaving Talleyrand remarked, 'What a pity that so great a man should be so ill-bred!'

In 1812, and again in 1813, Napoleon offered the Foreign Office to Talleyrand. He refused. On 31 March 1814 came the hour of his vengeance and of his greatest achievement. This was one of those rare occasions when an idea can shape the fate of nations. The Allies were about to enter Paris; the future of France was dark. Talleyrand saw the road to salvation: the Bourbons had to be restored. They had been forgotten; they were strangers to modern France, but

Europe needed them. What Europe had fought, and still feared, was the French Revolution and Napoleon. The Bourbons were a natural barrier against both, acceptable, or at least tolerable, to France. Napoleon was Emperor of the French, successor to Caesar and Charlemagne; they were Kings of France, heirs to Louis XIV. With the Bourbons France could resume *les anciennes limites*. But the sins of the Revolution and Napoleon must not be visited on Bourbon France. Had not the Bourbons been the first sufferers and victims? The greatest transformation trick of history was played. France was absolved of guilt and escaped punishment.

It was not mere cynicism in Talleyrand to come forward as the apostle of *légitimité*. A tired, ageing man, he tried to gather up broken threads. At the Congress of Vienna he worked with the pacific and conservative Powers, Great Britain and Austria. Europe was not to be remodelled when France could not profit by it. This opposition to Russia counted against Talleyrand when, after Waterloo, France required her protection. A few months later he retired into private life.

He emerged once more after the July Revolution. Between 1814 and 1940, France, victorious, tried to establish her own system on the Continent; defeated, or in times of weakness, she turned to England or Russia, the choice being largely determined by conditions at home. In 1830 help had to be sought in London, and Talleyrand became the maker of the first Franco-British Entente, in defence of French liberalism and of the Belgian revolution. He established close co-operation with British statesmen. 'We have to deal here with timid people,' he wrote. '*Ils arrivent un peu lentement, mais enfin ils arrivent.*'

Talleyrand on his death-bed accepted the rites of the Church, but he remembered the privilege of his pre-Revolution state. He received the holy oil with his hands closed and his palms turned downwards, murmuring, 'Do not forget I am a bishop'.

# III

# METTERNICH

A HEGELIAN once described the Napoleonic period as the sixth day of Creation, for a man had arisen; it was followed by the Sabbath Day of history when all creative power seemed at rest. A cold shadow lay over Europe for thirty-three years, the active life of a generation, and people connected it with the person of Metternich and called it his 'system', though they never ceased to wonder how that rococo figure in porcelain, stylish and nimble, and in appearance hollow and brittle, could last so long and keep off the light from tens of millions of men. In his youth described as *le ministre-papillon*, in his old age as a blind, senseless fossil, he was none the less credited with the power to stop the stars in their courses. It is this incongruity between Metternich's personality and his reputed achievements that constitutes the seeming enigma.

He himself denied having devised any 'system'—it was '*eine Weltordnung*' ('a world order'), based on deep immutable laws which his own clear spirit had merely discerned and laid bare to the eyes of men. The aristocrat and the diplomat, the professor and the prophet, and finally the old actor and buffoon, were quaintly blended in the person of Metternich when, in discourses and despatches of ever-growing length, year after year, he propounded his doctrines to a world over which his master-mind seemed to preside. But the more he talked and wrote, the less apparent were the positive contents of his teaching, till people began to doubt whether there were any. The mistake was in accepting the would-be philosophic and scientific character which Metternich gave to his harangues; these were songs, in which the music mattered and not the text.

Conservatism, of which Metternich was an exponent, is primarily based on a proper recognition of human limitations, and cannot be argued in a spirit of self-glorifying logic. The history of the French Revolution and of Napoleon had shown once more the immense superiority which existing social forms have over human movements and genius, and the poise and rest which there are in a spiritual inheritance, far superior to the thoughts, will or inventions of any single generation. It was the greatness and strength of Metternich during these fateful years to have foreseen that human contrivances, however clever and beneficial, would not endure, and to have understood the peculiar elasticity with which men would finally revert to former habits. The failure of striving, struggling men brings the heir of ages back into his own. The fine and, in its own way, unique diplomacy of Metternich, during both the Napoleonic era and the years which followed, was based on this deep, almost instinctive, understanding of Conservatism. He annotated the margins of the great book of human insufficiency and inertia—interesting work indeed, which requires a strong and free mind, but which ought to be undertaken in a spirit of humility. Of this there is no trace in Metternich. He was essentially of the eighteenth century, a disciple of Voltaire rather than of Rousseau. He shared its belief in the infinite power of the human mind (exemplified to him in his own person), though not in the unlimited perfectibility of human nature; much interested in science, he liked to treat of society and politics in terms of immutable, abstract laws, and, unaware of the inadequacy of the data we possess, allowed a sterile, doctrinaire logic to repress psychological perception. His scientific interests themselves had the typical eighteenth-century turn towards things curious and extraordinary rather than towards the basic average, and mainly served to supply him with a pseudo-scientific jargon and with what a bitter critic once called his 'five metaphors'. He was sentimental, but disliked melodrama; he professed feelings, but shrank from enthusiasms; he could loathe, but not hate. He remained classic in an age of romantics, and worshipped reason, but denied creative power to human thought. He, for one, certainly lacked it; he was a *raisonneur* rather than a thinker—'*Je raisonne sur tout et en toute occasion.*'

Like the eighteenth century, he knew States and not nations. He abhorred the idea of the sovereignty of the people and failed to see that, after all, it was just an abstract idea, incapable of full realization, and therefore doomed to compromises. It has been alleged that his ideas were based on the needs and calculated to serve the peculiar interests of Austria; but it is hardly in the power of man successfully to develop *ad hoc* systems. Metternich was sincerely attached to the Habsburg Monarchy because, like no other State, it was bound up with the time and world in which he would have chosen to live, and because its very existence was a denial of nationality and popular sovereignty; he rose to the first place in it because his ideas so completely answered its needs and nature. He was not an Austrian by birth, but from the Rhine, and he was twenty-one when he first came to Vienna. In fact, he was a Rhenish *émigré*, with the intellectual outlook of the French *ancien régime*; but, not being a Frenchman, was even less capable than the average French aristocrat of sharing in the national developments of revolutionary and Napoleonic France. These antecedents, coupled with the world-wide interests of his class and the non-national character of Austria, made him a true European. '*C'est que depuis longtemps l'Europe a pris pour moi la valeur d'une patrie,*' he declared in 1824 to the Duke of Wellington. With revolution lurking everywhere, he preached international comity to princes and favoured treaties of mutual guarantee for the existing frontiers, which to him, who knew no rights of nationality, presented no other moral problems than those of a private estate. He insisted on the full sovereignty and independence of every State, however small, but as the balance of power required the centre of Europe to be strengthened against France and Russia, he sought to establish the Germanic Confederation, and even dallied with the idea of a *Lega Italica*, paradoxically conceiving both as mere groups of States. Precluded from appealing to the national consciousness of the Germans or Italians, which alone could have supplied the proper basis for such unions and imposed them on recalcitrant princelings, he naturally and necessarily failed in his attempts.

Strictly speaking, Metternich was not the reactionary as which he is usually represented; for this he was too intelligent, too cautious, and too conservative. He honoured all prescriptive rights and vested interests. For him the British Parliamentary system was proper in its own home, but not a panacea for nations which had not developed it. Within the Habsburg Monarchy itself he tolerated and protected Hungary's old constitution, based though it was on a Parliament; it was not for him to destroy the growth of many centuries. But he seemed unable to conceive how anything new could ever be safely attempted without leading to the collapse of the entire social fabric; his own logic was too rigid and destructive. Theoretically he argued that stability was not synonymous with immobility; but in practice he loathed even the change of years, having by December become attached to the four figures of the date. Metternich was not an administrator, and did not claim to be one; he lacked the necessary energy, perseverance, and mastery of practical detail. But he cannot truly be held responsible for the administrative chaos and decay of

Austria during the years of his Chancellorship. He merely enabled her to exist so long being what she was; though it was no accident that he was riveted to such a State, since his fundamental ideas excluded the new elements of national life. Nor can he be blamed for Austria's intellectual backwardness; with him or without him Vienna has never produced anything truly great or creative, only a fine blend of a peculiar internationalism with an intensely local colouring—somewhat like Metternich himself.

The real strength and dignity of his nature revealed itself in the days of his fall and the years of his retirement. '*Eh bien, est-ce que nous sommes tous morts?*' asked his wife as he returned from the Imperial Palace after the revolution in the streets of Vienna had forced his resignation. '*Oui, ma chère, nous sommes morts.*' Unmoved and unshaken, he accepted his moral death. But when on the steps of the British Museum he met another great exile, Guizot, he remarked with a smile: '*L'erreur n'a jamais approché de mon esprit.*'

# IV

# PRINCESS LIEVEN

PRINCESS LIEVEN was the wife of a Russian Ambassador, a companion of the Imperial Family, and the intimate friend first of Metternich, next of Lord Grey, and finally of Guizot. 'I quite like Prime Ministers,' she wrote to Metternich in 1820. Prussia was the only Great Power whose policy she never tried to run.

She is often cited as a 'Russian'. But her father, Baron Benckendorff, was of a Prussian family settled in Estonia, and her mother, Baroness Charlotte Schilling, came from Württemberg: Princess Lieven had not a drop of Russian blood, nor had her husband; and both were Lutherans. They were of a Court which moved between St. Peters*burg* and Peter*hof*: Tsarism and its power-politics were their home and realm. There was no feeling in her for real Russia nor understanding of its Slav, Greek-Orthodox people. She thought of the world in terms of her own small circle. And if the German Nesselrode, the Greek Capo d'Istria, or the Corsican Pozzo di Borgo ('his presence lent great distinction to Russian politics,' she wrote to Lady Palmerston in 1842) could speak for Russia, and the Rhinelander Metternich personify Austria, why should not the Lievens play a part in Hanoverian London? She boasted: 'I am treated so much as an Englishwoman . . . that nobody minds talking in front of me.' She advised Wellington and patronized Palmerston ('Lord Grey praised Palmerston to me yesterday,' she wrote on 27 October 1831 to Lady Cowper, an intimate friend and subsequently the wife of Palmerston; 'an excellent Secretary of State'). When Grey had become Prime Minister she wrote to Lady Cowper:

> I see Lord Grey every day—I try to give him courage—he must feel himself strong. One must assume a certain pomposity when one is in power—it inspires confidence in other people.

And a fortnight later:

> Lord Grey . . . has responded nicely to my constant repetitions that he must be and show himself proud. . . . I endeavour to instil as much pride as possible into you.

But there were things touching her person and position which that quasi-Russian, acclimatized in England, did not fathom. Wellington wrote about the Lievens on 24 August 1829: 'They have played an English party game instead of doing the business of their Sovereign'; and later on, expressed surprise that 'so long employed in public office in this country' they should 'have committed the extraordinary indiscretions of which they have been guilty'. Palmerston, in 1834, managed to rid himself of them. 'Lord P. found my husband a stumbling block,' wrote the Princess to Lady Cowper on 7 October 1834. The husband?

Many friends preferred Princess Lieven at a distance. She seldom met Metternich even while she was his mistress. They corresponded: 'Some day, if our letters are read,' wrote Princess Lieven, 'people will wonder what they were about—love or politics. . . . In fact, I don't know myself . . .' Because her love affairs were so political. 'Personally I prefer weakness to strength in women. It is more feminine.' She herself was masculine and pursued a man's career in the only way open to her: a peculiar career, successively identifying herself with statesmen of different countries. Yet there was in her a deeper sense of frustration: her adjustments were superficial, and she venomously turned against husband and lovers whenever a rift opened. She had great social culture, and vulgarity underneath. Even her normal correspondence is rendered unpleasant by a strain of irritable disparagement. The Duchess of Wellington is 'stupid', Lady Grey 'a horrible woman, passionate, bitter, Jacobin, everything that is most detestable', Lady Conyngham 'a malicious fool', Countess Esterhazy 'a mediocre person . . . and what pretences to airs and graces!'; and the Duchesse de Berry 'a hopeless nonentity' whom 'nothing but the assassination of her husband before her very eyes could make... and object of interest'; etc. ('How much better the world would be', she wrote to Metternich, 'if people were kinder.') Men escaped censure so long as they served her purpose. But her interest was in situations and schemings, not in human beings.

'Some day, if our letters are read . . .' Hers, half-diary, were literature. She wrote to Lady Cowper, from Petersburg on 8/20 February 1835:

> I remain alone in my room writing, for I have strange tales to tell. I have seen much in my life. I have all my papers with me— it is a way of passing the time.

And to Lord Grey, on 6 October 1834:

> . . . as to my mental occupations, do you know what is the greatest source of my pleasure? It is putting in order of all my voluminous correspondence with my friends and among them all, the first place is taken by your letters. . . . Your letters are the history of the times we have lived through.

Grey protested that they were meant for her only: 'I have no desire that they should be preserved as materials for history.' Now her correspondence appears, one lot after another, and people are apt to overrate the historical value of such letters if they are spicy and 'high-lifey'.

Of the correspondence with Lady Cowper-Palmerston[1] five-sixths are subsequent to Princess Lieven's expulsion from the English paradise (which was drab and dull and cold and 'frankly depressing' while she inhabited it). 'Oh God! How I love everything that I have left behind!' '. . . not a day passes but I bemoan my separation from England'; 'England is always in my thoughts . . . never fails to interest me.' 'Everyone around me is enjoying life. I alone lie ill, sad, deserted.' 'Dearest, letters and again letters, these are what I need' (23 October 1834). 'My only joy is to read letters from England. And you know what a joy your letters are in particular' (6 January 1835). 'Dearest, how good you are to write to me so regularly. I beg you will continue to do so' (12 February 1836). And she repeats a dozen times throughout the years: 'Your letters are my greatest pleasure.' But to Grey on 9/21 November 1834:

> Lady Cowper writes to me very often, but then she is so hand in glove with the present Ministry that I do not learn much from her letters. I prefer hearing from outsiders, for they at least do not try to mislead. It is astounding how like bad faith this Ministerial prudence too often becomes.

And on 6 December 1834: 'Pray take pity on me and write, for it is only on you that I can count for getting at the truth.'

On the straight hedonistic view of life and of human pursuits one could truly wonder why these two women continued their correspondence; it is sometimes like cats screaming at each other in the night—rising in pitch or dropping to hostile purring. When Princess Lieven in July 1835, having lost two sons ('there has never been a greater grief than mine'), wanted to seek comfort in England ('your politics still interest me more than any others'), Lady Cowper replied:

[1] *The Lieven-Palmerston Correspondence, 1826–1856*, ed. Lord Sudley.

> I really believe that I should choose Paris . . . you need to live where there is constant news and political activity—and in Paris there are more travellers than anywhere else—and more owners of country houses; I do not think that England would suit you at all . . . you would be dreadfully bored here. . . . It is much better to keep England in your mind's eye as a place to return to when your grief has abated. The Duke of Wellington, my brother, all your friends advise you to go to Paris. . . .

And when the Princess dropped into (temporary) silence: '. . . can it be possible that you are offended . . . you could not be so unjust towards me . . . thus misinterpret my friendship and devotion.' And on another occasion: 'I love everyone who is kind to you.'

Princess Lieven would express fears of revolution in England, decry the Whigs (Lady Cowper was Lord Melbourne's sister), assure her (from Paris) that the Tories were firmly established in office, and greatly respected abroad, or tell her how much the English were disliked in France. Lady Cowper would, in reply, beg her 'not to worry about the peerage', which was 'stable and deeply rooted'; assure her that Peel was 'embracing liberal ideas . . . to gain popularity', and losing credit with his own party; that the Whigs were grand when in office, and happy when out of it; and that the things which made Palmerston unpopular in France 'made him popular in England', etc. She demurred: 'You can always count on my affection, although you certainly are a *trifle* unkind towards my friends.' The Princess retorted: 'I deny absolutely your accusation . . . with one exception I like them all'—the exception being Palmerston! And Lady Palmerston, when sending her congratulations on a Parliamentary success of Guizot's, regretted 'that a Minister who is usually so dignified should have lost his dignity to the extent of confessing such petty motives'.

'I agree with you, dearest, that our friendship should be able to withstand all political changes. . . .' No matter which of the two said it.

# V

# 1848: SEED-PLOT OF HISTORY

THE men of 1848, victorious in Paris, Vienna, and Berlin, stood amazed at their own success and moderation. A revolution had swept over Europe, wider than any before it, but eminently humane in its principles and practice. It had its dead but no victims; it made refugees but no political prisoners. Louis-Philippe crossed the Channel—not the first French ruler nor the last to take to that route. The other sovereigns remained, shaken but not overthrown. Metternich, Guizot, and the Prince of Prussia (the later William I) one by one arrived in London: exponents of three systems, disparate in nature and aims, but seemingly obliterated by the same storm. The strongholds of reaction had fallen, rubble had to be carted away, new structures were to arise; there was a great void, filled by sun and air; and over it brooded a singularly enlightened *Zeitgeist*. Men dreamed dreams and saw visions, and anything the spirit could conceive seemed attainable in that year of unlimited possibilities. Next year the light and airy visions had faded, and it was as if they had never been.

A gale blows down whatever it encounters, and does not distinguish. Revolutions are anonymous, undenominational, and inarticulate. If there is an inherent program, as in agrarian revolutions, it is of a most primitive character. The elemental forces of a mass movement can be made to do the work of men whose quest is alien to them. Most revolutions are filched or deflected: groups or parties with elaborate programs—panaceas or nostrums—try to stamp them with their own ideology and, if successful, claim to be their spokesmen or even their makers. But revolutions are not made; they occur. Discontent with government there always is; still, even when grievous and well founded, it seldom engenders revolution till the moral bases of government have rotted away: the feeling of community between the masses and their rulers, and in the rulers a consciousness of their right and capacity to rule. Revolutions are usually preceded by periods of high intellectual achievement and travail, of critical analysis and doubt, of unrest among the educated classes, and of guilt-consciousness in the rulers: so it was in France in 1789, in Europe in 1848, and in Russia in 1917. If such corrosion of the moral and mental bases of government coincides with a period of social upheaval, and the conviction spreads, even to the rulers themselves, that the ramshackle building cannot last, government disintegrates and revolution ensues. Revolutions, as distinct from mere revolts, usually start at the centre of government, in the capital; but the nature of the actual outbreak and its purpose almost invariably escape analysis. What aim did the labouring poor of Paris pursue in the Great Revolution, and what did they attain? What was it that made them fight in July 1830, or in February 1848? And what would they have done had they been successful in the June Days or in the Paris Commune? Agrarian movements are far more articulate in form and aim, and therefore, if extensive and determined, are usually successful. The village is a living organism and its communal consciousness transcends other loyalties; and the peasants' demand to be relieved of dues, or to be given the land of the nobles and the Church, can be met or enforced overnight. The weakness of agrarian movements usually is in that they break out sporadically, and therefore can be suppressed. But if linked with a rising in the urban centres and with self-doubt in the upper classes, if fanned by generalizing factors, such as *la grande peur* in 1789 or the effect of war in 1917, they become overpowering; and then urban groups or parties graft on to them their own programs.

The revolution of 1848 followed on a period of intellectual efflorescence such as Europe has never known before or since; it supervened at a time when the Governments themselves came to feel unequal to the new circumstances and problems; in a period of financial crisis and economic distress, but of disjointed, or even contradictory, social movements. A numerous urban proletariat gathered in the rapidly growing capitals; the independent artisans were fighting a long-drawn losing battle against modern industry; the factory workers started their struggle for a human existence; while the incidence of the agrarian problem was uneven and varied. In France it had been solved by the Great Revolution; in Germany it was confined to several large areas; in the Habsburg Monarchy it was general and acute: there the peasants were determined to sweep away the surviving feudal burdens and jurisdictions. Before the first gusts of the revolutionary storm the Governments collapsed without offering serious resistance; there was a paralysis of will and a consciousness of defeat almost before the fight was joined. But there was no uniform or unified social-revolutionary force to continue the struggle; and the educated middle classes, the successors or new partners of the princes, from an exaggerated fear of the Reds quickly turned counter-revolutionary, though they still counted on preserving the conquests of the initial victory which they had appropriated. The peasants were bought off by timely and extensive concessions; the proletariat was defeated in Paris in the June Days, in Vienna in October, while in Berlin (as in 1933) it succumbed without fighting. In France, where 1789 had done most of the work which still awaited accomplishment elsewhere, 1848 followed a path apart; in the rest of Europe the conflict was between the principle of dynastic property in countries and that of national sovereignty: from which devolved the problems of self-government and self-determination, of constitutional rights and of national union and independence.

The year 1830 had brought a reaction against ingenious solutions which the Congress of Vienna had devised for France, Belgium, and Poland; outside France, 1848 was largely an endeavour to find solutions where the Congress had not seriously attempted any. The movement of 1848 was European, yet consciously French in origin. In 1847 Karl Mathy, a Baden bookseller and publisher, had planned a pamphlet putting forward the demands of the German people, to be distributed broadcast on the death of Louis-Philippe: for this was expected to set the European revolution going. 'Our revolutions, like our fashions, we were wont to receive from Paris,' wrote in 1849 his partner, F. D. Bassermann, a leader of the moderate liberals in the Frankfurt Parliament. The European revolution, when it came, operated within the area of Napoleon's work and influence; for he had sapped inherited forms and loyalties, regrouped territories, established modern administrations, and familiarized tens of millions of men with change in political and social conditions—and new ideas are not nearly as potent as broken habits. When Napoleon was overthrown there had to be restoration. Even had the monarchs and ministers assembled in Vienna wished to reconstruct Europe on a rational basis, how could they by agreement have squared Austrian and Prussian aims and claims in Germany, solved the problem of the Papal State in Italy, or resettled the Habsburg Monarchy on any but dynastic foundations? The failures of 1848 go far to justify 1815. Incapable of devising, men are forced back to the *status quo ante*; and with the pristine facts return ideas in which men no longer wholly believe: in every restoration there is an element of make-believe. The Vienna Congress reaffirmed the idea of indefeasible monarchical rights—and over wide areas failed to restore the previous rulers. Nor were the proprietary and quasi-contractual rights attributed to dynasties or Estates compatible with the new social and economic conditions: for those ideas were connected with the land; they were alien to the intelligentsia (including the bureaucracy which supplied a remarkable percentage of members to the Parliaments of 1848) and to the modern cities. With them conceptions of the neo-horde replace those of rooted populations. In 1848 a considerable advance was made towards the State untrammelled by contract and custom; and a non-territorial, linguistic nationality asserted its sway. The privileged orders entered into partnership with the educated middle classes, accepting their intellectual lead. As early as 12 December 1847 the Prince Consort advised the King of Prussia to meet the coming onslaught by attaching 'the well-to-do and intelligent sections of the population—that is, the real people (*das eigentliche Volk*)' to the Government by a share in the administration of the country.

Guizot and Metternich had voluntarily left their countries. Prince William had to be persuaded, nay, made to leave in order to put an end to rumours that he was about to march on Berlin. They quitted, and he did not—and all three proved right; their systems were dead, his was to be the foremost beneficiary of 1848. There was philosophic elevation and spiritual pride in the fallen Ministers, while the Prince was single-minded and *borné*. 'Je ne connais guère l'embarras et je ne crains pas la responsabilité,' was Guizot's dictum. 'L'erreur ne s'est jamais approché de mon esprit,' said Metternich with a faint smile when in March 1848 he met Guizot on the steps of the British Museum. But Metternich, on the night of his fall, had replied to his wife: 'Oui, ma chère, nous sommes morts'—and never again did he try to force his way among the living. Nor did Guizot: in France, he wrote, in great crises the vanquished *deviennent des morts*. Neither was quite of the country he had governed. Metternich, a Rhinelander, the exponent of a non-national ideal, tried to uphold the Habsburg Monarchy, that dynastic creation *par excellence*, by tying all Europe to the principle which alone could secure Austria's survival. Internal reform he never seriously contemplated: he apprehended its hopelessness—'je passe ma vie à étayer un édifice vermoulu.' When asked by Guizot to explain how it was that revolution had spread to Austria governed by him, he replied: 'J'ai quelquefois gouverné l'Europe, l'Autriche jamais.' Guizot, on the other hand, was a Protestant attracted by British institutions and ideas, and self-nurtured on them, who tried to establish constitutional monarchy in France. Under Louis-Philippe France had enjoyed what the rest of the Continent aspired to in 1848: a Parliamentary régime, equality before the law, civic freedoms. And what Guizot's *toryisme bourgeois* tried to cultivate in France were the civic virtues of Victorian England: 'l'esprit de famille, le goût du travail régulier, le respect des supériorités, des lois et des traditions, les sollicitudes prévoyantes, les habitudes religieuses.' For him French history neither stopped nor started in 1789; he wanted to secure the achievements of the Revolution and lay its ghosts. He thought of 'ces millions d'existences qui ne font point de bruit mais qui sont la France.' But beyond these were men he combated and feared:

> The French Revolution and the Emperor Napoleon I have thrown a certain number of minds, including some of the most distinguished, into a feverish excitement which becomes a moral and, I would almost say, a mental disease. They yearn for events, immense, sudden, and strange; they busy themselves with making and unmaking governments, nations, religions, society, Europe, the world. . . . They are intoxicated with the greatness of their design, and blind to the chances of success. To hear them talk, one might think that they had the elements and ages at their command . . . and that these were the first days of creation or the last days of the world.

And Louis-Philippe would say to Guizot:

> You are a thousand times right; it is in the depth of men's minds that the revolutionary spirit must be fought, for it is there that it reigns; *mais pour chasser les démons, il faudrait un prophète.*

*Le juste milieu* was uninspiring, and no compromise, for neither wing accepted it: to the Legitimists the July Monarchy was a 'profanation of monarchy', to the Republicans a perversion and usurpation of national sovereignty. Sainte-Beuve wrote in 1861:

> The Orleans dynasty were neither a principle nor a national glory; they were a utility, an expedient; and they were taken for what they were.

And this was his account of the period:

> I appreciated the joys of that reign of eighteen years, the facilities it afforded to the mind and for study, for all pacific pursuits, its humanity, the pleasures offered, even to those not possessed of a vote, by the wonderful display of Parliamentary talent and of eloquence from the tribune. . . . Yet it was impossible to view that régime, in its spirit and ensemble, as in any way grand . . . as something of which one could be proud to have been a contemporary.

Guizot himself writes:

> It makes the greatness of our nation . . . that purely material and immediate success does not suffice, and that the mind has to be satisfied as much as the interests.

When the revolution started in the streets of Paris even those who valued the July Monarchy as a 'utility' would not die for it. As Tocqueville puts it 'the government was not overthrown, it was allowed to fall'. It flopped.

The February Revolution had been universally expected, and after it had occurred no one could account for it. Its course was meaningless, or at least unproductive of immediate results. Memories were relived, and the circle of repetition was completed by the Second Republic, the Presidency of Louis-Napoleon, and the Second Empire. Only in the June Days a new reality pierced through the counterfeit displays; the people of Paris, with a tradition and consciousness of power, but without clear aim, took action. In 1848 the French monarchy was consigned to the grave, and with it an element essential to the proper working of the Parliamentary system was lost. Since then France has faced an uneasy choice between a Parliamentary Republic in which President and Prime Minister to some extent duplicate each other, and a system based on an independent Executive which is a cross between the American Presidency and the Napoleonic dictatorship. The principles of equality and national sovereignty, bequeathed by the Great Revolution, found in 1848 their logical fulfilment in universal suffrage and the Republic, two principles not contravened even by a plebiscitarian Empire. While British radicals adhered to the tenets of classical economy and free trade, French thought in 1848 moved towards new social concepts: the organization and protection of labour, 'the right to work' (with its concomitant: relief for the unemployed), universal education as a citizen right, a graduated income-tax—most of which were realized in Britain before they were in France. To begin with, the February Revolution was not anti-clerical, still less anti-religious: the revolutionaries were romantics rather than free-thinkers, while the clergy were largely Legitimists. Lammenais and Lacordaire were forerunners of a socially radical Catholicism. It was only after the June Days that the cleavage between the Church and the radicals reopened, while the big bourgeois drew closer to the Church in a political clericalism. The problem of Church and State was now sharply put, and the battle joined which was to reach its climax fifty years later.

When Metternich fell, aged seventy-five, he was replaced by Kolowrat, aged seventy, and at the Foreign Office by Ficquelmont, aged seventy-one; in May, Pillersdorf, an official aged only sixty-two, became Prime Minister; but on 8 July he was succeeded by Wessenberg, aged seventy-five, who continued the septuagenarian set-up of Austria's 'rejuvenation' till after the October rising in Vienna. And when Bach (aged thirty-five), a politician of revolutionary origin, attained office, within a few weeks he turned into a heavy-handed reactionary. The Vienna revolution was indeed a peculiar affair. But any radical handling of the situation was bound to endanger Austria, immediately or ultimately. Joseph II, Schwarzenberg and Bach, and the men of 1906–14, were exponents of sharp, centralizing authoritarian systems; Maria Theresa, Metternich, and Francis Joseph in his later years temporized; *immer fortwurschteln* ('always muddle along') was the precept of the Emperor's most accordant Premier, Count Taaffe. Where historic survival is both *raison d'être* and aim, logical conceptions are a deadly poison. And Austria survived because of the inherent impossibilities and contradictions of the situation. Metternich knew it, but preferred to bedeck the dismal truth with philosophical dissertations.

The pattern of Austria's existence becomes patent in 1848, though it takes time before it is discerned and the consequences are drawn. There were four dominant nationalities within the Habsburg Monarchy whose upper and middle classes covered also the territories of the subject races: Germans, Italians, Magyars, and Poles, *versus* Czechs, Slovaks, Yugoslavs, Ruthenes, and Rumans. The four master races demanded a united Germany, a united Italy, an independent Hungary, and a reunited Poland, including between them all the territories of the subject races inhabiting the Monarchy. Their programs carried to their logical conclusion implied the complete disruption of the Austrian Empire, and were therefore opposed by the dynasty, and by those among the Austrian Germans who were more Austrian than German. The subject races, too, desired national unity and independence, but they preferred the rule of the non-national Habsburgs to that of the master races. Some of their leaders, especially among the Czechs, went the length of developing a program of 'Austro-Slavism'—of an Austria reconstructed on a Slav basis. But this was a phantasm: for it offered no possible basis for the existence and survival of the Habsburg Monarchy. In the long run the dynasty had to take for partners nationalities which shared their proprietary interests in their territories, as did the Germans, Magyars, and Poles, and which, therefore, were prepared to defend every square mile. But the Germans, inside and outside Austria, would only accept her continued existence in lieu of complete national unity if the German predominance within Austria was maintained and reinforced by a German alliance, which in turn the Habsburgs themselves required to safeguard their dominions; and the Magyars and Poles would only accept it provided it did not touch, and indeed safeguarded, their dominion over Hungary and Galicia. Socially also the German-Magyar-Polish basis best suited the Habsburgs: an ancient dynasty cannot permanently ally itself to peasants against their masters. In 1848–9 the peasant nations supported the dynasty; in 1867 they were abandoned by it to the dominant races. In 1866–7 the German, Italian, and Magyar programs of 1848 were realized in modified forms, and the Polish, in so far as this was possible within the framework of the Habsburg Monarchy alone. In 1918–19 came the time for the subject races of the German and Magyar spheres, and for the Poles; in 1939–45, for the Yugoslavs and Ruthenes in the Italian and Polish spheres. Every idea put forward by the nationalities of the Habsburg Monarchy in 1848 was realized at some juncture, in one form or another.

With 1848 starts the German bid for power, for European predominance, for world dominion: the national movement was the common denominator of the German revolution in 1848, and a mighty Germany, fit to give the law to other nations, its foremost aim. *Einheit, Freiheit, und Macht* ('Unity, Freedom, and Power') was the slogan, with the emphasis on the first and third concepts. 'Through power to freedom, this is Germany's predestined path,' wrote in April 1848 the outstanding intellectual leader of the Frankfurt assemblies, Professor Dahlmann. Even some of the Republicans were Republicans primarily because they were Nationalists: the existence of thirty-odd dynasties and the rival claims of Habsburgs and Hohenzollerns were the foremost obstacles to German unity, easiest removed by proclaiming a German Republic, one and indivisible. The movement for German unity originated in 1848 in the west, south-west, and in the centre of Germany, in the small States which gave no scope to the German *Wille zur Macht*, and in the newly-acquired, disaffected provinces of Prussia and Bavaria. But although the aim of the Frankfurt Parliament was a real Pan-Germany, not a Great Prussia, or Great Austria, one of the two German Great Powers had to be the core of the new German Federal State. And here started the difficulties: Austria was the greatest State within the Federation and its traditional 'head', but of its thirty-six million inhabitants less than six were German; while of sixteen million in Prussia, fourteen were German. Austria obviously could not merge into a German national State, whereas Prussia could—theoretically. It became clear in 1848–9 that a united Greater Germany (*Gross-Deutschland*), comprising the German provinces of Austria, implied the disruption of Austria; otherwise it had to be a Lesser Germany (*Klein-Deutschland*). With an undivided Austria within Germany, the German Confederation could not change into a Federal State; but a Federation of States offered no prospect of real national unity or of power. The Frankfurt Parliament therefore finished by accepting *Klein-Deutschland*, and offered its Crown to the King of Prussia; who refused from respect for Austria and because he could only have accepted the Crown if offered to him by his fellow-sovereigns. Nor would the new Empire as planned at Frankfurt have proved acceptable to the true Prussians: Frankfurt, not Berlin, was to have been its capital, and Prussia was 'to merge into Germany' (there was intense jealousy at Frankfurt against the Berlin Parliament, and as a safeguard against Prussian predominance in a *Klein-Deutschland* it was planned to break up Prussia into her eight provinces, each about the size of a German middle-sized State). When in March 1848 Frederick William IV sported the German tricolour and made his troops assume it, the Second Regiment of the Guards replied by a song about 'the cry which pierced the faithful hearts: you shall be Prussians no longer, you shall be Germans.' When Bismarck showed its text to the Prince of Prussia, tears ran down William's cheeks. But it was his system based on Prussia, her army and administration, which was to be established by the man who showed him the song.

The year 1848 proved in Germany that union could not be achieved through discussion and by agreement; that it could be achieved only by force; that there were not sufficient revolutionary forces in Germany to impose it from below; and that therefore, if it was to be, it had to be imposed by the Prussian army. Again the future was mapped out. There were four programs in 1848–9. That of *Gross-Oesterreich*, a centralized Germanic Austria retaining her traditional preponderance in Germany, was realized by Schwarzenberg in 1850, after Olmütz. That of a Greater Prussia was realized in the North German Confederation of 1866, and was extended in 1870–1 to cover the entire territory of the Frankfurt *Klein-Deutschland*. That program itself, with the capital removed from Berlin, was haltingly attempted under the Weimar Republic; while the other Frankfurt program of *Gross-Deutschland*, including the German and Czech provinces of Austria, was achieved by Hitler in 1938–9.

In 1800, after some forty years in politics, Lord Shelburne wrote in his memoirs:

> It requires experience in government to know the immense distance between planning and executing. All the difficulty is with the last. It requires no small labour to open the eyes of either the public or of individuals, but when that is accomplished, you are not got a third of the way. The real difficulty remains in getting people to apply the principles which they have admitted, and of which they are now so fully convinced. Then springs the mine of private interests and personal animosity. . . . If the Emperor Joseph had been content to sow and not to plant, he would have done more good, and saved a great deal of ill.

Most of the men of 1848 lacked political experience, and before a year was out the 'trees of liberty' planted by them had withered away. None the less, 1848 remains a seed-plot of history. It crystallized ideas and projected the pattern of things to come; it determined the course of the century which followed. It planned, and its schemes have been realized: but—*non vi si pensa quanto sangue costa.*

# VI

# NATIONALITY AND LIBERTY

LIBERTY was claimed in 1848 for the individual and liberty for nations, and a natural, wellnigh intrinsic connexion was assumed between the two; to be consummated—so the theory ran—in a peaceful fellowship of free nations. But there was a deeper antinomy between constitutional development in most of the States concerned, and the postulates of the new national movements. Individual and civic liberty requires a stable, uncontested political framework: internal freedom is best secured where the communal consciousness coincides with the territory of the State, that is, where nationality is territorial in character and the existing frontiers do not give rise to claims by, or against, neighbours. But the politically minded cannot feel truly free except in a State which they acknowledge as their own, and in which they are acknowledged as indigenous: that is, in their own national State; and the nationalisms which in 1848 entered the political arena, and held it during the next one hundred years, were primarily linguistic. 'The sole idea now fruitful and powerful in Europe is the idea of national liberty; the worship of principle has begun,' wrote Mazzini in 1832.[1] And further: 'The nation is the universality of the citizens speaking the same tongue.'[2] Territorial nationality is essentially conservative, for it is the product of a long historical development; nationalisms which place the emphasis on language almost invariably seek change, since no existing satiated community singles out one principle for its basis—the demand that the State should be coextensive with linguistic nationality was an internationally revolutionary postulate which, seeing that nations are seldom linguistically segregated, proved destructive both of constitutional growth and of international peace. National feeling was hailed in 1848 as a great and noble force which was to have regenerated Europe, and is denounced today as an obsession

[1] *Life and Writings* (1864), vol. i, p. 147. [2] Ibid., vol. i, p. 167.

which has brought ruin upon her: but from the outset it was the expression of social and political maladjustment, and has since been at least as much the vehicle as the source of destructive passions.

## I

The British and Swiss concepts of nationality are primarily territorial: it is the State which has created the nationality, and not *vice versa*. A historical process, operating within a geographically determined framework, has produced a British island nationality which comprises the English, Scots, and Welsh, and to which Ulster adheres; and neither within the island, nor in the English-speaking world outside, could language be the criterion of nationality, or else Scotland and Wales would each be split internally, while, for instance, Irishmen and Americans would have to count as 'English'. Liberty and self-government have moulded the territorial nation of Britain, and given content to its communal nationality. The political life of the British island community centres in its Parliament at Westminster, which represents men rooted in British soil. This is a territorial, and not a tribal, assembly; it was for centuries the representation of freeholders and householders, of men with a share in their native land; and 'every blade of grass in Great Britain' was said to be represented in it. Bound to the soil of Britain, it is limited to it: by now the British Parliament does not claim authority over communities even of British origin and English speech once they are rooted in other soil. And so close is the nexus between territory and nationality in English law that a child of whatever parentage if born under the British flag can claim British nationality. Indeed, the English language lacks a word to describe a 'nationality' distinct from, or contrasted with, the citizenship derived from territory and State; and the meaningless term of 'race' is often used for what in Continental languages is covered by 'nationality'.

The island character of Britain and the 'genius' of its people are acclaimed as factors which have produced that rare entity, a real, and not merely nominal, territorial nationality. But the argument must not be pressed too far: for in the adjoining island a similar mixture of Celt, Anglo-Saxon, and Norman has failed to evolve an Irish territorial nationality. Even unity of language has failed to bring its inhabitants together; and now the political dissonance has resulted in a deliberate and laborious attempt to revive linguistic separateness. The geographical factor is obvious also in the rise and development of the Swiss nationality, yet the frontiers of Switzerland are by no means preordained, nor amenable to a strict rational explanation. Undisputed territory has rendered possible the growth of orderly self-government and of civil liberty, which in turn has heightened the national consciousness and coherence of the community: so that any desire for territorial expansion, still more for merging into another State, is completely absent. In and even before 1848, the most far-sighted among the German nationalists desiring a union of all Germans, feared the growth of civic liberty and self-government in the separate German States as liable to consolidate and crystallize them, and thereby to hinder unification. Fichte wrote:[3] 'One might say: gradually a German nation will come to be. But how can the conception of one nation arise at all? (Nor was Greece ever united. What prevented it? Answer: the single State prematurely grown solid).'[4] Men cannot fit themselves into a new nation 'once a communal existence [*das Volkseyn*] has entered their natural existence and consciousness'. All men desire civil liberty, and mutual understanding and trust between representatives and represented is the basis of national life: 'Therefore a people can no longer be reformed, or added to another, once it has started steadily to progress towards a free constitution.'

## 2

The Germans, more than any other European nation, had emptied the territorial State of communal contents and converted it into sheer dynastic property; and they brought forth dynasties without roots or substance, ready to rule over any country or people. The denationalized State with an unpolitical population was the product of German political incapacity and deadness, and of German administrative efficiency. The Habsburg Monarchy, an almost unique phenomenon in history, rooted in the German hereditary provinces, the *Erbländer*, yet seemingly unrelated to any land or people, unrestricted in its acquisitive ambitions and singularly successful, variegated and ever changeable, was private dynastic domain, and so were the innumerable German pygmy States, too small to rank as political entities. Even Prussia, a military and administrative organization turned State, was ready to absorb territory and population of any language or race. In such dynastic proprietary or organizational

[3] 'Politische Fragmente aus den Jahren 1807 und 1813' *Werke*, vol. vii, p. 549. [4] *der schon zu feste Einzelstaat.*

creations German and non-German provinces were frequently yoked together, while the German dynasties and bureaucracies of Vienna, Berlin, and St. Petersburg encouraged fresh German settlements in non-German lands, adding considerably to the residue left by earlier, medieval, migrations. Lastly, Habsburg non-national territorialism extended the contradiction between nationality and State to other parts of Europe, especially to Italy; and when in 1848 the demand arose for national liberty and self-determination, it was against the Habsburgs that it was primarily directed.

The highest forms of communal life became the basis of West European nationalisms, the myth of the barbaric horde that of German nationalism.

> Nationalism in the West was based upon a nationality which was the product of social and political factors [writes Professor Hans Kohn[5]]; nationalism in Germany did not find its justification in a rational societal conception, it found it in the 'natural' fact of a community, held together . . . by traditional ties of kinship and status. German nationalism substituted for the legal and rational concept of 'citizenship' the infinitely vaguer concept of 'folk', which, first discovered by the German humanists, was fully developed by Herder and the German romanticists.

With roots which 'seemed to reach into the dark soil of primitive times', that concept 'lent itself more easily to the embroideries of imagination and the excitations of emotion'. Moreover, the Germans transferred 'to the field of society and nationalism' Rousseau's ethical and cultural antithesis between the primitive and artificial.

> They established a distinction between State and nation : they regarded the State as a mechanical and juridical construction, the artificial product of historical accidents, while they believed the nation to be the work of nature, and therefore something sacred, eternal, organic, carrying a deeper justification than works of men.[6]

Here it was not the State which moulded nationality, but a pre-existent nationality which postulated a State. The German concept of nationality is linguistic and 'racial', rather than political and territorial, and it finds its final expression in the doctrine of the *Volksdeutsche* which claims that anyone of German 'race' and language owes allegiance, first and foremost, to his German Fatherland, of whatever other State such an *Ausland-Deutscher* may claim to be a citizen. Nor is that idea a mere Nazi invention: for instance, in the

[5] *The Idea of Nationalism* (1946), p. 331. [6] Ibid., p. 249.

Frankfurt Parliament of 1848 the suggestion was made that Germans resident in Paris should be represented in it; this patently absurd and impossible proposal received no support, yet it is symptomatic of certain trends in German thought that it should have been made at all. And though no other European nation has gone the same length as the Germans, the German concept of nationality, largely through the influence which German political formations and deformities had on Central and Eastern Europe, has become dominant on the Continent.

## 3

The French Monarchy was based on territory with a common literary language and a national culture and consciousness; the elements of a rich nationality were present, but the welding force of active civic development was wanting; and no synthesis was reached between the power of the State, the growing influence of Paris, and the vigorous life of the provinces. The final unification of France was achieved not through an organic growth preserving the historical individuality of the component parts but in the cataclysm of the Great Revolution: by abstract thought setting out to build on a non-historical basis. A new principle of unity was found in the community of men declared free and equal; the liberty of the individual and his rights were placed in the forefront, yet he was completely integrated into the sovereign nation. The emphasis in the concept of nationality was shifted from the land to the people; the component countries and populations were merged into the Republic, one and indivisible: *la patrie* became a dogma and a principle. To the French people, coincident with the territory of its State, was ascribed a non-territorial and a-historical existence: it was as if the French nation had shaken off the bonds of locality and time, and taken wing. 'In the words of Siéyès,' writes Lord Acton,[7] 'it was no longer France, but some unknown country to which the nation was transported. . . . The idea of the sovereignty of the people, uncontrolled by the past, gave birth to the idea of nationality independent of the political influence of history. . . . Every effaceable trace and relic of national history was carefully wiped away—the system of administration, the physical divisions of the country, the classes of society,

[7] In his essay on 'Nationality', published in the *Home and Foreign Review*, July 1862; reprinted in *The History of Freedom and other Essays* (1909), pp. 277–8.

the corporations, the weights and measures, the calendar.' Here was a break in historical continuity which has left deep rifts in the nation; and the French, passionately attached both to nationality and liberty, have to this day failed to evolve political forms that would provide the consensus and stability which these two require. But so dazzling in its spiritual magnificence was the opening of the new era, so convincing intellectually the argument, so powerful the surge of the movement, and so generous and universal was the message of the Revolution, that men were slow in perceiving the losses which were suffered even in the realm of ideas. From the French Revolution dates the active rise of modern nationalism with some of its most dangerous features: of a mass movement centralizing and levelling, dynamic and ruthless, akin in nature to the horde.

It was the agrarian movement that rendered invincible the French Revolution of 1789 and the Russian of 1917, but it was the cities which supplied these two revolutions with their ideology and their striking force; and a metropolitan population is the common denominator of the nation detached from its lands. Michelet, himself a Parisian, extolled Paris as 'the great and complete symbol' of France formed into one city.

> The genius of Paris is a most complex and at the same time the highest form of France. It might seem that something which resulted from the destruction of all local spirit, of all regionalism, must be something that is purely negative. It is not so: of all the negations of material, local, particular ideas results a living generality, a positive thing, a life force.[8]

Indeed, Michelet rejoiced at the rapid effacement of the 'French provincial distinctions' (*nos provincialités françaises*).

> That sacrifice of the diverse interior nationalities to the great nationality which comprises them, undoubtedly strengthens the latter. . . . It was at the moment when France suppressed within herself the diverging French countries that she proclaimed her high and original revelation.[9]

And he reached the significant conclusion that 'nations will endure . . . if they do not take thought to suppress the towns, in which the nationalities have condensed their self-expression' (*ont résumé leur génie*).[10] Rousseau, on the contrary, 'hated the great metropolitan capitals which seemed to him to destroy the individuality of nations'.[11]

[8] Quoted after Hans Kohn, *Prophets and Peoples* (1946), p. 53.
[9] Michelet, *Le Peuple* (1946), p. 286. [10] Op. cit., p. 288.
[11] Kohn, *The Idea of Nationalism*, p. 254.

'It is in the distant provinces', he wrote, '. . . where the inhabitants move about less, and experience fewer changes of fortune and status, that the genius and customs (*le génie et les mœurs*) of a nation have to be studied.' Yet the contradiction between Rousseau and Michelet is more apparent than real, for they were speaking about different things: Michelet had in mind the modern nationalist movements, now so curiously alike all the world over, while Rousseau thought of the distinct contents of each nationality.

## 4

For men rooted in the soil there is, as a rule, a hierarchy of allegiances: to their village community or estate, to their district, to their 'country'[12]—for them the nation is of a naturally federal structure. Traditional beliefs and hereditary ties persist; class and the way of living determine alignments; things are individual and concrete in the village or the small, old-fashioned town. But in the great modern cities men grow anonymous, become ciphers, and are regimented; thinking becomes more abstract and is forced into generalizations; inherited beliefs are shaken and old ties are broken; there is a void, uncertainty, and hidden fear which man tries to master by rational thought. He starts by proudly asserting the rights of the abstract average individual freed from the bondage of tradition, and then integrates him into the crowd, a collective personality, which unloads itself in mass movements. The mass is the refuge of the uprooted individual; and disintegration of spiritual values is as potent a process as the splitting of the atom: it releases demonic forces which burst all dams. The program may be social revolution, or national revolution, or both; the aim may be to right wrongs or to sweep away stultifying encumbrances; the result can be liberation, but it can hardly be liberty which is founded on restraint and not on force, even if genuine idealism guides it. 'Whenever a single definite object is made the supreme end of the State,' wrote Lord Acton,[13] 'be it the advantage of a class, the safety or the power of the country, or the support of any speculative idea, the State becomes for the time absolute. Liberty alone demands for its realization the limitation of the public authority. . . .' Liberty is the fruit of slow growth in a stable society; is based on respect for the rights of the

[12] In France *pays* is used to this day for various provinces; in eighteenth-century England, 'country' was still frequently used for 'county'.
[13] Op. cit., p. 288.

individual, deeply embedded in the life and habits of the community; is in its origin an aristocratic idea: of the self-conscious individual, certain of himself and his position, and therefore perfectly at ease. It spreads when every man's house becomes 'his castle': yet he must have a house and be safely rooted.

In 1848 the political insufficiency of the existing States of Central and East-Central Europe was rendered even more glaring by a peak period in intellectual development. Cultural entities were forming which transcended meaningless frontiers or disrupted territorial agglomerations. British political practice and French revolutionary doctrine provided the runways for the new movements, and the work of the Napoleonic period, uncompleted or reversed, their starting-points; while the Metternich régime, negative and uncreative, had hollowed out still further the forms which it endeavoured to maintain, for it had impeded within them the growth of an active political life such as is apt to evolve nationality even within accidental territorial frameworks. The conception of dynastic property in States was of feudal origin and derived from property in land: it fitted into the ideology of a community whose relations and connexions were bound up with the soil. But it no longer made sense in urban communities: and it was these, with their strong educated class and their new proletariat, which were now coming to the fore. The uprooted individual becomes conscious of his personal rights, rational rather than traditional; and so does the crowd detached from the soil. There is a profound difference between a King of France and an Emperor or King of the French—but what if the territorial term does not even correspond to a human aggregate?

The first logical inference of individual liberty and popular sovereignty is the claim to national self-determination: 'One hardly knows what any division of the human race should be free to do, if not to determine with which of the various collective bodies of human beings they choose to associate themselves,' wrote J. S. Mill in 1861.[14] And he rightly concluded that 'it is in general a necessary condition of free institutions, that the boundaries of governments should coincide in the main with those of nationalities'.[15] Liberty and nationality, especially when opposed to the concept of dynastic property in States, seemed therefore to be concordant ideas. The national movements demanded the union of nations disrupted between dynastic domains, and the independence of other nations engulfed in dynastic empires. It was taken for granted that representative and responsible government would be practised by the

[14] *Considerations on Representative Government*, p. 289. [15] Ibid., pp. 291–2.

sovereign nations, with full guarantees of the rights of the individual; and it was hopefully assumed that no free people would ever attack another people. The problem of the territorial squaring of intersecting national circles did not as yet vex the minds of the theoretical exponents of the creed of nationality.

## 5

A foremost position among the prophets of nationality is due to Mazzini, a man outstanding for spiritual integrity and single-minded devotion to the cause he preached. A sincere lover of liberty, he believed in the rights and dignity of man, in the 'law of progress', and the joint destiny of humanity; and he adhered passionately to the tenets and postulates of a truly humanitarian liberalism. 'Liberty is sacred, as the individual is sacred.' 'Without liberty there is no true morality.' And on what principle can an association of free men be founded except on 'that of the rights of the individual'? Yet he never wearied of contrasting the age which had placed rights in the forefront with the new age centred on duty—the doctrine of individualism with that of nationality. 'The epoch of *individuality* is concluded'; it has been 'replaced by the epoch of the peoples'; 'the question of nationalities is destined to give its name to the century.' 'Individuality' was 'a doctrine useful perhaps . . . in securing the exercise of some personal rights, but impotent to found nationality or association'; and 'it is the duty of reformers to initiate the epoch of association. Collective man is omnipotent upon the earth he treads.' Mazzini yearned for a collective life which would reveal itself 'in regular and progressive development, similar to the gradual evolution of vegetation in the new world, wherein the separate trees continue to mingle their branches, until they form the gigantic unity of the forest'. Even art, 'vital art', must be a collective performance, inspired by the collective purpose and serving it. He was prepared to subordinate the entire life of the community to a political aim—thus Young Italy was 'to comprehend all the various manifestations of national life in one sole conception, and direct . . . them all . . . towards one sole aim, the emancipation of our country and its brotherhood with free nations'. He saw Europe being transformed 'into vast and united masses'.

Mazzini himself said that his heart was stronger than his head; and the moral fervour, purity of purpose, and religious sincerity which pervade his writings—words of faith and action rather than of thought—were apt to conceal from contemporaries how deficient his teachings were in substance correlated to everyday reality, and what dangerous germs they contained. National self-glorification and claims to moral superiority were of their core: which entails a measure of depreciation of other peoples, and is not conducive to international comity. Nor are self-conscious apostles of an exalted creed easy to work with at home. Liberty calls for sanity, a modicum of scepticism, and tolerance: a man must be prepared to believe that he may be mistaken, if he is to treat others as equals. Mazzini was not; he had faith and was intolerant of 'opinions'; his aim was action which ill accords with doubt. He retained his contempt of the 'moderates' even after the goal of a united Italy had been achieved by them; and he never showed real understanding for the nature of Parliamentary government, which rests on a good many seeming absurdities but so far has proved the most efficient system for safeguarding civic liberty.

Mazzini claimed for Italy a position of primacy in the world, and assigned to her a unique mission. There was 'a void, a want in Europe'; 'no power of initiative' existed in any of its peoples; a 'regenerate Italy' could alone initiate a new and superior life and unity among them. Twice before has the world been united by Rome, Imperial and Papal; and the tradition of those two epochs bears witness to a further mission.

> Why should not a new Rome, the Rome of the Italian people . . . arise to create a third and still vaster unity; to link together and harmonize earth and heaven, right and duty; and utter, not to individuals but to peoples, the great word Association—to make known to free men and equals their mission here below?

But first, Italy had to be reconstituted 'as one independent sovereign nation of free men and equals'; and the basis was to be republican and unitarian, not monarchical and federal.

> Because without unity, there is no true nation.
>
> Because without unity, there is no real strength; and Italy surrounded as she is by powerful, united, and jealous nations, has need of strength before all things.
>
> Because federalism, by reducing her to the political impotence of Switzerland, would necessarily place her under the influence of one of the neighbouring nations.

Mazzini insisted that the first thing was 'to put an end to our servile subjection to French influence', intellectual as much as political; and he seemed hardly aware of how much his 'unitarian' program was a response, both defensive and imitative, to the national France of the Great Revolution. 'I could wish', he wrote in 1861, 'that all the artificial territorial divisions now existing were transformed into simple sections and circumscriptions.'

'Young Italy', when he started organizing it in 1831, was to be the instrument of Italy's regeneration: it was to be 'neither a sect nor a party but a faith and an apostolate'; and the emphasis was not on numbers but on the homogeneous character of the movement. 'I still believe', he wrote on another occasion, 'that next to the capacity of rightly leading, the greatest merit consists in knowing how and when to follow.' During the period which might elapse before the movement achieved 'the complete liberation of Italian soil', it would have to be directed 'by a provisional dictatorial power, concentrated in the hands of a small number of men'.

The banner of Young Italy was to bear 'on the one side the words —*Liberty, Equality, Humanity*; and on the other—*Unity, Independence*'. 'What is it we want?' wrote Mazzini in 1832.

> We demand to exist. We demand a name. We desire to make our country powerful and respected, free and happy . . .
>
> In other words, we demand independence, unity and liberty, for ourselves and for our fellow-countrymen.
>
> . . . All are agreed in the cry of *Out with the foreigner*.

The same process of unification Mazzini desired for other nations. He saw the future 'arousing extinct peoples, uniting divided races, proceeding by masses, and making individuals the mere stepping-stones to their ascent'. 'To reconstruct the map of Europe . . . in accordance with the special mission assigned to each people by geographical, ethnographical, and historical conditions, was the first step necessary for all.' 'Lasting liberty can only be achieved and maintained in Europe by strong and compact nations, equally balanced in power.'

Here was real vision of the future though not of its dangers, and high idealism not devoid of elements which have since become dominant in nationalist movements. He wanted to see his country 'powerful and respected', not merely free and secure: 'the political impotence of Switzerland' would not have been acceptable to his feelings. His conscious thought turned towards humanity and embraced the whole; but when stigmatizing an answer given in 1831 by the Provisional Government of Bologna, he says that they spoke 'like foreign barbarians'. He disliked Italy's two neighbours, France and Austria; his demand of an equal balance in Europe was directed against the French 'instinct of domination,' and his program of redrawing the map of Europe against Austria's survival. He spoke of 'the special mission assigned to each people', but would hardly have endorsed those claimed by the nations themselves: they might not have left the 'mission Italy is destined to accomplish towards humanity' quite as great as Mazzini conceived it.

For in the romantic era the prophets of each nation found that it was destined to play the noblest part. 'La patrie, ma patrie peut seule sauver le monde,' wrote Michelet in 1846. The history of all the nations was 'mutilated', that of France alone was 'complete': 'avec elle, vous sauvez le monde.' But France, after some experience in the redeeming of nations, knew that such attempts do not necessarily earn the love of those to be 'saved'. 'Children, children,' wrote Michelet, 'I say to you: ascend a mountain, provided it is sufficiently high; look to the four winds, and you will see nothing but enemies.'[16] Poland 'the Christ among the Nations' was at the time the doctrine of Polish Messianism propounded by her greatest poet, Mickiewicz; all the other nations were described as worshipping false gods who were no gods, while the Poles alone were 'from first to last faithful to the God of their fathers'.[17] Russia as 'the God-bearing nation' was the creed of her most inspired writers from Khomiakov to Dostoyevsky, coupled with contempt for the 'decaying West' (which did not impair their admiration for its achievements). Fichte, one of the discoverers of *Germanentum*, found that the Germans alone were a real nation, *ein Urvolk*, speaking a living language—the other languages were 'dead in their roots', mere echoes. He thus apostrophized the Germans in 1808: 'Of all the modern nations it is you who carry most clearly the germ of human perfection, and it is your mission to develop it. Should this perish in you, all hope of humanity for salvation from the depths of its evils will perish with you.'[18] And the much applauded poetaster Geibel, wrote in 1861 on 'Germany's Calling':

> Und es mag am deutschen Wesen
> Einmal noch die Welt genesen!

Thus every nation was exalted above the rest: compensatory dreams of grandeur dreamt by suffering or afflicted nations and uprooted individuals—immature, comparable to the day-dreams of adolescents. Nations unified, regenerated, or resurrected, have since proved to be in no way better than other nations—there is a limit to

[16] *Le Peuple*, p. 35. [17] *Ksiegi narodu polskiego i pielgrzymstwa polskiego* (1832).
[18] *Reden an die deutsche Nation* (1808).

miracles even in Wonderland, as Alice discovered when she ate cake. And what remains after the idealistic gilt of nationalism has worn off is the claim to superiority, hence to dominion.

## 6

The impact of France on Europe during the Revolutionary and Napoleonic periods was the chief political factor in the arousing of its nationalisms. In France, united even before 1789, the process of revolutionary transformation had released forces which deluged Europe: a nation welded into an ideological entity, and freed from the bonds of territory and tradition, offered a spectacle of power of which the nature, cost, and consequences men did not as yet probe, but which evoked the wonder, envy, and fear of its neighbours. The Germans, superior in number to the French, and the Italians, not very much inferior, realized to what disadvantage they were put through the political fragmentation of their countries. Napoleon himself started the work of territorial 'rationalization' in both; and the fall of many governments and the frequent redistribution of territory 'deprived the political settlement of the dignity of permanence'—'tradition and prescription', writes Lord Acton, 'ceased to be guardians of authority.' In Italy most of the previous States were re-established in 1815, but the foreign origin of so many of the rulers and the foreign support on which they relied, the foreign occupation of Lombardy and Venetia, and the oppressive character of most of the Governments rendered the territorial divisions even more galling. Genoa was merged into Piedmont; and one wonders how much this may have contributed to Mazzini's 'unitarianism'—if his native city had still been the glorious ancient republic, would he have wished to wipe out its identity? But after it had been placed under a dynasty strange to it, was it not more reasonable to go the whole length in national unification? In his 'General Instructions for Members of Young Italy' he used against a monarchical constitution for a united Italy the argument that 'while the populations of the various Italian States would cheerfully unite in the name of a principle which would give no umbrage to local ambition, they would not willingly submit to be governed by a man—the offspring of one of those States'.

In Germany the territorial resettlement of the Napoleonic period was much more extensive and more permanent. More than two hundred small principalities, ecclesiastical States, and Free Cities were incorporated in the big and middle-sized States whose character was thereby changed very considerably. After the Rhineland and Westphalia had in 1815 been included in Prussia, the Roman Catholics came to form more than one-third of her population; the inclusion of Franconia and the Palatinate in Bavaria raised the proportion of her Protestants to over one-fourth of the whole; in Baden, originally a Protestant country, the Roman Catholics now formed two-thirds of the population, and in Württemberg one-third. The West-German Roman Catholics felt no affection for the Hohenzollerns, nor the Protestants, say, of Nuremberg for the Wittelsbachs, etc. And both in 1814–15 and in 1848, the small mediatized princes or Knights of the Empire were among the foremost champions of a united Germany: Stein, the Gagerns, Leiningen, and Chlodwig zu Hohenlohe-Schillingsfürst are outstanding examples. Men whose old territorial rights had been extinguished, or whose allegiance had been changed, wished to see all territorial rights merged in a Great Germany: in 1848 *Stock-Preussen* or *Alt-Bayern* showed a high degree of *Partikularismus* (local territorial consciousness), especially in the rural districts, but the newly acquired provinces clamoured for German national unity, the Roman Catholics hoping for a Habsburg Empire, and the Protestants for one under the Hohenzollerns. The territorial shufflings and reshufflings in the Napoleonic period and at the Congress of Vienna facilitated the rise of a movement for a united Germany.

'The German people wanted a strong and free State: this is the content of the German revolution of 1848–9,' writes its historian, Veit Valentin, in the first volume of his work;[19] but by the time he reached the second, 'free' dropped out: 'The strong national Reich was the foremost aim of the German revolution.'[20] And while Mazzini's counterpart to the watchwords of the French Revolution was *Independence, Unity, Liberty*, that of the German revolution of 1848 was *Einheit, Freiheit, und Macht* ('Unity, Freedom, and Power'); which was soon abbreviated to *Einheit und Macht*. Bassermann, one of the foremost leaders of the South-Western Liberals and Chairman of the Constitutional Committee, said in the National Assembly on 16 February 1849: 'If I knew the unity and future greatness of Germany were to be attained through a temporary renunciation of all the freedoms (*sämmtlicher Freiheitsrechte*), I should be the first to submit to such a dictatorship.' And Stremayr, an Austrian member of the Left, said on 27 October 1848: 'Were

[19] *Geschichte der deutschen Revolution von 1848–49*, vol. i, p. 246.
[20] Ibid., vol. ii, p. 31.

Slavia to offer me freedom, and Germania to put me in chains, I would still follow Germany, for I am convinced that a united Germany will lead me to freedom.' Thus the emphasis was on nationality rather than on liberty, and even where liberty was placed in the forefront, it was not always for its own sake but rather as the means for realizing the overriding purpose of national unification. As dynastic interests and rivalries were the main obstacle, and it was not possible to square them by negotiation or compromise, national unity could have been easiest achieved in a German Republic, one and indivisible; and even to the moderates the doctrine of a joint German national sovereignty, superior to the claims of dynasties and constituent States, supplied the basis for their endeavours to achieve unity. But everywhere 'the German revolution stopped at the steps to the thrones'; and not one dynasty was overthrown. Indeed, again for the sake of unity some republicans considered it necessary to renounce their program: 'I desire German unity,' wrote Heinrich Simon, a leader of the Left, in April 1848, 'but it would be impossible if in a few places the republic was now proclaimed.'

Aggrieved national feelings were perhaps the greatest and most universal force behind the revolution of 1848. Here are two passages from the oath to be taken by members of Young Italy:[21]

> By the blush that rises to my brow when I stand before citizens of other lands, to know that I have no rights of citizenship, no country and no national flag . . .
>
> By the memory of our former greatness, and the sense of our present degradation . . .

And Prince Chlodwig zu Hohenlohe-Schillingsfürst wrote in December 1847:[22]

> *One* reason for dissatisfaction is universal in Germany, and every thinking German feels it deeply and painfully. It is the nullity [*Nullität*] of Germany vis-à-vis of other States. . . . It is sad and humiliating not to be able to say proudly abroad: 'I am a German', not to see the German flag flying on ships, nor find a consul, but to have to say: 'I am a Kurhesse, Darmstädter, Bückeburger, my Fatherland was once a great, powerful country, but is now split into thirty-eight fragments.'

And a Memorandum presented on 19 October 1848 by the Radical minority on the Constitutional Committee (including H. Simon and

[21] Mazzini, *Life and Writings*, vol. i, p. 111.

[22] *Denkwürdigkeiten des Fürsten Chlodwig zu Hohenlohe-Schillingsfürst*, edited by F .Curtius (1906), vol. i, p. 38.

Robert Blum) declared that the German Revolution had been provoked as much by the princes suppressing popular freedom as by their 'failing to unite with a view to establishing Germany's power'. Germany's *Macht* was a concern of the Left no less than of the Centre and Right.

The longing for German unity was strongest where the State could not endue its educated and semi-educated classes with a 'consciousness of power' (*Machtbewusstsein*), which is the German substitute for freedom, as the organized violence of war is the German version of revolution: a commutation of particular importance in a study of liberty and nationality, many other nationalisms having since developed along similar lines. South-western, Western, and Central Germany were most solidly behind the endeavours of the Frankfurt Assembly: these were regions of small or middle-sized States and of disaffected provinces, where the most extensive territorial reshuffles and transfers of allegiance had occurred, and where the impact of France—the influence of French ideas, and the fear of a new French invasion—was felt most acutely. Austria and Prussia, or even Bavaria and Hanover, had developed a 'State consciousness' (*Staatsbewusstsein*), the territorial nationality of 'subjects'; but their 'nationality' being of dynastic or organizational origin, and not based on a free communal life, was as acquisitive as the dynasty or organization which had created the State.[23] Yet, their territorial ambitions being more realistic (they had existing States for basis), were moderate when compared with the formless, unmeasured, visionary Pan-Germanism of more or less stateless Germans: most of the extravagant German claims of the two World Wars were raised and applauded by the 'freedom-loving' *idéologues* of the Frankfurt Parliament of 1848.

'What is the German's Fatherland?' The Frankfurt Assembly, being the parliament not of an existing State but of one to be created, had to decide the question. And a double, contradictory answer was given: *Was deutsch spricht, soll deutsch werden* ('Whatever speaks German, shall become German'), and *Was deutsch ist, soll deutsch bleiben* ('Whatever is German, shall remain German'). Thus linguistic claims were combined with another set based on history and the *status possidendi*, and each in detail was further garnished and extended—strategy, geography, the presumed wish

[23] The German language has no word to describe the 'nationality' of the separate States, and in 1848 the term employed for those territorial nationalities was *Stämme*, which means 'tribes' and was originally employed for the Franks, Swabians, Saxons, etc. To attach it to territorial formations, some of as recent origin as 1815, is rather comic.

or interest of some 'inferior' race, or the 'needs' of German expansion supplying the arguments. Even the linguistic test, *wie weit die deutsche Zunge klingt* (as far as the German language resounds) was indefinite, for it was left open how many Germans had to speak at the top of their voices for the claim to be established. Poland, martyred, partitioned Poland, the victim of Tsarism, enjoyed quite exceptional popularity with the exponents of liberty and nationality in 1848; and the Frankfurt Pre-Parliament started off with a resolution declaring the dismemberment of Poland a 'shameful wrong', and her restoration 'a sacred duty of the German nation': but at no time did it occur to anyone that the Polish-speaking districts of West Prussia and Upper Silesia were due to the Poles, while in Posnania, recognized as Polish, a demarcation line was drawn between German and Polish districts which, after several consecutive corrections each favouring the Germans, gave the Poles less than one-fourth of a province in which they formed two-thirds of the population.

Even less liberal was the attitude of the Frankfurt Parliament concerning Trieste and the Trentino. Schuselka, a leader of the Left, thus defended the *Territorialpolitik* of the National Assembly in July 1848: 'Such must be our basis, for a great nation requires space (*Raum*) to fulfil its world destiny (*Weltberuf*), and I would rather die a thousand times than, for instance, renounce Trieste because they speak Italian.' Don Giovanni a Prato, a leading figure in the Trentino, had, against the opinion of the Trentino *émigrés* who had left with the Lombard *insorti*, persuaded the population to take part in the elections to the Frankfurt Parliament in the hope of having the national claims of the Trentino endorsed by it:[24] he left Frankfurt in December 1848 a deeply disappointed man. (Giovanni de Pretis, Count Festi,[25] and G. Vettorazzi had done so before him.)

When the Czechs, under Palacky's leadership, refused to send representatives to the German National Assembly, their refusal produced a storm of indignation among the Frankfurt 'Liberals': it was described as 'a direct challenge to the territorial integrity of Germany', and their absence as in no way affecting the right of the Assembly to legislate for the Czech provinces. There was unanimity in condemning any possible claim of so-called 'a-historic' nations to an independent national existence. Heinrich von Gagern, an outstanding personality who dominated as no one else the Frankfurt Parliament, thus defined on 26 October 1848 Germany's 'task in the East': 'to include as satellites nations on the Danube which have

[24] See M. Manfroni, *Don Giovanni a Prato* (1920), pp. 50–1.
[25] See Livio Marchett, *Il Trentino nel Risorgimento* (1913).

neither a call nor a claim to independence.' And Wilhelm Jordan, one of the first on the Left to translate his political radicalism into ultra-nationalist terms, spoke on 20 June 1848 of 'the attempts of puny nationalities [*Nationalitätchen*] to found their own lives in our midst, and like parasites to destroy ours'. Even Marx and Engels admitted the right only of 'the great European nations' to 'a separate and independent national existence', but not of 'those numerous small relics of peoples' which have been (or should have been) absorbed by the 'more powerful nations'. But as they did not deny that right to the Magyars, who were hardly equal in number to the Czechs, and much inferior to the Yugoslavs and Rumans, one must presume that, unconsciously, these German middle-class prophets of class-war assigned the privilege of nationhood to peoples with a well-developed upper and middle class, and denied it to such as consisted almost entirely of 'a-historical' peasants and workmen.

## 7

The linguistic nationalism of the Germans, through its lore and example as well as through its impact, in turn stimulated the growth of linguistic nationalisms among their eastern neighbours, especially in the Habsburg Monarchy. But as Austria's *Staatsidee* was territorial, the Czech or Slovene cultural revival, so long as it remained a-political, received lenient, or even friendly, treatment from the dynasty and the feudal aristocracy, whose territorial concepts it did not as yet contravene. 'There is no such thing as an Austrian patriotism,' declared a speaker in the Hungarian Parliament in 1848. 'It is as unthinkable as a specific patriotism on the various estates of Prince Esterhazy.' Wherein he was wrong: every territorial unit is capable of developing a specific patriotism[26] in those truly rooted in it; which non-territorial mass-formations may, however, in time cut across, overshadow, or even destroy. 'Patriotism' need not be one of 'storm and stress'; there can be also a patriotism interested in what exists, and desirous of preserving it: such conservative sentiment, of varying intensity, gathers round every existing territorial formation.

The nationalities of the Habsburg Monarchy, barring the Italians and Serbs, all had, at one time or another, some interest of their own in its survival, developing accordingly their specific type of 'Austrian

[26] An amusing example of 'estate patriotism', amazing in its inhumanity, occurs in Bismarck's early correspondence. On 9 April 1845, at a time of great floods, he wrote to his sister: 'I am proud to be able to report that my rivulet [*Nebenfluss*], the Zampel, has drowned a carrier and his horse' (see Horst Kohl, *Bismarckbriefe* (7th edition, 1898), pp. 24–5).

patriotism'. This was strongest and most permanent among the Austrian Germans: German was the official language of the Monarchy, they held the central position within it, supplied the largest proportion of administrative officials and army officers, and felt as if they were partners of the dynasty—even a democracy is apt to assume the role or inheritance of its late rulers.[27] But the fact that the Habsburg Monarchy tended to show tolerance to nationalities which did not threaten its territorial integrity, even in 1848 very much sharpened the hostility to it of the extremer German nationalists, especially in the Czech provinces, and enhanced their desire to break up the Monarchy and engulf its western provinces in a united Germany, which would enable them to crush completely the Czech national movement: a program openly avowed in the Frankfurt Parliament. Naturally the danger of such inclusion made the Czechs wish for Austria's survival: they developed the idea of 'Austro-Slavism' of the Habsburg Monarchy reconstructed on a Slav basis. This program enjoyed the support of a great many aristocrats who were of very mixed national origin and talked at home German or French, but developed a Bohemian territorial nationality, favoured the Czech national movement (as dynasties, whatever their origin, assume the nationality of the country over which they rule), and demanded within the framework of the Habsburg Monarchy, autonomy for the Czech provinces, expecting to maintain their own primacy in the provincial self-government. When the Czech national movement assumed during the next fifty years a markedly democratic character, the Bohemian territorial nationalism of the magnates steeply declined.

The Magyars were at all times opposed to a federalist reconstruction of the Habsburg Monarchy which would have conceded territorial or linguistic rights to any of the 'subject' races, since freedom for the Czechs (the nearest kinsmen of the Slovaks), the Yugoslavs, the Ruthenes, or the Rumans in Austria, would have encouraged parallel movements in Hungary; and the Magyars, who insisted on Hungary's right to an independent State existence, within that State insisted on their own absolute dominion over Slavs and Rumans. They were bitterly hostile to the concept of a *Gesammtmonarchie* (a monarchy embracing all Habsburg dominions) upheld by the Vienna centralists, for which these tried to enlist the support of Hungary's subject races. Yet while all Magyars were united in the

[27] When in 1536 the citizens of Geneva drove out the Bishop and the Vidomne, they cried with joy, 'Nous sommes princes,' and proceeded to rule in an autocratic manner thirty surrounding villages.

defence of Hungary's constitutional rights and territorial integrity, the views on how best to secure them ranged from those of nationalists even more *enragé* than Kossuth, to those of the Old-Hungarian magnates who on a conservative basis wished to arrive at a compromise with the dynasty and the Vienna Court; and the less radical a group was politically the more tolerant it was as a rule towards the non-Magyar nationalities of Hungary: an early example of conflict between nationality and liberty, and, in the case of Kossuth, of a spurious reputation for liberalism.

In 1848 most of the Poles were hostile to the Habsburgs and the Vienna Government. They still expected an early restoration of a free and united Poland; in 1846 they had experienced the catastrophe of the West Galician *jacquerie* in which Polish peasants, incited by Austrian officials, turned on the Polish gentry as these were about to start an insurrection of a national and, in fact, democratic, character; and in East Galicia they were faced by an alliance of the Vienna Government with the Ruthene peasants on a socially and nationally anti-Polish basis. But even then there was a group of Polish aristocrats and Conservatives who aimed at a co-operation with the Habsburgs such as was established afterwards. And while the Poles continued to suffer persecution under Russia and Prussia, in Austria they attained a privileged position, enjoying after 1867 self-government and dominion over the Ruthenes. Consequently during the fifty years preceding the First World War, they developed a remarkable Austrian patriotism.

The Slovenes, Croats, Rumans, Slovaks, and Ruthenes or Ukrainians in various periods developed varying degrees of pro-Austrian feeling; but in time all these Austrian 'patriotisms' were disappointed, barring that of the 'partners' of the dynasty. No civic territorial nationality could unite the different nationalities of Austria-Hungary, for such community is possible only between linguistic groups acknowledging each other as equals, whereas the Germans, Magyars, and Poles claimed cultural, social, and political superiority over those on whom they looked down as 'a-historic' subject races, not entitled to an independent national existence. The Compromise of 1867 resulted in a division of the Habsburg dominions into three distinct domains: Western Austria of the Germans—approximately the territory which in 1848 these had wanted to see included in the Frankfurt Parliament; Hungary of the Magyars; and Galicia, which in 1919–20 the Poles managed to carry over entire into the restored Poland against the armed opposition of the Ruthenes.

## 8

In 1789 two nations on the European continent, Poland and Hungary, could look back to an unbroken tradition of Parliamentary Government, with a concomitant territorial nationality and a high degree of personal liberty for their citizens; these, however, in contrast to England, were of a single Estate or caste: the gentry, a very numerous body comprising about one-tenth of the population, yet an exclusive, privileged class. Towards the end of the Middle Ages, under the impact of German aggression or infiltration, the Poles had developed an early form of conscious linguistic nationality. But in their own subsequent expansion to the east they changed their concept of nationality: Poland and Lithuania, constitutionally united, became a gentry-Republic (under elected kings), based not on a common language or religion but on caste: the gentry-nation spoke Polish, White and Little Russian, and Lithuanian; in some western and northern districts also German and Swedish; and it comprised even Moslem Tartars, Armenians, and baptized Jews. Citizenship depended on being of the gentry, or being received into it. In Poland, in the sixteenth century, the official language was Latin, in Lithuania it was White Russian; and the Greek Orthodox and Protestants together may at one time have equalled in number the Roman Catholics. But gradually, across Reformation and Counter-Reformation and the Uniat Church, the overwhelming majority of the gentry joined Rome, and with Polish superseding Latin as the literary language, became Polonized. Similarly in Hungary the gentry-class was of very mixed national extraction, and its nationality was originally territorial rather than linguistic; the language of State and Parliament was Latin, and so remained till the nineteenth century, when a growing Magyar linguistic nationalism transformed the nature of the Hungarian State.

Had the landed gentry of the non-Polish or non-Magyar provinces remained united to the peasants in language and religion, the territorial nationality of the two realms might possibly have been capable of modern development and readjustments, and might consequently have survived. But when the deep cleavage of the agrarian problem became exacerbated by differences in language and religion, a joint territorial nationality became utterly impossible: Poland and Hungary could claim their historic frontiers only so long as the peasant masses did not count politically. Consequently the modern Polish and Magyar nationalisms, which were no longer those of 'single-class' communities but which none the less aspired to taking over the territorial inheritance of the gentry-nations, were driven into hopeless contradictions and manœuvres. In 1848 these two nations were looked upon as foremost champions of liberty and nationality: they had had within their historic frontiers a fuller and freer political life than most Continental nations, and therefore a stronger civic consciousness and patriotism; and now they were fighting the despots of the Holy Alliance to re-establish those free and independent communities; that these had in the meantime become social anachronisms and could not be rebuilt on modern foundations, was realized by very few among the men of 1848 in Western and Central Europe, and was never acknowledged.

## 9

The revolution of 1848 was urban in its character and ideology. It started in the capitals, spread to other towns, and was directed or turned to account by the urban middle-class intelligentsia. The countryside remained indifferent or hostile, or, if revolutionary, pursued aims extraneous and alien to the distinctive purposes of that year. In France it was Paris which made the February Revolution without encountering any active opposition from the provinces; but the June Days and the Presidential election of December 1848 disclosed the social conservatism of the peasantry. In Italy the peasants gave no support to the liberal and national revolution which remained entirely urban, while in Sicily and Naples the rural movement bore a purely agrarian character. In northern Germany the countryside was almost entirely conservative, far more so than appeared in the April elections, and Prussian Junkers, like Bismarck, chafed to lead their peasants against Berlin. F. Th. Vischer, a Württemberger who in the Frankfurt Parliament belonged to the Left, wrote to a friend on 28 May 1848: 'Here are Pomeranians and East Prussians, some of them hefty fellows with the best will who say that if we proceed too sharply, we shall provoke a reaction not from the Government but from the provinces. . . . A German Vendée.'[28] And there was more than one potential Vendée in Germany; while revolutionary agrarian movements—in Silesia, Baden, Württemberg, or Hesse—threatened to result in *jacqueries*, but were com-

[28] 'Achtzehn Briefe aus der Paulskirche', edited by Engelhaaf, *Deutsche Revue* (1909).

pletely indifferent to national or constitutional ideas. In the Habsburg Monarchy there was a strong peasant movement but again of a purely agrarian character: the leaders in the Austrian Parliament clearly realized that once the peasant was freed from the remainders of servitude and from feudal rights and dues, and was given his land, he would turn reactionary. On the whole Governments and Oppositions alike avoided appealing to the peasants, a dark, incalculable force which, if roused, could not easily be directed or mastered. Thus neither the landed classes nor the peasants had a share in determining the character of the revolution of 1848 which used to be described as 'the awakening of the Peoples'.

## 10

The year 1848 marks, for good or evil, the opening of the era of linguistic nationalisms shaping mass personalities and producing their inevitable conflicts: a nation which bases its unity on language cannot easily renounce groups of co-nationals intermingled with those of the neighbouring nation; and an alien minority within the State, or an intensely coveted *terra irredenta*, are both likely to distort the life of the nation, and impair the growth of its civic liberty. The alien community within the disputed borderland, hostile to the State and possibly plotting against it, provokes repressions which are apt to abase the standards of government; while fellow-countrymen across the border awaiting liberation keep up international tensions, which again are destructive of a free civic life. Moreover, the strongly knitted mass formations of the neo-horde are based on positive feelings which keep the nation together; but the negative feelings, which have to be suppressed within the group, turn with increased virulence against 'the stranger in our midst', or against the neighbour. Freedom is safest in the self-contained community with a territorial nationality; and where this has not by some miracle or the grace of God grown up spontaneously, it might perhaps best be secured by a transfer of populations. But it serves no purpose to expostulate with history: *on ne fait pas le procès aux révolutions*, nor to any other historical phenomena.

## VII

# THE FIRST MOUNTEBANK DICTATOR

Recurrent situations in history reproduce analogous forms; there is a morphology of politics. But to the basic repetition and the individual variations of organic growth an element is added peculiar to man: imitation engendered by historical memory. The modern dictatorship arises amid the ruins of an inherited social and political structure, in the desolation of shattered loyalties—it is the desperate shift of communities broken from their moorings. Disappointed, disillusioned men, uprooted and unbalanced, driven by half-conscious fears and gusts of passions, frantically seek a new rallying point and new attachments. Their dreams and cravings projected into the void gather round some figure. It is the monolatry of the political desert. The more pathological the situation the less important is the intrinsic worth of the idol. His feet may be of clay and his face may be a blank: it is the frenzy of the worshippers which imparts to him meaning and power.

Such morbid cults have by now acquired a tradition and ideology, and have evolved their own routine and political vocabulary. With Napoleon I things were serious and real—the problems of his time and his mastery of them; he raised no bogies and whipped up no passions; he aimed at restoring sanity and at consolidating the positive results of the Revolution; and if, in superposing the Empire on the Republic and in recreating a Realm of the West, he evoked the memories of Caesar and Charlemagne, the appeal was decorative rather than imitative. There would have been no occasion for his dictatorship had not the living heritage of French history been obliterated by revolution; but his system has left its own unhealthy legend, a jackal-ghost which prowls in the wake of the 'Red spectre'. Napoleon III and Boulanger were to be the plagiarists, shadowy and counterfeit, of Napoleon I; and Mussolini and Hitler were to be unconscious reproducers of the methods of Napoleon III. For these are inherent in plebiscitarian Caesarism, or so-called 'Caesarian democracy', with its direct appeal to the masses: demagogical slogans; disregard of legality in spite of a professed guardianship of law and order; contempt of political parties and the parliamentary system, of the educated classes and their values; blandishments and vague, contradictory promises for all and sundry; militarism; gigantic, blatant displays and shady corruption. *Panem et circenses* once more—and at the end of the road, disaster.

The first coups of Louis-Napoleon, at Strasbourg in 1836 and at Boulogne in 1840, were miserable failures, like Hitler's Munich *Putsch* of 1923. Both men were treated with humane and neglectful forbearance, and in the enforced leisure of their comfortable prisons they composed their programmatic works—*Des Idées Napoléoniennes* and *Mein Kampf*. Not even at a later stage did the political leaders realize the full gravity of the situation—thinking in terms of their own and not in those of the masses, they could not descry either in Louis-Napoleon or in Hitler a possible ruler or dictator. Louis-Napoleon escaped from his prison at Ham in 1846, and settled in London. On the outbreak of the February Revolution he hastened to Paris, a professed supporter of the Republic; but when requested by the Provisional Government to leave the country, he complied, and the Chartist crisis of April found him acting the special constable in London. In the by-elections of 4 June he was returned to the Constituent Assembly by four *départements*, but rather than face an imbroglio, he withdrew. 'When one is weak, one has to submit and await better days,' he wrote to his cousin Napoleon ('Plonplon') in 1844; and on 5 June 1848: 'In these moments of exaltation, I prefer to remain in the background.' Re-elected in September by five constituencies, he took his seat, and read out a brief address affirming his devotion 'to the defence of order and the strengthening of the Republic'. 'These correct words, spoken in a toneless voice, were received with perfunctory applause,' writes his latest biographer, Mr. Albert Guérard.[1] He looked

> disarmingly unobtrusive. His torso was long and his legs short; he moved awkwardly, with a shuffling gait; his head sat heavily on his broad and round shoulders; his countenance was pale and immobile; his eyes were small, heavy-lidded, of an undefinable grey. . . . He was not downright ludicrous; he was not exactly commonplace; he certainly was not impressive.

[1] Albert Guérard: *Napoleon III*. Harvard University Press, London: Cumberlege, 1945.

When the Assembly, enmeshed in constitutional doctrine and democratic dogma, decided to have the President of the Republic elected by popular vote, and not by the Legislature, the door was opened for a Bonapartist restoration. To preclude it, an amendment was moved debarring members of former ruling families.

> Every eye turned towards Louis-Napoleon, for the amendment was aimed at him alone. He went up to the tribune and, in a few halting sentences, uttered with a strangely un-French accent, he protested against 'the calumnies constantly hurled at his head', stammered, ended abruptly and shuffled back to his seat.

The amendment was withdrawn, its mover himself describing it, 'after what we have just seen and heard', as superfluous. On 10 December 1848, in the Presidential election, Louis-Napoleon received 5,400,000 votes against the 1,800,000 of his four opponents; Lamartine—poet, orator, and leader in the Provisional Government—found himself at the bottom of the poll, with a mere 17,000. 'The world is a strange theatre,' remarks Alexis de Tocqueville; 'had Louis-Napoleon been a wise man or a genius, he would never have become President of the Republic.'

'The remote lack-lustre gaze of his grey eyes, now that it was fraught with destiny, could be declared sphinx-like or prophetic,' writes Guérard. And Pierre de La Gorce, historian of the Second Empire, says that the change which success produced in the public estimate of the same traits of Louis-Napoleon's character was like a picture advertising a hair-restorative: 'before' and 'after'. Between these two appraisements, the taciturn, shadowy, impassive figure of Napoleon III has puzzled the century which has gone by, as the shrieking, convulsed, hysterical figure of Hitler will puzzle the one to come. 'A sphinx without a riddle,' was Bismarck's summing up of Napoleon III; 'from afar something, near at hand nothing'; 'a great unfathomed incapacity.' And N. W. Senior reports Tocqueville having said to him in January 1852:

> Louis-Napoleon is essentially a copyist. He can originate nothing; his opinions, his theories, his maxims, even his plots, all are borrowed, and from the most dangerous of models—from a man who, though he possessed genius and industry such as are not seen . . . once in a thousand years, yet ruined himself by the extravagance of his attempts.

But Napoleon III, said Grimblot to Senior in 1855, 'lacked industry and capacity'—and on this point most contemporaries are agreed.

> When we were together in England [continued Grimblot] I saw much of him. We have walked for hours in the Green Park. His range of ideas is narrow, and there is always one which preoccupies him . . . and shuts out the others. . . . He learns little from his own meditations, for he does not balance opposite arguments; he learns nothing from conversation, for he never listens.

And an unnamed friend of Senior's, in 1858: '. . . as he is ignorant, uninventive, and idle, you will see him flounder from one failure to another.' Guizot, Thiers, Montalembert, Falloux, Duvergier de Hauranne, Victor Hugo, Ampère, Beaumont, they all despised *celui-ci*; but the opposition of the intellectuals was tolerated because, as Tocqueville put it, their writings were not read 'by the soldier or by the *prolétaire*'; and 'the principle of his régime was to rest on the army and the people, and to ignore the existence of the educated classes'.

'Within the last fifty years', writes Guérard, 'Napoleon III has won the respect and sympathy of practically every critical historian.' Sympathy, perhaps; but respect is based on a man's actions, and not on his dreams and intentions. La Gorce, summing up a life's work, wrote about Napoleon III in 1933: 'Baleful (*funeste*) he was: still, hardly have I written the word than I would like to soften it, for he was good and even enlightened; but no sooner did the light break through than it was clouded.' Nor does Guérard's book, the product of years of study, yield a very different result, though the story is often lyricized, especially in an attempt to represent Napoleon III as a far-sighted reformer, a 'Saint-Simon on horseback' whose régime is of the most 'vital importance'. Moreover praise is offered of his plebiscitarian dictatorship, of 'direct democracy' as contrasted with 'parliamentary practices'. None the less, the picture which emerges of Napoleon III is hardly fit to inspire respect in the reader.

Guérard seeks to understand Napoleon III, but finds no solution to the enigma. 'His elusive physiognomy changes altogether with the light that is turned upon it.' His mind was 'complex, perhaps tortuous'; 'perhaps unfathomable, perhaps simply nebulous'; there was 'no flash of intuition, no capacity for sudden decision'. Princess Mathilde, Louis-Napoleon's cousin and at one time his betrothed, exasperated by his taciturnity, wished she could 'break his head, to find out what there is in it'; and both she and her brother, Prince Napoleon, 'ascribed his caution to mental hesitancy or flabbiness of will'. He had grown up 'in an atmosphere of elegiac resignation,' writes Guérard; and in his youth he was 'retarded in development, "gently stubborn", as his mother called him'. He was a 'damaged soul'. But, like La Gorce, Guérard stresses Napoleon III's 'profound and unaffected kindliness', his gravity, courtesy, and gentleness—'a man of '48', 'a democratic humanitarian'. In his own eyes Napoleon III was 'a providential man', 'an instrument of the Divine Purpose'; but even that faith 'was "gently obstinate", not blatant'. 'I am sure that the shade of the Emperor protects and blesses me,' he wrote from Ham in 1842. Even in his obsessionist ideas he lacked energy and ruthlessness. How then did such a man succeed?

By the time the Napoleonic disaster had assumed 'dramatic value and epic grandeur', in the late 'twenties, Romanticism adopted 'the Napoleonic theme', writes Guérard; and in the 'thirties the Emperor turned 'into a hero of folk-lore'. The July Monarchy, prosaic and dull, could not afford to dramatize conservatism without playing into the hands of the Legitimists, nor move to the Left, for fear of the Republicans; but they tried to surfeit France with Napoleon's glory, 'retrospective, and therefore safe'. As was proved by Louis-Napoleon's failure at Boulogne, this was then 'but a legend . . . something to be enjoyed rather than to be believed in or acted upon . . . a sufficient motive for a pageant, but not for a revolution'. How did it ever come to life? Even in the early months of the Revolution 'Bonapartism was advancing . . . with a strict minimum of ideology, organization, and expenditure'—'it held itself in reserve'. But had it ever more than a minimum of ideas and resources? To Guérard, Louis-Napoleon is not 'merely the passive heir of the Legend'—he reshaped it 'in his own image' and by his pamphlets

> created in the public mind that paradoxical association between Bonapartism and humanitarian democracy which was Louis-Napoleon's special contribution to politics. It was not exclusively the Emperor's nephew, it was also the man who had written *On the Extinction of Pauperism*, who was chosen by the people in December 1848.

'The chief quality in Louis-Napoleon's style is its directness. . . . His words are historical documents.' Not many who have read those pamphlets are likely to endorse such praise. La Gorce says that they are neither good nor bad, but significant; turgid, contradictory, and baffling, both naive and cunning; they develop commonplaces 'with a sustained solemnity'; but occasionally, he claims, there occurs an original idea. Some of us have failed to discover any. In fact, had the electorate been sufficiently advanced to read Louis-Napoleon's writings, fewer might have voted for him—but what percentage is likely even to have heard of them?

According to Guérard, Louis-Napoleon was elected on his own

program of 'authoritarian democracy', known, understood, and 'freely endorsed by 5,400,000 votes'. All political parties stood for 'the privileges of some élite': with the Legitimists the criterion was social superiority, with the Orleanists property, with the Republicans profession of their creed. Bonapartism, it is claimed, brushed aside the 'intermediate powers and special interests'—Parliament and plutocracy—in order to realize the 'unformulated doctrine' of the people: 'direct contact between sovereign and masses.' This kind of argument formed indeed the stock-in-trade of Louis-Napoleon. In his *Idées Napoléoniennes* 'the tutelary and democratic power of the plebeian hero . . . who was the true representative of our revolution' is contrasted with the aristocratic or oligarchic character of the British Parliamentary system; 'aristocracy requires no chief, while it is in the nature of democracy to personify itself in one man'. And the Second Empire in its depreciation of *les anciens partis*, its strictures on 'sectional interests', and its bombast about the integration of all truly national interests and 'the organization of modern society', is a forerunner of the single-party totalitarianisms.

But such animadversions on Parliament call for no rebuttal. Oligarchy is of the essence of Parliament which requires an articulated society for basis. Elections presuppose superiorities; these may be based on birth, wealth, education, service, personal standing; or the rise may be achieved through local bodies, party organizations, trade unions, etc. But acknowledged superiorities there must be: and these were much impaired in the France of 1848. Three years later their absence was adduced in justification of the *coup d'État*; Louis-Napoleon, in a pamphlet 'La Révision de la Constitution', which he sent to the British Ambassador, Lord Normanby, naming himself as its author, denounced Parliamentary Government as 'totally unfit for a country like France, without aristocracy, without bodies politic, in short without any local sources of influence or power except the creatures and instruments of the Central Executive'.

With such 'official candidates' he himself managed in time to pack his Assemblies. But in May 1849 the electorate, which had given him an overwhelming majority half a year earlier, returned an Assembly consisting of some 300 Orleanists, 160 Legitimists, 160 Republicans, and a mere handful of Bonapartists; 'partisan elections, worse confounded by local influences and local issues,' writes Guérard, 'were but a shattered mirror, and could not reflect the country as a whole.' Obviously millions of men, politically unschooled, will in a free election put their mark against the name they happen to know. Of the five names in the Presidential election 'Napoleon' alone had nation-wide currency; in Parliamentary elections a similar advantage accrued to the local notables. Louis-Napoleon's person mattered little, his pamphlets even less, and of his program only as much as could be read into his name, a greater engine of propaganda than even the modern Press and the wireless. Through the freak of a plebiscite the ghost of Napoleon entered the body politic of a sick, deeply divided community: the peasants were hostile to the big landowners and their exiled kings, and had no use for the urban bourgeois and *intelligentsia*; the Legitimists loathed the Orleanists; and everybody abhorred and feared the 'Reds', so much so that even of those who knew Louis-Napoleon in the flesh and despised him—the politicians—many supported him. They thought that because he was intellectually their inferior, they would be able to run him or get rid of him; the German Conservatives—Junkers, industrialists, generals, Nationalists—thought the same about Hitler. 'The elect of six millions executes, and does not betray, the will of the people,' declared Louis-Napoleon, nicely rounding off the figure. But too much should not be read by historians into that verdict.

'The workmen of the great cities', writes Guérard, '. . . refused to recognize the Empire as a genuine form of democracy.' Their strength and spirit were broken in the June Days of 1848, long before Louis-Napoleon appeared as the 'saviour of society' (Cavaignac was his Noske). But exploiting the feeble riots of June 1849, engaged in *par acquit de conscience*, Louis-Napoleon proclaimed: 'It is time that the good be reassured, and that the wicked should tremble.' And after the *coup d'État* his shady associates staged their own Reichstag Fire. There had been hardly any opposition, the workers refusing to fight; but as some kind of insurrection was required to justify the coup and extensive repressions, resistance was encouraged and beaten down. Next, an accidental shot on the boulevards provoked a fusillade; the ground was strewn with dead. 'These were not insurgents,' writes Guérard; 'it was a quiet, well-dressed crowd, which was watching the military parade as a show.' And the sequel? 'Mixed commissions', often of an atrocious character, condemned thousands of innocent men to death, transportation, or exile. Where was then, one may ask, Louis-Napoleon's renowned kindliness? He had written in his *Idées Napoléoniennes*: 'The Imperial eagle . . . was never stained with French blood shed by French troops. Few governments can say as much about their flag!' Not he about his own any longer.

The plebiscitarian Caesar 'had not grown up with the French aristocracy, the French court, the French army, the French people,' writes Guérard. 'He remained on the throne an enigma, an adventurer, an exile.' And like Napoleon I, he 'was saddled with the Bonapartes'. One of them, Pierre son of Lucien, was 'a fit subject for a picaresque romance'. But Louis-Napoleon himself and his favourite cousin, Napoleon, 'in their exalted sphere had in them something of the Pierre Bonaparte element: they too are disquieting, they elude normal classification; they are both Caesars and *déclassés*'; while Morny, an illegitimate son of Napoleon III's mother, and Walewski, a bastard of Napoleon I, both leading Ministers of the Second Empire, were 'the perfect models of aristocratic adventurers'. Morny was a man of affairs—promoter, speculator, and profiteer *par excellence*—'his secret information and his great influence as a statesman were freely used to foster his private schemes'. And he was not the only one of that type in the doubtful *équipe* of the Second Empire, which, says Guérard, 'was free from bourgeois pettiness, but also lacked some of the bourgeois virtues'. The view that it was not a régime but a racket is not altogether unfounded.

The gaudy Empire 'on its glittering surface . . . was a military régime'; 'the great reviews . . . were an essential part of its political strategy'; 'the days of bourgeois drabness were over'; gold braid and epaulets, much martial display, conspicuous waste and maladministration. 'War was made into a blend of the circus, the tournament, and the quest. There was a dash of gaiety about it all . . . the spirit of Cyrano and d'Artagnan.' Louis-Napoleon 'believed in the army, but not in war. . . . He believed implicitly that he was born a soldier . . . it was faith without works.' His technical knowledge did not prevent him from fumbling even in peace-time manœuvres. 'At Magenta . . . he was sluggish, almost paralysed. When Frossard came with the news: "Sire, a glorious victory!" the queer "victor" could hardly credit his luck: "And I was going to order a retreat!"' 'The Empire . . . in its warlike aspect was an imitation, and feeble at the core.' Napoleon III 'was unmilitary in his ineradicable gentleness. . . . A philanthropist at the head of any army is a pathetic absurdity.'

A 'philanthropist' and a 'policeman': for the army at home was 'a vast police force in reserve', 'held in readiness against any possible uprising of the democratic great cities'. 'Napoleon III the Policeman was not in contradiction with Napoleon III the Socialist'; 'racketeer, policeman, reformer . . . were mingled in that equivocal figure'. In the social reformer, 'the romanticist whose dreams were of the future . . . and translated themselves into terms of engineering', who realized that 'modern industry is collectivistic' and through the Imperial power wanted to give it a collective sense,

Guérard tries to find atonement for Napoleon III's failure in all other spheres. Still, the *éloge* is hardly convincing; Napoleon III talked the humanitarian jargon of his generation and shared its mechanic interests and hobbies, but no convincing evidence is adduced of original ideas or personal achievements. And, intermixed with vast unproven claims, appears the admission that his economic and social policies 'are no less perplexing than his management of foreign affairs'—which is saying a great deal.

For Napoleon III's foreign policy was shallow and utterly confused. He believed in peace and was out to tear up the Treaty of Vienna; he believed in nationality and claimed for France her 'natural frontiers'; he wanted Italy free but not united; in eighteen years he waged three major European wars and sent three expeditions overseas, without ever seeming to know what he was after. At first luck covered up, to some extent, his muddles and blunders. But after 1860 'the series of setbacks, wrong guesses, false moves on the part of the Government was unbroken'—Poland, Denmark, Sadowa, Queretaro, Mentana; the Emperor and his people were losing faith in his star. There was perplexity, aimless drift, and obscure dismay. By 1867 French hegemony was at an end; France felt intolerably humiliated, the Emperor was infinitely weary. 'L'Empire a été une infatuation,' writes La Gorce, 'il a été l'incohérénce, il a été aussi . . . l'imprévoyance.'

But here is a last attempt at justification: 'Everywhere', writes Guérard, 'in Paris, in provincial France, in Algeria, the true monuments of the Second Empire are its public works.' (Faust, who sold his soul for power, concludes his life over public works.) 'The transformation of Paris, his personal conception . . . was so nobly conceived that after half a century it was still adequate.' The pulling down and rebuilding of capitals is again a recurrent feature in the history of despots and dictators, from Nero to Mussolini and Hitler. Self-expression, self-glorification, and self-commemoration are one motive. But there is also a deeper, unconscious urge, born of fear: of things lurking in the dark, narrow streets of old cities, the product of organic, uncontrolled growth. Let in light and air and suffer nothing which is not of the despot's will and making! With Napoleon III such fears found a conscious rationalization: open spaces were needed for a 'whiff of grapeshot'. When his empire fell not one shot was fired.

The careers of Napoleon III and Hitler have shown how far even a bare minimum of ideas and resources, when backed by a nation's reminiscences or passions, can carry a man in the political desert of 'direct democracy'; and the books written about Napoleon III show how loath posterity is to accept the stark truth about such a man. And yet a careful examination of the evidence merely confirms the opinion of leading contemporaries about him: the enigma was not so much in him as in the disparity between his own spiritual stature and the weight of the ideas centred on him. Dream pictures are best projected on to a blank screen—which, however, neither fixes nor brings them to life.

How much can be safely said of Napoleon III? Biographers agree that there was something in him which defies definition and description: obviously the unstable, the shapeless, the void cannot be delineated. He was reticent, secretive, conspiratorial; at times his power of silence created the appearances of strength. Narrow and rigid in his ideas, out of touch with reality, he was a dreamer entertaining vast, nebulous schemes, but vacillating, confused, and therefore complex and ineffective in action. There was in him a streak of vulgarity. He was sensual, dissolute, undiscriminating in his love-affairs: his escapades were a form of escapism, a release. He was benign, sensitive, impressionable, suggestible, yet 'gently obstinate'. He talked high and vague idealism, uncorrelated to his actions. He had a fixed, superstitious, childish belief in his name and star. Risen to power, this immature weak man became a public danger. His silence was self-defence: to cover up his inadequacy and to preserve him from the impact of stronger personalities, of demands which he would have found difficult to resist, of arguments to which he had no reply; it also helped him to avoid commitments. Ampère describes him as 'what is called a good-natured man' in that 'he likes to please everyone he sees'. Tocqueville, for a few months his Foreign Minister, and Beaumont, an ambassador, were aghast at his vast chimerical, unscrupulous, confused schemes and ideas; when argued with he would keep silent without giving in—'he abandoned nothing'. He would bide his time—which with him meant inactive waiting without any approach to reality. He tumbled into situations, neither designed nor deliberately created by him. When forced to act, the day-dreamer would try to draw back: so it was before the *coup d'État*, and again in 1859—in fact in almost every crisis. But if the initiative had passed out of his hands he would drift anxiety-ridden, fumbling, wishing to call a halt, and mostly unable to do so. Under stress his personality seemed to disintegrate.

With all the pretence to destiny, he was personally modest, for he himself was anonymous under his great name. La Gorce wrote about him in 1933:

> He advanced towards greatness with a blind assurance which resembled both the dreams of a somnambulist and the mysticism of the predestined. And this prodigious infatuation offended less than one might have expected, for so much did this heir of the Bonapartes efface himself in order to derive everything from the rays of his name!

'Quand on porte notre nom' is a recurrent phrase in his letters to Prince Napoleon; but in one, written some time in 1848, he thus expostulates with his cousin:

> . . . you have sense and tact, and you ought to realize that it is hardly suitable for you to sign yourself publicly Napoleon Bonaparte, without any other Christian name, for you sign yourself like the Emperor, with nothing to distinguish you. And no one seeing your signature knows who it is. I always have myself called Louis-Napoleon, to distinguish me from my relatives. I wish I could call myself Louis-Napoleon Nabuchodonosor Bonaparte in order better to mark my identity [*afin d'avoir une personification bien marquée*]. . . . To sign Napoleon Bonaparte looks unspeakably pretentious—that's all. . . .

Two things emerge clearly: Louis-Napoleon's annoyance at his cousin's identifying himself with the Emperor, and the consciousness of himself being in danger of losing his own identity in such an identification. And indeed as Emperor he was like an actor surrendering his own personality. He became a screen for memories and dreams, with the caption: Napoleon.

# VIII

# UNE AMITIÉ AMOUREUSE

## FRANCIS JOSEPH AND FRAU SCHRATT

PRINCE BÜLOW wrote in his *Memoirs, 1897–1903*:

> Francis Joseph was human only in his relationship with Frau Katharina Schratt. I will add at once that the relationship was purely one of friendship. Frau Schratt was not merely a talented actress; she was also an amiable and agreeable woman, sprightly, gracious, and above all natural as Viennese women are. She kept aloof from politics completely, a fact which did not keep the industrious envoys of the smaller Powers from paying zealous court to her and with grave importance reporting her harmless chatter to Dresden and Munich. Frau Schratt stood in completely good relations with the Empress Elizabeth who was genuinely glad that her exalted spouse found, in conversation with Katharina, the relaxation and compensation for the checks to his policy and the terrible ordeals which he had to undergo in his private family life. In his letters to her, Francis Joseph always addressed Frau Schratt ceremoniously. In her drawing-room hung a large picture of the Empress Elizabeth who had sent it to this friend of the Emperor's.

But Bülow's account, which deals even with the style of the Emperor's letters to Frau Schratt, seems to suggest that 'the industrious envoys of the smaller [German] Powers' were not alone in cultivating her acquaintance. And indeed, Francis Joseph wrote to her from Cap Martin, on 5 March 1896:[1]

> My dear, good Friend,
>
> . . . I received your dear letter just as I was starting with the Empress for Mentone, to lunch at the Perimont Rumpelmeier, and so could not read the second half till in the pastry-shop, and when I communicated its contents to the Empress, who sends you her most cordial greetings, she immediately remarked that Count Eulenburg

[1] *Briefe Kaiser Franz Josephs an Frau Katharina Schratt*, ed. Jean de Bourgoing.

> [German Ambassador in Vienna] will prove dangerous to me. As you know, I have long feared it, for the Ambassador is very amiable, and much cleverer and more amusing than I, and will soon have ousted me from your heart. Thus I am constantly beset by grievous thoughts, and it is indeed high time for you to reassure me by giving me a chance to look into your dear clear eyes. . . .

And four days later: 'That Count Eulenburg should have seen you three times is too much for my taste.' Count (subsequently Prince) Eulenburg himself admits in his diary that at times he

> communicated with the Emperor through Frau Kathi in short questions and answers: whether this or that would be pleasing, or displeasing, to him.

The Emperor's letter of 5 March to Frau Schratt contains this further remark:

> Your views on the line to take about the Vienna [communal] elections pleased me very much as fresh evidence of your clear and sound political judgment.

Thus even at that time politics were not absent from their talks and correspondence; and with the passing years they fill more and more space in the Emperor's letters.

*Fragments of a Political Diary* of Joseph M. Baernreither, a Minister in Count Thun's Cabinet, 1898–9, is one of the few published memoirs of Austrian statesmen or politicians; he writes on 5 February 1913:

> Marchet [another ex-Minister] telephoned me today that he had told Frau Schratt about the warlike plans of the military party and she had said to him that she would speak to the Emperor about it at 5 o'clock today.

And on 8 November 1913, while the Emperor was in search of a new Prime Minister, Baernreither wrote:

> Frau Schratt proposed to the Emperor Baron Beck and myself. About the former, the Emperor's tone was not at all sympathetic. Of me, he remarked that I was a very intelligent man, and had many friends, but also many enemies.

'Frau Kathi' was not so completely a-political after all.

The first meeting between her and the Emperor occurred apparently on 20 May 1886, in the studio of the painter von Angeli and in the presence of the Empress Elizabeth, who had commissioned him to paint for the Emperor a portrait of Frau Schratt—a singular opening to a strange relationship. He was fifty-five, and she thirty-two; and their friendship continued for thirty years, till his death. The published correspondence consists of some 560 letters from him, which cover about 400 pages, though only very few are printed in full. But none from her appears in the book, except one, of February 1895, found in draft among her papers; yet they are essential to a full appreciation even of his part in the correspondence and friendship. Have they perished? The Emperor kept and treasured, numbered and counted them. By 15 January 1888 he had forty, and hoped that they would 'grow into a voluminous library of letters'. 'I employ my leisure in rereading your entire correspondence from the beginning,' he wrote on 28 January. By November 1888 he had one hundred, and still addressed her as *Meine liebe gnädige Frau*; but at last she changes into *Meine liebe Freundin* (and a few years later small crosses begin to appear at the end of his letters). On 10 June 1890 he announces receipt of her 200th letter. 'Your letters are my greatest joy,' he wrote on 9 May 1888. 'I await them always with longing and impatience, and always read them several times.' His own are worth reading for their cumulative effect, though except one or two, none, deserves being reread. 'You might ask why I write again, and I could really give no sufficient answer' (19 May 1887). 'I close this letter as I have nothing sensible (*nichts Gescheidtes*) left to say, and in fact what I have written is not very sensible either' (5 July 1888). He praises her letters for being 'so pretty and delightful', and apologizes for the 'deficient form' of his own (5 October 1888)—'I have no time to correct them', he explains on one occasion, and on another puts *pardon* against a blot. 'And now my paper has come to an end, and also my anyhow not very profound thoughts' (10 October 1889). 'I am constantly amazed at my ability to produce such long and empty letters, and apologize for their lack of contents' (10 November 1889). A correct appreciation—but what unfeigned modesty in one who had been Emperor for more than forty years.

Lonely, never sure of himself, and very seldom satisfied with his own performance, he worked exceedingly hard from a compelling sense of duty, but without deriving real satisfaction from his work. Shy, sensitive. and vulnerable, and apprehensive that he might cut a poor or ridiculous figure, he took refuge in a still and lifeless formalism, which made him appear wooden, and in a spiritual isolation, which made him seem unfeeling or even callous. Never in all these letters is there the least trace of pride in the part he had to fill, and hardly ever any sign of pleasure in it, except when he thought he met with genuine attachment from his people: human warmth and sympathy touched him deeply, and he seemed in need of them. But human contacts were difficult for him; and he disliked social gatherings and shunned 'clever conversation'. He could not, and would not, 'improvise': everything had to be fixed beforehand, and no freedom was given to thought or to impulses. This was not the rigid 'Spanish etiquette', as which it is sometimes described, but the self-imposed slavery of one painfully aware of his own insufficiency: and the heavy burden of the task, to which he felt unequal, he had to carry for sixty-eight years. But the things eliminated from his own life attracted him: frivolous gaiety, carefree enjoyment, sensuality, volatile moods, especially if rendered innocent by a basic decency. He found an unwonted release in his relationship with Kathi Schratt: and his deeper self—tender, immature, frustrated, and impoverished by lifelong imprisonment—appears in these letters.

How he loathed the publicity which attached to his every word and movement! At parliamentary dinners or public receptions he had to be amiable and talk 'with sparkling intelligence' (*und geistreich sprechen soll man auch mit den Leuten*), for 'all the twaddle I talk appears in the Press'. His one wish on such occasions was to escape—*aussi möcht i*, is his stereotyped phrase in Vienna dialect. Even more trying were the visits of brother-sovereigns. In October 1888 he had to entertain the speechifying William II: 'My toast at yesterday's dinner, which I dreaded terribly, I managed to deliver without getting stuck, and yet without a prompter. . . .' Similarly, when 'ordered' to give the toast at a family wedding—'I did it very briefly and, thank God, without coming a cropper' (5 July 1892). However pleasant his 'exalted guests' may have been, he felt ill at ease—*gemütlich ist die Sache doch nicht*. But the visit of the King of Serbia, in October 1894, was excruciating—'he continually asks questions and repeats the same thing ten times over'. (For once Francis Joseph did not realize that he was portraying himself—though on innumerable occasions he avows that asking tiresome questions was his own 'bad habit', for which he was 'constantly pulled up by the Empress'. 'Again a question,' he wrote on 5 March 1893. 'The Empress says that it may be an honour to be my lady-friend, but that it is *assommant*. . . .') Most of all he disliked the visits of women with a claim to intellectual distinction. 'I shall have to pull myself together; and appear highly intelligent and educated.' The wife of Charles I of Rumania was an authoress writing under the name of 'Carmen Silva', and she managed to inflict one of her plays on the Vienna Court Theatre: what Francis Joseph dreaded most was that she might come to its production. Her highfalutin exhibitionism grated upon him; he writes a few years later from Budapest (1 October 1897):

> The Rumanian visit passed off well and according to program, but was very exhausting. Carmen Silva, who was most amiable and very friendly, got on my nerves with her ecstatic delight at the truly excellent reception with which they met here. I naturally grew colder and colder, and almost uncivil. . . .

He squirmed at any display of feelings—what would he not have endured had he known that the story of the *amitié amoureuse* of his old age would one day be exhibited in print?

Frau Schratt, an actress of the Court Theatre subsidized from the Emperor's Civil List, tried even early in their acquaintance to gain his support in an argument with its director. The Emperor wrote to her in January 1886:

> I had meant . . . to speak about your business, but did not dare, since so far I have never meddled with the repertory or the casting of parts, as I consider that the theatre is for the public and not for me, and besides I do not trust my judgment in these matters. Moreover, I feared that my interference might place you in a false position, and do harm rather than good. But to please you I shall state your wishes at the next opportunity. . . .

A few weeks later Frau Schratt fainted in church in the Emperor's presence, and the next day he wrote to apologize for not having stayed after she had regained consciousness: 'I wanted to avoid a sensation.' In the same letter he reproached himself with not having had the courage to speak to her at a ball but he was watched from all sides 'through, or without, opera glasses, and the Press hyenas were about who get hold of every word I say. Well, I did not dare.' And on 21 April 1887:

> Forgive my having troubled you with my views about our friendship and the chatter of our dear fellow-men. I felt a real need to speak frankly to you about it. . . . Your honour and reputation are sacred to me above all, and I wanted to tell you how I endeavour to make our friendship, in which I see nothing wrong, appear in a proper light before the world, and wanted to hear what you think of my failure to do so. What you said the other day, and wrote yesterday, reassures me, and is new proof of your goodness and indulgence toward me.

30 May 1887: 'the three weeks since I saw you, seem to me an eternity.' 29 November: 'I would be happy to see you again, but of

course only if it pleases you, if you feel well, and can spare the time.' 6 January 1888: he saw her cross the square in front of the Imperial Palace without her seeing him, 'but to my joy you looked up several times, to my window'. 20 January: 'I could shout with joy at the idea that tomorrow I shall probably meet you again.' And next came a clarifying talk, followed by two letters. 14 February 1888:

> This morning I was overjoyed to receive your dear, good, long letter of the 12th. . . . The enclosed 'Letter of Meditations' made me immeasurably happy, and if I did not know that you always tell me the truth, I could hardly believe it, especially when I see in the mirror my wrinkled old face. . . .
>
> That I adore you, you must know or at least guess, and in me that feeling grows steadily. . . .
>
> So now it is out, and it may be as well, for out it had to come.
>
> But that's enough, and our relation must remain the same as till now, if it is to last, and last it should, for it makes me so happy. You say that you will hold yourself in hand, and I shall do the same on my part, even if it is not easy, for I don't want to do anything that is wrong. I love my wife, and do not want to abuse her confidence and her friendship for you. . . .

And on 18 February:

> . . . you again have scruples and a *panicky* fear that I shall think you a seductress and be angry with you. The latter is impossible, and as for the first, you are indeed so beautiful and lovable and good that you could be dangerous to me, but I shall remain firm, and since I have your 'Letter of Meditations' I am happy and reassured. Clarity is best, and even if it is perhaps not altogether proper, still it is better so, and it saves me now from my stupid jealousy, which often plagued me.
>
> . . . It has been snowing all day, and the mood is melancholy; but how jolly all this snow would be if we were walking in Schönbrunn, and if the slope above the Tyrolese Garden is again slippery, I might perhaps be allowed to take your arm!

A most satisfactory existence *à trois* ensued: the Empress publicly avowed friendship for Frau Schratt, while the Emperor revelled in the calf-love of a mid-nineteenth-century adolescent. 20 May 1888: 'Tuesday afternoon I had luck. Thinking that this was about the time for you to drive to the theatre, I kept careful watch'—and he saw her pass in her carriage: 'I then laughed with joy over your friendly greeting.' 24 May: 'The last two days were lucky for me, because . . . at last I saw you again from a distance, and I am most grateful to you for having rendered this possible by clever manœuvring. . . .' The moment he caught sight of her grey hat or her red umbrella in the square in front of the palace he would try quickly to get rid of whoever was with him and rush to the window to greet her. 'I remain in longing (*Sehnsucht*), attachment, and most devoted love, yours. . . .'

Then, in January 1889, the Mayerling tragedy broke upon them: the suicide of his only son, the Archduke Rudolph, together with Baronesse Mary Vetsera. Frau Schratt drew even nearer to the Imperial couple. 12 February 1889:

> I often think of you with deep love and gratitude, and we often talk of you. The Empress was glad to hear that you propose to come in the spring to Hietzing, because, she says, you will be nearer to us.
>
> I again thank you with all my heart for your intention to go to Lourdes. Pray there above all for our poor, dear Rudolph, the best of sons, and pray to the Mother of God, our Lady of Dolours, for the poor mother whom Heaven has visited with the greatest imaginable pain.

16 February 1889: 'Outwardly the Empress is quiet and only concerned for my health and distraction, but I can see she is filled with deep, silent pain. A great, rare woman!' 28 February: 'The sad mood continues. . . .I begin to worry about the Empress. She daily grows more sad and silent. . . .' The Empress had been ordered to go to Wiesbaden for a cure, but, wrote the Emperor on 12 March, 'stubbornly refuses to leave me before you are back in Vienna'. On the 16th, having transmitted theatre news to Frau Schratt (a frequent subject in their correspondence), he remarks: 'You see that I again take some interest in gossip. . . .' Next he went to Budapest for 'the manufacturing of new Ministers'; and in April to Ischl, to recuperate and 'shoot capercailzie'.

> So I drift back into my old habits and resume the old life, though things can never be the same.

She had her difficulties in the theatre, and he with his Ministers and Parliaments. The Hungarian crises loom large in his correspondence: a genuinely Parliamentary system rendered them more difficult to settle than in Austria, where Parliament, paralysed by inter-racial divisions, left the Emperor free to make his own choice; moreover, while in Budapest he had to communicate with her by letter. 'It would of course be splendid', he wrote on 13 February 1890, 'if you could come here, but how to find a plausible excuse, and our dear fellow-men would say that you have followed me, and probably invent some additional stories.' And another time about Press reporters: 'These reptiles are even worse here than in Vienna.' Frau Schratt did not share the Emperor's dislike of publicity and occasionally caused him worry by indiscretions. Thus she went up in a balloon with Alexander Baltazzi, a relation of Baronesse Mary Vetsera. The Emperor wrote on 7 June 1890:

> I cannot get over your flight. It is the first time . . . I could be angry with you, but as this cannot be, I am merely aggrieved (not offended). That flying is very rash, I told you before, and even the Empress, who fears nothing, thought it dangerous and wrong. Moreover, I immediately apprehended that the newspapers would not keep silent.

Here followed a selection from the Press.

> I know you too well to doubt that for you this was merely an amusement to satisfy your curiosity, but the papers . . . make it look like self-advertising and a bid for renown in an alien field, which fits neither your style nor your natural simplicity, for which I have the greatest regard. . . . I have never objected to your social relations with Alexander Baltazzi . . . on the contrary, I was grateful, for it enabled me in a difficult period to learn through you things which were of importance to me. That you should have undertaken the flight under his auspices is truly indifferent to me, but in the eyes of a wicked world this fact, picked out by the Press, will harm you. . . . If you should ever again think of such a silly prank, please let me know beforehand.

He was much relieved at her mild reception of what he later described as his 'wicked letter and bold remarks'.

Even ordinary forms of active sport worried the timid Emperor. The yacht of the Empress, he wrote on 5 September 1890, 'is already at Bordeaux, and so restarts the sea-voyaging, but for me constant anxiety and worry. . . .' When she reached Oporto he was relieved. When she left Algiers in a rough sea: 'I shall have no peace till I learn that she has arrived safely.' And hearing of some boating accident: 'It is terrible, and further proof of how careful one should be on the water.'

Frau Schratt's mountaineering, however mild, filled him with similar dread. 'No more glacier expeditions,' he begged. And next bicycles were invented: Frau Schratt and one of his daughters started cycling. 'A real epidemic!' he groaned. 'Naturally I worry constantly because of your cycling and other dangerous pursuits.' A few years later spiritualism and hypnotism became the fashion. 'This can only harm you and affect your nerves still more.' By 1907 there were motor-cars. 'I am less pleased with your having hired a car,' wrote the Emperor on 18 March, 'this causes me constant anxiety.' 7 April: 'That you should have met with a motor accident is disturbing, but was to be expected. . . .'

There was another side to mountaineering and cycling: slimming had become the craze among women. 'Don't forget to report whether cycling has de-fattened our friend (*die Freundin*),' wrote the Empress. Baths, waters, gymnastics, massage, patent medicines, glandular extracts, milk and fruit cures, diets, fasting—everything was tried by the two women: and detailed information was exchanged through the Emperor. There was daily weighing: 'I consider the weighing-machine nonsense and a misfortune.' Or again: 'I reported to the Empress that your weight has remained the same, whereupon she immediately inquired whether you were taking certain dangerous medicines, which unfortunately I had to confirm. . . .' Another time he begged Frau Schratt not to talk too much to the Empress about health, 'and above all not to recommend any new cure or remedies'.

On the other hand, a wellnigh comic importance was attached to eating. Thus with an invitation to tea: 'The Empress . . . asks you not to have too much for lunch, so that you should have a good appetite at five. Like all *Hausfrauen*, she has a passion for stuffing her guests as much as possible.' (On another occasion Frau Schratt is told beforehand that the afternoon tea will consist of cold meat and chocolate ice!) And when the Imperial couple went to Territet (his letters sound as if he had never been abroad, at least not outside courts), there were continuous reports on the quality of food and the dishes consumed. 12 March 1894, from Cap Martin:

> We are well, although we try all kinds of restaurants, and really eat far too much and too varied a fare. . . . The main purpose of life here is after all only in eating. With this sparkling remark I conclude my letter.

Altogether his accounts are of an engaging naivety. This from Cap Martin, in March 1896, *æt.* 65, in the forty-seventh year of his reign:

> The interview with President Faure passed off very well. . . . When I visited him in the morning at Mentone, rows of Chasseurs des Alpes stood from the Cap to the Hotel de Ville at Mentone, and cuirassiers paraded in front of it. . . . When he came to return my visit, he was escorted by a squadron of the cuirassiers who paraded in front of the hotel. The trumpeters blew their trumpets. It was magnificent. . . . At 7 I went with my three companions to the Hotel

de Paris, where we had an excellent dinner, as per enclosed menu, much better than at Noel's or Patard's.

On 10 September 1898 the Empress Elizabeth was murdered by an anarchist at Geneva. 11 September: '. . . with whom can I talk better about the noble dead (*die Verklärte*) than with you.' 16 October: 'I feel best in your company, for I can talk so well with you about the unforgettable one, whom we both loved so much, and because I love you.' He needed Frau Schratt more than ever. But soon shadows fell on their friendship. On the fiftieth anniversary of the Emperor's accession, 2 December 1898, an 'Elizabeth Order' was to be founded, and the Empress had promised it to Frau Schratt, who failed to understand that the Emperor could not now fulfil that promise without causing a painful sensation. Archduchess Valerie, because of a promise given to her mother, invited Frau Schratt to her country house, but the Emperor, who knew the real feelings of his daughter and her husband, advised Frau Schratt to decline the invitation—which she resented. Lastly, over some differences with the director of the Court Theatre, she sent in her resignation; and the Emperor allowed it to be accepted. She would now absent herself from Vienna, in bad health and worse humour, and make the Emperor pay for having displeased her. Undoubtedly he must often have been very trying—even *assommant*. He was an old dear but a bore. He was exacting in a naive way—he would, for instance, rise at 4 a.m. to get through his work, and then think nothing of asking Frau Schratt to receive him between 7 and 7.30 a.m. In Austria, on all levels, matters were settled by *Protektion*—but the Emperor, even if appealed to by Frau Schratt, would strive to decide them in accordance with justice. When the director of his own Court Theatre was allowed to flout her wishes, how much prestige could attach to being the Emperor's friend? Besides, their relationship, notwithstanding its innocence, appeared equivocal; and the Emperor was visibly embarrassed by what people might think of it: indeed, but for the encouragement and sanction given to their friendship by the Empress, he would never have dared to enter upon or to proceed with it. His attitude must have irritated Frau Schratt, free and easy in outlook and manner. And yet it is difficult to justify the callous and whimsical ill-humour with which she treated the poor old man when he needed her most.

He wrote on 17 January 1899:

> I have just received your note which distresses me all the more as I fear that it is I who have caused your nervous depression, and yet my intentions toward you are so good, and I love you more than I

can say. But I hope that you will soon regain equanimity and I shall be permitted to see you, for the hour which I spend with you is the only relief and comfort I get in my sadness and worries. With a heartfelt prayer to love me still a little bit and not to be so very angry with me,

I remain, in faithful devotion,

Yours,

FRANCIS JOSEPH

But her bad mood continued, and throughout 1899 meetings seem to have been comparatively rare. 14 November 1899: 'Your nerves must be in a truly bad condition if it took you so long to make up your mind to open my last letter. Did you expect something so awful in it?' On 27 December he asks her, if she feels 'a little more friendly and kindly' toward him, to send round her servant with a message about her health. Early in March 1900 his refusal to intervene in her conflict with the director of the Court Theatre seems to have produced a painful scene between them—Frau Schratt 'passionately and obstinately' rejected the Emperor's arguments and suggestions, and left him in an 'abrupt and deeply hurting manner'. He appealed to her once more:

> Think of the long years of our unclouded friendship, of the joys and pain which we shared—unfortunately more pain, which you helped me to bear—think of the beloved, unforgettable one whom we both loved and who is like a guardian angel above us, and then I hope you will incline toward reconciliation. . . . May God protect you, and turn your heart to mercy and reconciliation. . . .

Another year went by: highly strung, she travelled about Europe, planning more distant journeys—perhaps unconsciously imitating the late Empress. She had even 'the awful intention of going to Egypt', but first meant to come to Vienna. Overjoyed, the Emperor wrote on 9 December 1900:

> . . . if only it was possible to keep you here and put an end to your nomadic life, if only a way could be found to meet your—unfortunately undeclared—wishes, and to quieten you. . . . Your journey to Egypt you must drop in any case, and think a little of me, of my sorrows and anxiety, were you to go so far and was I to be without news from you.

After a separation of five months, he merely hoped that he would not irritate and annoy her again. But apparently they did not meet, and when in March she was once more in Vienna, he wondered whether he would be permitted to see her or even to write to her in future. And when in a letter of 5 April she asked 'why had it all to happen in that way', he replied that it was rather for him to ask that question, 'for you yourself had wanted things to happen as they did'. At last, in June 1901, he saw her 'dear, though not friendly face'; and once more he appealed to the love which they had both borne to 'our dear dead one'—'the last tie between us'. There was some improvement that summer; but she continued her travels, going even to the Canaries. He wrote before her return, on 12 May 1902: 'I am sad and tired, and you will find me much aged and enfeebled in mind.' He was not quite seventy-two, and had still fourteen years to live and rule. Yet he was old and weary. Their relations now resumed a more steady character. But the once frequent and chatty letters seem to have become fewer and shorter. Perhaps what had once been a passionate longing was now a settled habit.

# IX

# MEN WHO FLOUNDERED INTO THE WAR

## I. PRINCE VON BÜLOW

### I

THE German editor of Prince Bülow's *Memoirs*[1] writes in his preface:

> Prince Bülow devoted five years to dictating his *Memoirs*, and three further years to the careful, laborious revision of the text. . . . There was not a name, not a date, not a quotation, that was not verified repeatedly by the use of reference books. There was not a sentence that was not carefully weighed and pondered again and again. The growth of the work was considerably facilitated by the Prince's unusually powerful memory . . . a memory that hoarded not only historical persons and events, but significant quotations. . . . Of documents in the strict sense of the word there were very little. There were in particular few letters.

The dire meaning of this passage gradually dawns on the reader as he ploughs through the 620 large pages of the first volume. It contains little original material; either Prince Bülow failed to preserve it, or the choice he made for reproduction was singularly poor. Congratulatory messages from august personages and letters of adulation from subordinates take up at least as much space as historical documents; and the Prince's 'unusually powerful memory' fills the book with masses of insipid anecdote, of irrelevant information, and of tiresome literary quotations—the narrative stagnates, while the smooth *causeur* chatters.

[1] *Memoirs, 1897–1903*, vol. i., by Prince von Bülow, trans. F. A Voigt.

> Even when I was at school I had a taste, or a weakness, for quotations. When an idea came into my head I preferred to leave it in the form which some great prose writer or poet had discovered before me.

Throughout the book futile erudition is more apparent than thought—here is a typical passage, presumably 'verified by the use of reference books':

> The Cyclades and Sporades were settled by Ionians, the Thracian Islands successively by Athens and Sparta, Macedonia and Rome, Byzantium and Venice, and finally by the Osmans, and now a German ship was carrying the German Emperor past them to the former residence of the Emperor Constantine and Sultan Soliman.

The book might well have been written by an elderly lady-in-waiting, originally chosen for her looks, noble birth, social polish, and liberal education, qualities in which she herself took considerable pride; being observant, she picked up a certain amount of information, which, when carefully collated with more authoritative materials, may prove of some historical value; and having been dismissed from Court, she takes her cattish revenge by ridiculing her late masters and reviling her successors. But the author is the statesman who for twelve years controlled the policy of Imperial Germany, first as Secretary of State, and next as Chancellor. Something of this incredible production may be ascribed to senility, but most of it undoubtedly reflects the man's normal self. He had seemed important when in charge of one of the most powerful political machines ever constructed—but then how superhuman some one switching on electric light would appear to a man who had never seen it done, and knew nothing about the mechanism.

Of political thought and penetration, of a critical analysis of events there is nothing in this fat volume; nor is there a trace of real wit, amusing malice, or finesse. The account is crude, flat, and childish—an unconscious exposure of a pitiful set which ruled and ruined a nation, hard-working and intelligent, though uncouth, and, in a deeper sense, not altogether civilized. The insincerity of the author is transparent, and even more unpleasant than his incessant attacks on William II are his attempts at camouflaging them. Here is his account of a cruise with the Emperor:

> The weather was beautiful; the Baltic as calm as an inland lake, which was just what the Kaiser wanted. He was filled with a passionate love for the sea, but, like his mother, the Empress Frederick, and also like Admiral Nelson, he was plagued with seasickness.

Yes, exactly like Nelson. And then:

> . . . every naval officer would tell me that no one knew the naval signals better than the Kaiser, that no one knew the technical vocabulary of navigation so well as he, yet that he was quite incapable of sailing the tiniest vessel. . . .
>
> William II loved display; he used . . . to wear as many orders as he could. His self-esteem rose when he took a field-marshal's baton in his hand, or, on shipboard, the admiral's telescope, which, on the high seas, replaces the marshal's baton.

Although in appearance Bülow defends the Kaiser against the accusation of cowardice, he does his best to cover the All-Highest War Lord with ridicule. Here are a few examples. William II was fond of making presents of a picture in which he appeared 'with sword uplifted, leading his Royal Uhlans in a manœuvre attack'.

> This picture showed what he really wanted: a smart 'conduct' and a 'dashing' manner, but no real danger, no serious test. He never wanted to ride in any attacks but those made in manœuvres.
>
> These attacks were specially prepared for His Majesty. The ground was chosen months beforehand and put in order. The royal horses were taken over it till they knew it perfectly. As far as human calculation could foresee everything would go well.
>
> What William II most desired . . . was to see himself, at the head of a glorious German Fleet, starting out on a peaceful visit to England. The English Sovereign, with his fleet, would meet the German Kaiser in Portsmouth. The two fleets would file past each other, the two Monarchs, each wearing the naval uniform of the other's country, and wearing the other's decorations, would then stand on the bridges of their flagships. Then, after they had embraced in the prescribed manner, a gala dinner with lovely speeches would be held in Cowes.
>
> . . . this same Monarch, who . . . never had his fill of parades and parade marches, cavalry charges, and frontal attacks on the manœuvre ground, drew back when Bellona turned her stern face towards him and real war began.
>
> . . . a Prussian king who, in that moment, could do no more than apply his proved capacities to standing for hours at one spot in ignorance of all that was passing and in complete passivity, impresses one as a mockery of all Prussia's history.

Nor does Bülow, in a book which deals with the years 1897–1903, miss a chance of referring to the 'painful' subject of the Emperor's flight to Holland in 1918.

He makes fun of the Kaiser's 'unquenchable flood of eloquence', of the uneasiness felt by other sovereigns when exposed to his oratory, and of the way in which after every speech his entourage and Ministers had to try to prevent its being published as delivered. There are hints throughout the book that mentally the Kaiser was not altogether normal, but the suggestion is always ascribed to others, and loyally or charitably denied by Bülow. In 1897 Count Monts reported from Munich 'great joy . . . over the exalted orator . . . who is clearly no longer a responsible person', and the Chancellor, Prince Hohenlohe, anxiously inquired of Bülow whether he 'considered that the Kaiser was really absolutely sane'. At Jerusalem, when the Kaiser was about to deliver a speech in church, the Empress herself is described as casting 'anxious looks' at Bülow.

> She was evidently seized with fear lest her consort, overpowered by the solemnity of the moment and under the influence of the frightful heat, might no longer be quite in his right mind.

In 1900 Prince Philip Eulenburg, considered an intimate friend of the Kaiser's, feared 'a nervous crisis the character of which cannot be foretold', and in 1903, during a cruise 'on board this floating theatre' (the Imperial yacht), the Emperor 'made a terrible impression' on him—'pale, glancing about him uneasily, orating, and piling lie upon lie. Not healthy—this is probably the mildest verdict that can be given'. But Bülow defends his late friend and master:

> I feel bound to reiterate once more that I am firmly convinced that William II was not mentally deficient, but he was certainly superficial, hypersensitive to impressions, lacking in self-criticism and self-control.

The years of 1898–1901 were crucial in the history of Anglo-German relations. These were the years of Mr. Joseph Chamberlain's plans for a close understanding or alliance, of the agreements concerning Samoa and the Portuguese colonies, of England's search for a new orientation, 'splendid isolation' being no longer practicable. Bülow in his *Memoirs* refrains from giving an account of these talks and negotiations, nor does he explain his own, now published, despatches on the subject. But it is clear that he did not expect Great Britain to reach an understanding with France and Russia, that he suspected British statesmen of a design to use Germany as a cat's-paw against them, and that he meant to withhold German support till in a crisis Great Britain would have to pay for it any price which Germany might demand. Whatever part Holstein and the Emperor may have had in the rejection of the British advances, the final responsibility for it falls on Bülow. He prefers, however, to throw all the blame for subsequent development on his successors whom the Homeric scholar never names without an *epitheton ornans*—Bethmann Hollweg is always 'wretched and sanctimonious', 'clumsy', 'ineffective', 'awkward and simple', etc., etc. One wonders to what extent Bülow's description of other men is an unconscious, accurate estimate of his own self. He writes:

> When I look back upon these intrigues, so often petty, still more often spiteful and low, I understand everything said by great poets, from Sophocles to Shakespeare, and deep thinkers, from La Rochefoucauld and Montaigne to Schopenhauer, about the low instincts of mankind and the worthlessness of the world. Though here I must not forget to add that I believe things to be no better in other countries. . . . The reason of such occurrences lies as little in the form of government as in the climate or in the race; it is to be found in the baseness of human nature itself.

## II

The second volume of Bülow's *Memoirs*[2] is superior to the first. Some important documents are reproduced, and certain crucial transactions of his Chancellorship elucidated, while the worst literary tricks of the author are less in evidence than in the first volume; there are fewer tags and quotations, fewer irrelevant stories, and there is less of his loving abuse of William II.

Not that the tricks are dropped altogether. The Emperor, a 'gifted, nobly-endowed character', is shown sending the Tsar pictures by his favourite painter, Knackfuss, 'as his own works', or publishing under his own name Prince Eulenburg's song 'Aegir'. He was 'so lovable and so amiable, so natural and so simple, so large-hearted and so broad-minded'—'I loved him with my whole heart'. This does not prevent Bülow from gloating over his flight to Holland; from sneering at the 'Admiral of the Atlantic' who was unable to steer a yacht without bumping into something, and at the Supreme War-Lord who delighted in showy parades but feared war; and from describing him as a coward, a braggart, and a liar. One such lie Bülow, characteristically, reported to Dr. Renvers, against whom it was directed, asking for a medical explanation of the case.

> Renvers . . . answered: 'If the Emperor were an ordinary patient I should diagnose *Pseudologia phantastica*.' When I asked him to explain this technical term, he said with a laugh: 'A tendency to live in phantasy. Or, to put it quite bluntly, to lie.'

[2] *Memoirs, 1903–1909*, vol. ii, by Prince von Bülow, trans. Geoffrey Dunlop and F. A. Voigt.

But while critical of the Kaiser, Bülow seems unwittingly to emulate him in his conceit as orator, statesman, soldier on parade, and God's own chosen instrument. Here are a few examples:

> . . . the value of words is incalculable. I doubt whether, in 1906, we should have won such brilliant victories over Socialism if my Reichstag speeches of the previous months had not been circulated in millions of copies, and paved the way for our victory.

In a letter to the Minister for War on 1 July 1906:

> God's help has enabled me to guide Germany safely through the danger in Morocco.

To the Emperor, in November 1908, on the effect of some of his telegrams and speeches:

> The . . . distrust . . . evoked in all parties and classes of the nation, though it in no way shakes my confidence in God, in Your Majesty, and in Germany, compels me to use prudent tactics.

On a circular which Bülow had written and 'brought to the direct notice of the Emperor Francis Joseph':

> His Apostolic Majesty . . . certainly owed to it his power of resistance to the blandishments of the tempter Edward VII, whom he withstood on 13th August at Ischl far more successfully than did our mother Eve the serpent.

And here is Bülow at the Imperial manœuvres of 1905:

> To my joy, in the course of these manœuvres, the Kaiser permitted me twice to lead my old regiment past the flag—at the trot and the gallop. When after the march past I pulled up left of His Majesty with the regulation volt, Deines, who stood next the Kaiser, said to me: 'Your beautiful volt gives the Kaiser far greater pleasure than the longest memorandum you could draw up for him.' Later I greeted the officers of my regiment, many of whom, within ten years, were to seal with their blood their loyalty to King and Country. . . . At the end of these manœuvres, immediately after the defile, the Emperor handed me my brevet as General à la suite, with uniform of the Royal Hussars. Here is the text. . . .

These *Memoirs* are an incredible exposure, not of the Kaiser and of Bülow alone, but of Germany's pre-war policy. Were any justification required for Great Britain's attitude towards Germany during the years 1903–1909, none better could be found than in this volume. The exotic schemings of the Emperor, his offer of the old Kingdom of Burgundy to the King of the Belgians, his plan to force

Denmark into a political surrender to Germany, the German calculations how much longer they would have to mind their conduct towards Great Britain (*i.e.* how soon their fleet would enable them to assume a different tone), and, finally, the prospect of such power in the hands of a man whom Bülow himself describes as irresponsible and downright psychopathic—who, in view of these facts frankly admitted by the ex-Chancellor, can say that British suspicions and caution were unfounded? To the Germans, and especially to William II, the most innocent suggestion of an agreement for the limitation of naval armaments was an indignity touching their 'national honour'—the Emperor 'was set against all and every attempt at a naval understanding with England'. Meantime British statesmen quietly ignored German provocations and blunders. Thus Bülow himself writes after the Emperor's interview with the *Daily Telegraph*: 'I am bound to admit that, officially, the English remained correct and friendly.'

One of the most interesting chapters in the book is that on the *Daily Telegraph* interview—when the story is told in full, the Emperor comes out better than Bülow. The interview was written up, in the autumn of 1908, by an English friend from political pronouncements which the Emperor had made in private company, almost a year earlier during his visit to England, and it was sent to him for approval. The Emperor, very correctly, submitted it to Bülow who, instead of examining it himself, handed it on to some subordinates. These did not dare to raise objections to anything which came from the Emperor, and returned the paper without criticism to Bülow who released it without having read it. None the less he seems to have felt nothing more than a formal responsibility in the matter, and if hereafter he defended the Emperor, in however slighting a manner, he thought himself heroically loyal and made the Emperor submit to numerous lectures on his behaviour.

## 2. CONRAD VON HÖTZENDORF

FIELD-MARSHAL FRANCIS CONRAD VON HÖTZENDORF was born at Penzing, near Vienna, in 1852; he was educated at the Military Academy at Wiener-Neustadt, and as a lieutenant served in the Bosnian campaign of 1878. Subsequently, as a teacher at a military school, he wrote a book on infantry tactics which became a manual in the Austro-Hungarian army. In 1906 he was appointed Chief of the General Staff.

From the very outset he championed an aggressive policy, and hardly anyone in Europe in a responsible position during the decade preceding 1914 has an equal record of constant incitement to war. In 1907 he pressed for war against Italy, in January 1908 he declared that 'the problem of Serbia and Montenegro should be solved during the coming year by war; we could also deal simultaneously with Italy'. In 1909 he advocated the annexation of Serbia, and the fact that the Bosnian crisis passed without war and conquest left him with a rankling grievance on which he constantly harped. When in 1911 Italy had engaged on the Tripolitan expedition, Conrad demanded that advantage should be taken of her temporary weakness. Venetia should be annexed. Such a war, he argued, would raise the spirit of the Austro-Hungarian army, which 'has suffered from the policy of continuous compromise, hesitations, and concessions'. In the memorandum to the Emperor dated 15 November 1911, he demanded war against Italy for the Spring of 1912. Count Aehrental, though mortally ill, with all his waning strength opposed Conrad's policy of aggression. The Emperor Francis Joseph took Aehrental's side, and very sharply reprimanded Conrad for his 'continuous attacks against Aehrental', declaring the peace policy to be his own and telling Conrad that 'everybody has to accommodate himself to it'; however probable the war with Italy might be, it should not come unless Italy provoked it. The Emperor closed the talk with the pointed remark that 'up to now there never has been a war party in our midst'. Conrad drew the consequences, and his resignation was immediately accepted. On 30 November 1911 he was appointed Army Inspector.

In 1912 followed the Balkan wars, and on 6 December Conrad, who at that time had a warm supporter in the heir apparent, the Archduke Francis Ferdinand, was re-appointed Chief of the General Staff. He felt that now he had come into his own, and with increased zest resumed his war propaganda. In January 1913 he officially demanded a general mobilization against Serbia to be declared on 1 March and to be followed by war. He failed once more, as Germany refused to let herself be dragged into war, and even the Archduke Francis Ferdinand was opposed to it. Another 'chance' was missed to Conrad's intense grief.

When the news of the Sarajevo murder reached Conrad von Hötzendorf, he, for one, felt no need to inquire whether any responsibility for it rested with Serbia, or to make up his mind as to the course to be taken. On 29 June he told Count Berchtold, the Austro-Hungarian Minister for Foreign Affairs, that immediate action was required, and that it should be a mobilization against Serbia. Berchtold replied that he wished to await the result of the judicial inquiry; and this view, as he informed Conrad on 1 July, was shared by the Emperor, and by Count Tisza and Count Stuergkh, the Hungarian and the Austrian Prime Ministers. 'Tisza, he said, was opposed to war against Serbia, as he feared that Russia would attack and Germany desert us. Stuergkh, on the other hand, expected the inquiry to yield good grounds for action. I maintained that an energetic stroke alone could avert the danger from Serbia. The murder committed under her auspices supplied the ground for war.'[1]

'Material relating to time previous to murder yields no evidence of propaganda having been supported by the Serbian Government . . .', wired on 13 July from Sarajevo Herr von Wiesner, who had been sent by the Austro-Hungarian Foreign Office to inquire into the matter. 'Nothing proves, or even suggests that the Serbian Government had a hand in organizing or preparing the murder or that it supplied the arms.' But Conrad treated such evidence as nothing better than 'a preliminary account of the point then reached in the inquiry' into a question which he, from the very first, had settled in his mind, without any evidence whatever. In fact, his endless, wearisome, hackneyed references to Serbia's 'crime', to her 'brutal provocation' of the Habsburg Monarchy, etc., are nothing but his habitual cant.

His real reasons are acknowledged at the outset of this volume: 'Two principles were in sharp conflict: the maintenance of Austria as a conglomerate of various nationalities . . . and the rise of independent national States claiming their ethnic territories from Austria-Hungary.' Serb activities brought this conflict to a head, and 'for this reason, and not with a view to expiating the murder, Austria-Hungary had to go to war against Serbia'.

But even in the minds of those who professed the desire to await the results of the judicial inquiry (in the firm hope that it could be made to prove what they desired) the foremost question was whether, if Austria plunged into war, she could count on the absolute support of Germany—during the Balkan wars Germany had refused to support the war party in Austria. Berchtold's *chef de cabinet*, Count Hoyos, was therefore sent to Berlin; the German Emperor committed himself in his typically impetuous way, and an understanding was reached with Zimmermann, the Under-Secretary of the German Foreign Office, who henceforth co-operated with the most extreme war party in Austria.

[1] *Aus meiner Dienstzeit*, vol. iv, Conrad von Hötzendorf.

Tomorrow we shall have a reply [said Berchtold to Conrad on 6 July]. The German Emperor has said 'Yes', but he must still talk to Bethmann Hollweg. What will be the attitude of his Majesty [the Austrian Emperor]?

MYSELF: If Germany agrees his Majesty will be for war against Serbia.

. . . . .

COUNT BERCHTOLD: Tisza is against the war. He fears a Rumanian invasion of Transylvania. What happens in Galicia when we mobilize against Serbia?

MYSELF: In Galicia we shall not mobilize for the present. But if there is a threat from Russia we shall have to mobilize the three Galician Army Corps.

COUNT FORGACH: I do not doubt that Germany will go with us; it is her duty as an ally, and moreover her own existence is at stake.

MYSELF: When can I get the German reply?

COUNT BERCHTOLD: Tomorrow. But the Germans will ask us what is to happen after the war.

MYSELF: Tell them that we do not know ourselves.

But Germany asked no questions. Hoyos could report that she left Austria a free hand and would unreservedly stand by her. Tisza alone had doubts and asked questions. After the Cabinet Council of 7 July, in which all the others demanded war, he addressed a Memorandum to the Emperor registering his dissent. 'In all probability such an attack against Serbia would provoke the intervention of Russia and therefore a world war, in which case, in spite of Berlin optimism, I would consider Rumania's neutrality at least doubtful.' Altogether he considered the diplomatic position in Europe most unfavourable to Austria-Hungary, and urged that a moderate, not a threatening, Note should be sent to Serbia, and the possibility left to her to accept a diplomatic defeat. 'In spite of my devotion to your Majesty's service, or rather because of it, I am unable to share in the responsibility for an exclusively and aggressively warlike *dénouement*.'

Meantime the war party proceeded with its plans. On 8 July Berchtold informed Conrad that a short-term ultimatum would be presented to Serbia.

COUNT BERCHTOLD: What happens if Serbia lets it come to a mobilization and then gives in on every point?

MYSELF: Then we march into Serbia.

COUNT BERCHTOLD: Yes—but if Serbia does nothing at all?

MYSELF: Then we shall remain there till our expenses are paid.

COUNT BERCHTOLD: We shall put our ultimatum only after the harvest and the Serajevo inquiry are concluded.

MYSELF: Better today than tomorrow; so long as the situation remains what it is. If our opponents get wind, they will prepare.

COUNT BERCHTOLD: Care will be taken that the secret is preserved. . . .

MYSELF: When is the ultimatum to be sent?

COUNT BERCHTOLD: In a fortnight. On 22 July. It would be good if you and the Minister for War went on leave, so as to give the impression that nothing is happening.

Conrad cordially endorsed this view—'Everything has to be avoided which might alarm our opponents and make them take counter-measures; on the contrary, a peaceful complexion must be put on everything.' Therefore on 14 July he and the Minister for War went on leave, which was to be broken off in eight days, simultaneously with the presenting of the ultimatum.

Events and conversations are recorded in Conrad's book in a steady, indiscriminate flow, true to life; so that, just as in life, one finds it difficult to fix the moment when decisions ripened until suddenly they are treated as irrevocable. A week earlier the question of Germany's co-operation seemed in doubt; next the German Emperor was made to commit himself; and in the end his promise came to be considered binding on Austria. Berchtold, who went to see the Emperor at Ischl on 9 July, reported to have found him 'very determined and calm. His Majesty seemed for action against Serbia and merely feared possible troubles in Hungary [obviously from the non-Magyar nationalities]. Nor could one now draw back any more, be it merely because of Germany. Tisza pleads for caution and is against war; but Baron Burian has gone to Budapest to talk to him.' Finally, at the Cabinet Council of 19 July, Tisza agreed to war, merely demanding a solemn and unanimous resolution that no annexations would be made in Serbia—he feared for Magyar dominion should any further Slav territories be included in the Habsburg Monarchy.

The ultimatum to Serbia was postponed by a day because Berchtold preferred to wait until President Poincaré had left Petersburg. It was presented on 23 July at 6 P.M., and even before the prescribed 48 hours had elapsed, on 25 July at 8 A.M., on (uncertain) news of a Serb mobilization, Conrad was already pressing for a mobilization order: 'where strategic considerations arise, it is for me to make suggestions and the rest does not concern me.' The same night eight Army Corps—half the Austro-Hungarian Army—were mobilized. Then Russia on her part began to prepare for mobilization, declaring, however, that she would not actually mobilize unless the Austrian troops crossed the Serbian frontier. On 28 July Austria-Hungary declared war on Serbia, and Russia mobilized the military districts of Kiev, Odessa, Moscow, and Kazan.

On 30 July the German Ambassador informed Berchtold of the British offer of mediation *à quatre*, adding the urgent request of the German Cabinet that Austria-Hungary 'should accept England's mediation under these honourable conditions'. With this Note Berchtold, Conrad, and the Minister for War went to the Emperor. The question was discussed what demands should be put to Serbia.

> She would have to accept our ultimatum word for word and repay all the expenses arising from the mobilization.
>
> I added that territorial cessions would have to be demanded, such as would at least secure our military position: Belgrade and Sabac with the adjoining territory for the raising of extensive fortifications, for which, too, Serbia would have to pay.
>
> THE EMPEROR: They will never agree to that.
>
> COUNT BERCHTOLD: Further, Count Tisza has demanded that we should not ask for any cessions of territory.
>
> I rejoined that we could not stop operations against Serbia when all was in progress; it would be impossible as the Army would not stand it. We would have to tell Germany—if Russia mobilizes, we too, would have to mobilize.

The upshot of the talk with the Emperor is summarized as follows:

> War against Serbia is to be continued.
>
> The British offer is to receive a very polite answer but without its substance being accepted.
>
> General mobilization is to be ordered on 1 August with 4 August as the first day of mobilization; but this was to be talked over further the next day (31 July).

Yet it seemed for a moment as if the Emperor William thought of drawing back, and as if there had been a change in the attitude of Berlin owing to the dropping out of Italy. Conrad's representative in the Information Bureau of the German General Staff wired to him on 30 July after a talk with Moltke:

> Russian mobilization no reason yet for mobilizing; only on outbreak of war between Austria-Hungary and Russia. In contradistinction to the by now customary Russian mobilizations and demobilizations, German mobilization would unavoidably lead to war. Do not declare war on Russia but await Russian attack.

To this Conrad replied: 'We shall not declare war on Russia nor start the war.'

But a telegram received the same day at 7 P.M. from the Austrian Ambassador in Berlin 'dispelled our fears concerning Germany's attitude. We were informed that Germany had declared on Sunday at Petersburg that Russian mobilization would be followed by German mobilization.'

On the morning of 31 July I was informed by the Foreign Office that Germany would address an ultimatum to Russia concerning her military preparations. My above telegram to General von Moltke, dispatched on 30 July, crossed another telegram from Moltke received by us on 31 July at 7.45 A.M.; it ran as follows: 'Face Russian mobilization: Austria-Hungary must be preserved, mobilize immediately against Russia. Germany will mobilize. By compensations compel Italy to do her duty as ally.'

Further the following telegram was received from our Military Attaché at Berlin : 'Moltke says that he considers the position critical if Austria-Hungary does not immediately mobilize against Russia. Russia's declaration concerning ordered mobilization renders necessary Austro-Hungarian counter-measures, which is to be mentioned in published explanation. This would constitute treaty case for Germany. With Italy reach honest agreement by giving compensations so that Italy remains actively on the side of Triple Alliance, by no means leave a single man on Italian frontier. Refuse renewed English *démarche* for maintenance of peace. For Austria-Hungary enduring of European war last measure of self-preservation. Germany absolutely stands by her.'

I went with these wires to the Minister for War and with him to Count Berchtold, where we met Count Tisza, Count Stuergkh, and Baron Burian. After I had read out the wires, Count Berchtold exclaimed: '*Das ist gelungen!* (This is excellent!) Who rules: Moltke or Bethmann?'

Berchtold then read out the following telegram from the German Emperor to the Emperor Francis Joseph, received at Schoenbrunn on 30 July at 8 P.M.: 'I did not think it possible to refuse personal request from Russian Emperor to make an attempt at mediation with a view to avoiding world conflagration and maintaining world peace, and I have yesterday and today instructed my Ambassador to submit proposals to your Government. Among other things they suggest that Austria after occupation of Belgrade and other places should make known her conditions. I should be most grateful if you could let me have your decision as soon as possible. In most faithful friendship, WILLIAM.'

. . . . .

Count Berchtold having read the telegram turned towards me saying: 'I have asked you to come here, because I had the impression that Germany was drawing back; but now I have received from the most authoritative military quarter the most reassuring declaration.'

Thereupon it was decided to ask his Majesty to order a general mobilization.

This was issued the same day at 12.23 P.M. But meanwhile Conrad's telegram saying that Austria-Hungary would not declare war on Russia nor start the war had reached Moltke and elicited from him the following reply, received in Vienna on 31 July at 7.15 P.M.: 'Will Austria desert Germany?'

Conrad had, of course, no difficulty in answering this. Events had outpaced the wires.

For the time being Austria refrained from declaring war on France and England, not from any special sympathy, but from fear lest her own fleet should be caught unprepared. An interesting scheme was discussed of sending it, together with the *Goeben* and *Breslau*, into the Black Sea, where, by securing Rumanian and Bulgarian coasts and by attacking that of Russia, it was expected to help in getting these two Balkan States into the war on the side of the Central Powers. This scheme had, however, to be dropped because the Admiral commanding the Austro-Hungarian Fleet declared it impracticable and the fleet insufficiently prepared. Meantime Berchtold twice assured France (on 9 and 10 August) that no Austro-Hungarian troops had been sent to the Western front, though on the same days Moltke was thanking Conrad for the heavy howitzers sent to Belgium.

Moltke had recommended an 'honest arrangement' with Italy which would have secured her help at the price of the Trentino. At one time, but only for a moment, Conrad himself seemed to have dallied with the idea, adding that 'after a successful war one perfidy could be repaid by another and the Trentino could be retaken from the blackmailers'—with which the honest Moltke seems to have agreed: 'Once the war with Russia is finished you can always challenge Italy, and Germany will stand by you.'

On the outbreak of war, 5 August, Moltke addressed a cordial letter to Conrad which started with the admission that 'our proceedings in Belgium are certainly brutal, but it is a question of life and death, and who gets into our way has to bear the consequences', and finished with a hearty Teuton 'Mit Gott, mein Herr Kamerad!' The third postscript to this letter ran as follows:

> Gather all your strength against Russia. Even the Italians cannot be such mean dogs as to stab you in the back. Unleash the Bulgars against Serbia and let that rabble kill off each other. Now there is

but one goal for you: Russia! Drive these knout-bearers into the Pripet marshes and drown them.—Yours ever, MOLTKE.

In a letter of 13 August Conrad reciprocated these fantasies:

> Will Germany let the six English Divisions land on the Continent without a naval battle? It would be grand to catch the transports and sink them.

They were indeed to drown *currum et aurigam*; but failed to foresee which.

## 3. COUNT STEPHEN TISZA[1]

COUNT STEPHEN TISZA, Hungarian Prime Minister at the outbreak of the First World War, was the strongest man in the Habsburg Monarchy and one of the very few among its statesmen with whom even Germany had to count. He was at first opposed to the measures which brought on the war; what was it, that about the middle of July 1914, made him give way to Berchtold, Conrad, and other irresponsible warmongers? To this question even his letters fail to supply an answer; but they confirm—what was obvious to those acquainted with Tisza's views and mentality—that he did not object to a war policy as such, but to the moment chosen for action. He wrote on 27 August 1914:

> Twenty bitter years I was oppressed by the idea that this Monarchy, and with it the Magyar nation, were doomed, for the Lord means to destroy those whom he deprives of reason. During the last few years things began to take a turn for the better. Again and again joyous events awakened a hope of new life: a hope that history will not after all coldly dismiss us. Now, in these momentous days, the decision will be reached.

Thus to Tisza the old peace policy of Austria-Hungary, and not the turn which it had been given since 1908, appeared as demented.

Tisza, for one, clearly realized to what an extent the fate of the Magyar State was bound up with the survival of the Habsburg Monarchy. While the Dualist structure of the Monarchy and the Hungarian constitution effectively precluded any far-reaching Habsburg intervention in Hungary's internal affairs, it enabled Magyar

[1] *Graf Stefan Tisza: Briefe* vol. i, ed. Oskar von Wertheimer.

statesmen, leaders of a nation of nine millions, to rule the other nationalities of Hungary with a rod of iron, and at the same time to direct the foreign policy of a Great Power. One would search in vain in these letters for any trace of that 'bondage' which, after the war, the Magyars alleged they had lived in before 1918 so as to establish their alibi with regard to a policy crowned with disaster. It was the Magyars who directed Austria-Hungary's foreign policy; and, according to Tisza, they alone were fit to do so. Thus, on 11 August 1914 he wrote to Burian, his representative at Vienna (Hungarian Minister *a latere*): 'If the Monarchy is to preserve its capacity for action and its political quality, the deciding influence in foreign affairs has to remain with the Magyar nation.' But not in private letters alone did he state this view, which could hardly have been palatable to the Austrians; in a circular issued on 31 December 1914 to the heads of the Hungarian counties, Tisza inserted the following brief and significant statement: 'The power of the [Magyar] nation and its decisive influence on the fate of the Monarchy must grow in proportion to its sacrifices and exertions.' And at the end of April 1915, replying to an alleged message from Sonnino, he declared:

> The lasting friendship between Italy and Hungary is the natural outcome of common interests and feelings, and the preponderance of the Hungarian element in the direction of Austria-Hungary's policy ensures that her diplomatic and military actions will never be directed against Italy.

Magyar preponderance was the inevitable result of political conditions within the two Habsburg States. There were two Prime Ministers in the hyphenated Austro-Hungarian Monarchy and only one Foreign Minister, who was not a member of either Cabinet and in theory had to carry out the policy of both; but while Austria's internal incoherence and the decay of her Parliamentary institutions had reduced her Prime Minister to the level of an official (which he usually was by antecedents), the Magyars, by effectively depriving the other nationalities of Hungary of their due representation in the Budapest Parliament, had succeeded in preserving the appearances of a strongly-welded national State and in establishing a firm Parliamentary Government. The Foreign Minister could ignore the Austrian Prime Minister, but when on one occasion Burian, while he was Tisza's representative, was refused information even though merely about a matter of secondary importance (Berchtold feeling bound by a promise of absolute secrecy), Tisza wrote to Berchtold on 4 September 1914:

> I agree with you that the present case is of small practical importance. This does not, however, absolve me of the duty to emphasize that even the strictest discretion and secrecy cannot extend to the Hungarian Prime Minister. I, too, am responsible for foreign policy; it is my task, as representing the Hungarian State to exercise its legal influence, and I can serve only with a Foreign Minister whom I can fully trust to withhold nothing whatever from me.

By the beginning of 1915, in view of the negotiations with Italy, Tisza decided that a change was necessary at the Foreign Office. He therefore went to Vienna, and on 10 January informed Berchtold of what he was going to say to the Emperor: that a stronger, more determined man had to be put in his place. Thereupon Berchtold, 'in his usual manner of a good child . . . replied, laughing: "I shall be awfully grateful to you if you say it to him. I say it all the time, but he does not believe me. If you say so, he will".' The 'good child' now gaily left the Foreign Office, which was offered by the Emperor to Tisza. But Tisza thought: 'Also from my present position I can influence foreign policy,' and advised the Emperor to appoint Burian. 'I added, that it would perhaps reassure his Majesty . . . that he [Burian] agreed with me in all important matters, and was a close friend of mine, so that we were sure of intimate, harmonious cooperation.' And he advised Burian to have a special telephone connexion with him installed in the new office.

The war had broken out over the problem of the Habsburg dominions; both Italy and Rumania had territorial claims against them, but were bound by traditional friendships and economic ties to Germany. In these circumstances it was natural that the German Foreign Office should take the lead in the vital diplomatic negotiations with these two Powers; but if they were to be bought off, Austria-Hungary would have to foot the bill. Germany had no objection to sacrificing scraps of Austrian territory—the Trentino to Italy, and part of the Bukovina to Rumania; moreover, she desired concessions to be made by Hungary to the Transylvanian Rumans. Austria was a corpse, and the Habsburgs were always ready to barter territories—now they had their eyes fixed on Russian Poland. But Hungary was a historic and geographical unit, and to the Magyars every square foot of territory belonging to the Lands of the Crown of St. Stephen was sacrosanct; and though they had no feeling about Austrian territory, they resisted cessions to Italy and Rumania; for if once that game was started, what certainty was there that it could be stopped at the frontiers of Hungary? And as for interference in internal Hungarian affairs, Tisza, while assuring the Germans that he himself meant to meet the wishes of the Rumans of Transylvania, refused to have either the extent or the time of his concessions precribed by Berlin.

> I must ask you insistently [he wrote to Berchtold on 4 September 1914, in reply to German suggestions in that matter] not to take Tschirschky [the German Ambassador in Vienna] tragically. It is his custom to 'climb about on superlatives'. As far as I know, nothing as yet has come direct from Berlin, but even if it had, we could face matters calmly. Germany needs us as much as we need her. Threats between us are ridiculous. There is no occasion for fears. No one can value the German alliance higher than I do. We must render it most valuable to them by loyalty and the greatest possible exertions; German attempts at preponderance must, however, be met in a friendly, calm, determined manner.

In the dealings with Italy, the Central Powers had the active support of the Pope who, in conjunction with Prince Bülow and Erzberger, practically prescribed what cessions Austria-Hungary should make—not an easy position for the unfortunate Macchio, the Austro-Hungarian Ambassador to the Quirinal. On 9 May Erzberger wired from Rome to Berlin:

> Developments have convinced me of necessity definitely to exclude Macchio. Please insist that Vienna instruct him today to get ill. He must not leave his house nor receive visitors, or else he intrigues. . . . There can be no mercy or pity for Macchio, or regard for Vienna.

But next day, under pressure from the Germans, the Vatican, and Giolitti, Macchio made the concessions they demanded. These Tisza considered excessive; and, although they could not be withdrawn any more, he telephoned to Burian:

> . . . I request you to send immediately instructions to Macchio forbidding him to make further concessions beyond those authorized by us, and ordering him to try with all his strength to reach favourable results on open points, while maintaining positive promises he has made in our name.

And on 15 May Erzberger wired through the German Embassy to Father Count Andlau in Vienna:

> Best thanks for your successful endeavours. His Holiness thanks you most warmly. He has declared . . . that he must consider any withdrawal of these concessions by Austria as personally slighting him, for his Holiness has most particularly pleaded in favour of this Austrian offer.

After the efforts had failed and Italy had entered the war, the Germans accused Austria-Hungary of having lost the game by refusing cessions of territory when the Germans thought a bargain could have been struck; while Vienna and Budapest accused the Germans of having destroyed the value of any offer they could make by freely running ahead of it. It seems highly probable that this combination of Germany's eagerness to make concessions at the expense of her ally, and of Magyar stubbornness in refusing them, had the worst possible effect; but the game was lost beforehand. Small concessions could not satisfy Italy who looked to great gains, while large ones could not satisfy her either, as she could not have trusted a victorious Austria-Hungary to abide by such a settlement. Italy's entry into the war was merely a question of time, and it was likely to be encouraged by a Russian defeat, which would have endangered her chances. When once a problem reaches a stage at which contrary developments are apt to produce equally unfavourable results, it is doubtful whether any man can save the situation.

## 4. HERR VON KÜHLMANN

HERR VON KÜHLMANN, well known in London society during the years preceding the First World War, stepped for a while, in its last phase, into the very forefront of international politics, achieving considerable though ephemeral prominence. His *Memoirs*, published in 1949,[1] even in this country gained a measure of recognition apt to endow them with undeserved credence. In the *Spectator* of 24 June 1949, Sir Harold Nicolson attributed 'great historical importance' to 'this calm, serious, saddened, and in some way honourable book'; while the reviewer in *The Times Literary Supplement* of 30 September called it a 'revealing book which historians of the period 1905–18 cannot well leave unread'—'it shows how near its author came to the attainment of aims that would have left Great Britain friendless and discredited in a Europe and a world made safe for Germany.' Revealing this autobiography certainly is as a self-exposure, and as such deserves being read; but it cannot be admitted in evidence. Trifling and self-important, suffused with the malignancy of a frustrated intriguer, these *Memoirs* if accepted would be more damaging to the men Kühlmann commends than to those whom he tries to disparage. But his inaccuracy in matters big and

[1] *Erinnerungen*, Richard von Kühlmann.

small—the result of a failing memory, of slovenly workmanship, and of an innate disregard of truth—eliminates him as a witness: on closer examination many of the transactions remembered by him in great and lively detail, change into mere comic potpourris, which must not be allowed to gain currency even in the lighter type of historical literature. It is stated by the publisher that Kühlmann died before he could revise his proofs, and that only obvious errors were corrected ('and not nearly all of these', adds the reviewer in *The Times Literary Supplement*); but had all been removed, the remnants of the book might no longer have been fit for publication.

There is a deceptive façade to these *Memoirs*, as there was to their author. Contemporaries knew him for an 'entirely unscrupulous intriguer'[2]—a judgment confirmed by his autobiography; but they credited him with a first-rate brain—'of his ability as a diplomatist there can be no doubt,' writes Lloyd George in his *War Memoirs*.[3] Yet his contemporary dispatches, published in the *Grosse Politik*, are nowise remarkable, while even his earlier books lack poise, depth, and judgment, and sometimes descend to puerility. As an author he falls into one class with the Kaiser and Bülow: a representative of the *Wilhelminische Aera*.

Richard von Kühlmann, the son of a German director of the Anatolian Railways, was born in Constantinople, in 1873; entered the German diplomatic service in 1899;[4] was Secretary at the Tangier Legation, 1903–5; Counsellor at the London Embassy, 1909–14; State Secretary from August 1917 till 9 July 1918, and chief German delegate to the peace conferences of Brest-Litovsk and Bucharest. At these historical junctures in his career, his chiefs happened to be absent or weak, or at least not equal to their forceful assistant. At the age of thirty-one, as Chargé d'Affaires at Tangier, he played a busy part in the first Morocco crisis, and at forty-four virtually directed Germany's foreign policy, Kaiser and Army Command permitting. But dismissed in 1918, he lived another thirty years without re-entering politics: not for the lack of trying. One such attempt attained publicity. In 1929, while the Young Plan for

[2] See the note 'An Ephemeral Career', in *The Times* of 11 July 1918. On the role he played at the London Embassy see Asquith, *The Genesis of the War*, p. 105. Even Sir Harold Nicolson, though lenient to him, describes him as 'not too scrupulous'—'a remarkable man' possessed of 'intelligence unaccompanied by strength of character.'

[3] Vol. iv, p. 2082.

[4] Hardly any dates are given in Kühlmann's *Memoirs*, and his entry in *Wer ist's?* (the German *Who's Who*) supplies a list of his decorations, but no proper service record. The above date, computed on the basis of his narrative, may be merely approximately correct.

German reparations was being settled in Paris, Kühlmann approached the British Ambassador, Lord Tyrrell, with his pet idea of colonies for Germany. But he overreached himself when he followed up the talks with a letter; this, duly transmitted to London, produced an angry communication from Austen Chamberlain to Stresemann, who replied by completely disavowing Kühlmann's unauthorized activities and unwarranted intrusion.[5] It was perhaps the hope of a come-back, joined to easy financial circumstances, which made him keep silent in the 1920's when others rushed into print with their memoirs: the Kaiser, Bülow, Bethmann Hollweg, Hertling,[6] and Lichnowsky, Hindenburg, Ludendorff, Tirpitz, and Hoffman, Erzberger and Scheidemann, Czernin, Burian, and Conrad von Hötzendorf, or even secondary figures such as Schoen, Eckardstein, Musulin, J. Andrassy jun., Arz, Auffenberg, etc. All that Kühlmann published in the interwar period was several excursions into history and politics, superficial even when plausible,[7] flimsy,[8] or primitive to a staggering degree.[9] He prided himself on his historical erudition: 'I could never resist the temptation to get to understand the present in the light of the past.'

In 1943, at the age of seventy, he started writing his autobiography, finishing it in September 1944. By the time Hitler was tottering, Kühlmann obviously felt it opportune to relate how he had tried to stave off the First World War, and next to bring it to a timely close; how he had endeavoured to secure a glorious future for Germany in Central Africa; how he very nearly saved both her and the world from the disasters which have befallen them since; and how he was frustrated. It were a pity had he not gone on record: for at certain crucial moments he did get hold of the right end of the stick, and without knowledge of the man it might seem strange that after having risen so high he achieved so little, and that he went down never to emerge again.

So-called humour has its stereotypes. Some fifty years ago, Central European comic papers of the genteel, bourgeois variety went in for stories about the ageing spinster and the absent-minded professor, while inferior productions would sport, for instance, the vulgar figure of a semi-Balkanic commercial traveller. Herr von Kühlmann,

[5] See *Gustav Stresemann, His Diaries, Letters, and Papers*, vol. iii (1940), pp. 424–9.

[6] The book, *Ein Jahr in der Reichskanzelei*, is actually by Hertling's son.

[7] *Thoughts on Germany* (German editions 1931 and 1933; English edition 1932).

[8] *Die Diplomaten* (1939), with a chapter on duorations.

[9] *The Heritage of Yesterday* (German edition 1936; English edition 1938)

on his own level, somehow manages to recall that unattractive type and his enjoyments. Not that there is anything improper in his book —it is his personality, polished yet crude and gross, that offends. He unconsciously depicts himself in writing of a friend: 'When he spoke of truffles in red wine, his eye of a poet would shine just as when he described the beauty of a divine woman.' Food, women, and the splendour of rich houses and luxury hotels is what Herr von Kühlmann seems to remember best, seeing himself as a refined *bon viveur*, a sportsman and traveller, a man of the great world, and an art connoisseur and collector. In short, here are 581 pages of 'high life', decked with the appropriate adjectives and clichés. Every woman is beautiful and accomplished—*schön, reizend, charmant, elegant,* (though of one he says that she was 'really very beautiful'); the meals which his memory treasures are rich, succulent, delectable; while the houses he visited are described in the language of a classy house-agent or auctioneer. Nor is the reader ever allowed to forget Kühlmann's interest in art, 'which invariably absorbed a substantial part of my working powers'.

The least part of Kühlmann's laudations goes to his chiefs. His first post was St. Petersburg, where Prince Radolin, a friend of his father's, treated him with wellnigh 'parental kindness'. A *grand seigneur*, 'kind and soft, and without any sharpness or hard precisions', Radolin, according to Kühlmann, owed 'his, after all unusually brilliant career' to the sinister Holstein, whose confidential letters he would read out to Kühlmann 'under seal of secrecy'. Similarly, at a later date in Paris, Radolin is shown having regular confabulations with Kühlmann, kept secret especially from the Counsellor of the Embassy. With Kühlmann there is usually someone to be short-circuited or circumvented.

His next chief, Count Rex at Teheran, is merely seen worrying lest that 'exile' might be his last diplomatic post. In 1903 followed a short assignment to London, and Count Metternich, under whom Kühlmann was to serve again 1909–12, comes in for a first dose of disparagement. His week-ends lasted four or five days; he would take holidays to shoot in Scotland or recuperate on the South Coast; but packets of blank sheets, signed in various places, were left to be filled in with non-committal stuff by his officials. On his return he would dictate brilliant dispatches. 'Were it sufficient in a diplomatist to write courageous and accurate reports, Count Paul Metternich would have to be placed among the remarkable diplomatists of his time'; but 'the essential part of an Ambassador's task consists in inducing correct decisions at home', while, by gaining influence with the leading men where accredited, he should 'carry on an active, constructive, go-ahead policy'. 'In that matter an appraisal of Metternich's activities in England would yield less favourable results.'

Kühlmann's next post was Tangier. The Minister, Freiherr von Mentzingen, was 'an experienced, painstaking diplomat, probably too painstaking'—he lacked 'wider horizons' or any desire 'to assume responsibilities'. Instead of intriguing against France he tried to see justice done to German subjects by the Shereefian Government.

> All my endeavours to convince him how inopportune his policy was just at that time, and all attempts, partly made through his charming wife and his clever mother-in-law, to deflect him from that course, proved unavailing.

But Mentzingen soon went on leave, not to return. 'I never had . . . any conflicts with him'; but may not Kühlmann have had a hand in this timely disappearance?

1906: Washington. Freiherr Speck von Sternburg, a cavalry officer, had in 1898, as German Military Attaché, helped Theodore Roosevelt with his Rough Riders. To please him when President, Speck was appointed Ambassador. 'I was never able to detect a great politician in him.' 1907–09: at The Hague, where the Minister, Herr von Schlözer, was 'an amiable man, devoid of political passions'; and was rescued by Kühlmann from comic embarrassments caused to him by the Kaiser's visit to Holland.

And then back to London, to the lonely bachelor and morose hypochondriac Metternich, who, when things grew critical, would do nothing but 'sit passive with folded arms'. Hence a cleavage arose between them—but never 'any controversy or even argument'; Kühlmann would merely do things behind the Ambassador's back, or try to short-circuit him. Here is a typical tale. Kühlmann was attending a fashionable wedding in Berlin at a date unnamed, but ascertainable through the Gotha Almanac as 12 March 1912. During the 'excellent wedding dinner', he was summoned to the State Secretary, Herr von Kiderlen-Wächter, who made him report on the situation in London; and agreeing with his conclusions, took him, in spite of the late hour, to the Chancellor Bethmann Hollweg. It was decided that Kühlmann should the next day return to London and seek an interview with Haldane (this was a month after Haldane's 'mission' to Berlin). 'The Chancellor added quite casually: "Please also inform the Ambassador of what was settled today."' But on hearing Kühlmann's report Metternich's face darkened visibly, and

> he said somewhat abruptly: 'Obviously they told you that I myself should discuss the matter with Haldane.' I replied that nothing of the kind had been said. . . . Still, if he desired to make the communication, I would comply with his wish.

And next Kühlmann was reprimanded from Berlin for his claim to deal with Haldane himself—'which did not impress me with Bethmann Hollweg's strength of character'. The new draft for a German-British agreement, brought by him from Berlin, is printed in the *Grosse Politik*,[10] which also shows that on 14 March—possibly before his return—Metternich saw Grey in the presence of Haldane, and was given a draft approved by the British Cabinet:[11] it is difficult to see how he could have let Kühlmann handle the German counter-proposals.

Metternich was informed at the end of April 1912 that he would be recalled from London, and left early in June. His successor, Freiherr Marschall von Bieberstein, arrived at the end of the month, and in August went home for a holiday: he died in September. 'I am convinced even now', writes Kühlmann, 'that he would have been able to prevent the outbreak of the World War'—'he had the advantage of working in London on ground which was well prepared' (obviously not by Metternich). But then came Prince Lichnowsky, who had made his career 'under the wing of Princess Marie von Bülow'—

> a *grand seigneur* whose forte was magnificent entertainments and an amiable personality. . . . Brilliant dinners, and a number of footmen and butlers, surprising even for English conditions, dressed in splendid, absolutely correct, liveries, masses of silver and flowers, soon became the talk of the town among the upper classes.

But what were his qualifications as Ambassador? Sir Edward Grey, writes Kühlmann, once asked permission

> to put to me a somewhat delicate question, fully relying on my discretion. . . . He was in the habit of dictating minutes of conversations while these were fresh in his memory. . . . So he did also after visits from Prince Lichnowsky. But he thought he had noticed that the Prince was 'most inaccurate' about particulars, and therefore asked permission to submit to me his minutes of conversations with the Prince: I should tell him whether he had correctly understood the Ambassador. . . . I agreed to this being done. But in the few months which separated us from the outbreak of war, it never so happened that Grey asked me to examine his notes.

[10] Vol. xxxi, pp. 167–9.

[11] Ibid., p. 178.

The concluding statement would seem the most credible part of the story.

In August 1914 Kühlmann was sent to Stockholm, where the burden of work and responsibility seemed too great for the German Minister, Herr von Reichenau: while in Brazil he had suffered a severe sunstroke.

> I received a secret instruction to take as much as possible off his shoulders and to keep a watchful eye on him. Should I find that his nerves were no longer equal to the task . . . he would be sent on sick-leave and I would carry on as Chargé d'Affaires.

Two months later Kühlmann was transferred to Constantinople, only to find that his new mission resembled his previous one.

> Baron Wangenheim was apparently thought to be highly strung, and a robust assistant was deemed necessary. Much importance was attached in Berlin to bringing Turkey into the war, and it was felt that the Ambassador was remiss in pressing the matter. Still, to my great relief, I was not expected, as in Sweden, to take over if I thought it necessary, but to try, with the utmost consideration for Wangenheim, to overcome his inhibitions.

And so Turkey was brought into the war; 'the Ambassador was inwardly pleased when it was accomplished without his having had to take the crucial decision'; and Kühlmann's relations with him remained 'perfectly harmonious'. Wangenheim was Kühlmann's tenth and last diplomatic chief, and looking back at the series one can merely wonder at the dictum in his *Thoughts on Germany* (p. 68): 'Our pre-war diplomacy was at least equal to the average of the diplomats of other countries.'

Kühlmann's next post was that of Minister to The Hague, from April 1915 till September 1916, when he returned as Ambassador to Constantinople: but this period seems blacked-out or confused in his memory—he mumbles something about The Hague, and then passes straight on to the final phase of his career. Bethmann Hollweg and his Secretary of State having resigned in July 1917, the new Chancellor, Michaelis, 'persuaded' Kühlmann to accept the Foreign Office. 'After we had reached basic agreement on the broad principles . . . Michaelis, I can truly say, left me completely independent in the conduct of foreign policy.' Even so he does not escape censure for 'political disloyalty', which 'unfavourably affected' Kühlmann's judgment of his character. By October, Michaelis got into difficulties with the Reichstag, and asked Kühlmann, on the point of going with the Emperor to Constantinople, to intervene in a stormy debate. Kühlmann took the opportunity to deliver

> a serious and sharp speech about Alsace-Lorraine, which concluded with a most heartfelt 'never'. . . . The Reichstag was deeply impressed and seemingly reunited . . . by this appeal to its patriotic feelings. . . . As I descended the great staircase . . . I was surrounded by crowds of members . . . who excitedly . . . argued that the political position of the Chancellor . . was too seriously affected by that most unfortunate debate, for him to remain in office . . . and begged me to report to the Emperor accordingly.

At that time 'the idea seems to have arisen in certain Parliamentary circles, probably in connexion with my speech on Alsace-Lorraine, that I should be his successor. No such thoughts entered my head.' And so, wholly disinterested, Kühlmann took the first opportunity to report against his chief, and to tell the Emperor

> that the leaders of the most important majority parties had asked me, before I left, to submit to him that in their opinion there was no chance of further fruitful co-operation with Chancellor Michaelis.

His successor, Count von Hertling, like Kühlmann a Bavarian,

> from the first moment left me, I can truly say, in completely sovereign direction of foreign affairs, and never during the whole period of our collaboration was there the least, even momentary, clouding of relations between us.

These were 'absolutely harmonious'; 'the aged Chancellor', who complained that at such a time he, 'a worn-out Professor of Philosophy', should be burdened with that office, in private conversation frequently spoke of Kühlmann as his successor. But at the end of June the 'demi-gods' of the Army Command, Hindenburg and Ludendorff, demanded Kühlmann's dismissal. He, when told by the Emperor that their 'paths must part', pleaded the need of being allowed to bring to some conclusion secret peace talks which he claimed to have started with London. Finding that the decision was final, he felt that this would cost the Emperor his Crown.

Thus in a diplomatic career of almost twenty years, Kühlmann had but two chiefs he fully approved of: one who died soon, and the other who was 'dead above ground'.

In Kühlmann's subjective story it is his attitude and emotions that matter rather than his facts. But from the way he remembers things which are of common knowledge and can easily be checked, conclusions must be drawn for events of which he is sole witness.

Here are a few examples. In 1900, in St. Petersburg, Kühlmann was presented to 'the beautiful, melancholic-looking Empress' who 'was unhappy because her eldest son . . . was a so-called "bleeder".' Her only son was born in August 1904.

At the end of September 1914, Kühlmann learnt that he would be moved from Stockholm; 'some time later' he was transferred to Constantinople; he arrived in Berlin for instructions just when the Polish State was proclaimed by the Central Powers (which happened two years later, on 5 November 1916); in Vienna he discussed that proclamation with the Austrian Premier, Dr. von Koerber (appointed in October 1916); and having visited Sofia, spent a few days in Bucharest, where the German Minister told him that the anti-German elements would not prevail in the lifetime of King Carol (who died on 10 October 1914). Kühlmann has mixed up his first journey to Constantinople with the (forgotten) second journey.

Similarly confused is his account of his London negotiations. In September 1911 he went to stay with friends in the Isle of Mull, in order

> to recover somewhat after the exciting and exhausting days of the [Agadir] crisis. Sir William Tyrrell had been in attendance at Balmoral[12] during the visit of the Russian Foreign Minister, Isvolsky, and now likewise arrived at the house. . . .

As Kühlmann was leaving, Tyrrell offered to accompany him to the landing place; and having reviewed the events of the preceding few weeks, asked:

> 'Are you satisfied with the state of our relations?' I expressed my deep dissatisfaction, and he declared himself in complete agreement. He argued that radical measures were required to place the relations of the two great countries on a satisfactory basis. We reached agreement that proper positive negotiations were needed to achieve a *rapprochement*, and that the old Anglo-German treaty concerning the Portuguese colonies offered a suitable basis. Tyrrell asked me whether I was prepared and determined to throw in my weight in favour of a *rapprochement*, and I, in clear terms, promised my co-operation. He, for his part, assured me that he would not fail us.

Pondering over the talk, Kühlmann concluded that Isvolsky must have spoken at Balmoral about the Balkan League which was being formed under Russian patronage, and that Isvolsky's 'personal policy', actuated by a desire of revenge for his discomfiture in the

[12] Grey might have been 'in attendance' at Balmoral, but not his Private Secretary.

Bosnian crisis, must have moved Tyrrell to abandon his reserve and offer Germany a closer understanding. 'The great historical value of the conversation was that Tyrrell, who was nearly all-powerful in British foreign policy, favoured Anglo-German co-operation'; 'the true director of British foreign policy for the first time unreservedly showed me his hand'. Kühlmann's suppositions were soon confirmed by a talk with Grey, to which he was invited in Metternich's absence. Grey spoke of the need of Anglo-German co-operation to prevent the Great Powers from being drawn into the imminent Turco-Bulgar War.

Such is Kühlmann's story. But Isvolsky left the Russian Foreign Office for the Paris Embassy in 1910; he did not visit Balmoral in 1911; the Balkan League was started in the spring of 1912; and the Balkan War broke out in October 1912. Sazonov (not Isvolsky) was at Balmoral 23–29 September 1912; and Kühlmann's talk with Grey can be identified as that of 7 October 1912,[13] with another of 14 October added to it.[14] But then where does Kühlmann's historical conversation with Tyrrell come in? If it occurred in September 1911[15] it loses its connexion with Russia's Balkan policy and Kühlmann's talk with Grey. On the other hand, there is no room for such a walk and talk in September 1912: on the 24th, when the news of Marschall's death reached Kühlmann, he was shooting clay-pigeons in London,[16] and not deer in Scotland; and his wires and dispatches in the *Grosse Politik* place him in London throughout the period (unless signed blanks were used in his absence). Moreover, dating it September 1912 would make nonsense of a number of other statements in Kühlmann's account.[17]

'The foundation of my political creed' and 'the lodestar of all my diplomatic work', writes Kühlmann, was to gain for Germany a Colonial Empire in Africa 'commensurate with the power and the greatness of the mother country.'[18] Even Angola and Mozambique would have made that Empire 'sufficiently great and rich to give

[13] See Kühlmann's cipher-wire of 7 October 1912, *Grosse Politik*, vol. xxxiii, No. 12240, pp. 175–6.

[14] See No. 12276, pp. 221–2, and No. 12284, pp. 228–32.

[15] Grey was at Balmoral 11–14 September 1911, and Tyrrell may have accompanied him.

[16] See *Erinnerungen*, p. 373.

[17] For instance, that Tyrrell and he were by no means pleased with the Haldane Mission (of February 1912), because it was liable to break the 'fine silk threads' of their conversations; or that Tyrrell advised Külhmann to have a talk with the Colonial Secretary, Lewis Harcourt, when, in fact many talks between Harcourt and Metternich, Marschall, and Kühlmann himself about the Portuguese colonies and the Congo are recorded in March-July 1912.

[18] *Erinnerungen*, pp. 245–6.

scope to German energy for generations to come, and to lay solid foundations for Germany's economic well-being'.[19] This gives the measure of Kühlmann's judgment: Germany's pre-1914 Colonial Empire accounted for a half per cent of her foreign trade, and between 1887 and 1914 cost the German tax-payer about £100,000,000; doubling its size would probably have increased these figures proportionately.

Morocco supplied Kühlmann with his first chance: he quickly 'realized' the importance of Germany's economic interests, boosted them in Berlin, and tried to convince the French that Germany would uphold them; he claims to have instigated the Kaiser's visit to Tangier,[20] which ostentatiously acknowledged Morocco's independence, to Kühlmann an object of bargain to be used in a 'sharp and quick action'.[21] But Bülow and Holstein were out to humiliate France instead of blackmailing her; and even Kühlmann's last overtures which, he thinks, 'might well have led to a profitable understanding for the future', were frustrated by 'unfortunate influences in Berlin' when the work 'was nearly completed'.[22]

Here is the story as told in his *Memoirs*.[23] On leave in Paris he met by chance the Tangier correspondent of the *Agence Havas*, with whom he claims to have had a curiously close association,[24] and who now suggested a private talk between him and some representative Frenchman. Kühlmann picked for it Count de Chérisey, French Chargé d'Affaires at Tangier. They met, and over lunch roughed out the basis for an agreement with which, completed but unavowed, France and Germany were to go to the Algeciras Conference: Germany was to offer no serious opposition to a French mandate for policing Morocco, and in exchange was to receive the entire French Congo, and the French right to pre-emption over the Belgian Congo, besides certain economic rights in Morocco. With this splendid bargain Kühlmann rushed off to Berlin, merely to see it turned down by the nefarious Holstein. And next Kühlmann's report vanished from the German archives. All that appears in the *Grosse Politik* is a memorandum, whose 'very unclear tenor (*sehr unklare Fassung*) suggests that Holstein had but imperfectly informed his colleagues

[19] Ibid., p. 343.

[20] In his *Thoughts on Germany*, p. 183, Kühlmann includes that visit among Germany's untoward 'threatening gestures'.

[21] *Erinnerungen*, pp. 203–45, and *Thoughts on Germany*, pp. 225–6.

[22] *Thoughts on Germany*, p. 226.

[23] *Erinnerungen*, pp. 246–50.

[24] See *Erinnerungen*, p. 206: 'Hardly ever was a more important message sent to the semi-official French telegraphic agency without my having previously been given an opportunity to talk over its contents.'

of the matter'. (In stating the terms the memorandum speaks of 'compensation in the French Congo', and not of 'the French Congo as compensation', and while ascribing the initiative to the French, adds that 'it is not clear from whom on the French side it came'.) Next Kühlmann, having kept no copy of the text settled with Chérisey, asked him to obtain it from the Quai d'Orsay, only to learn that there, too, it had mysteriously vanished: 'the document obviously inconvenienced so many people that on both sides unscrupulous politicians decided to suppress it.'

A very different story was told by Chérisey to the French Commission on the Origins of the War.[25] He had made merely a verbal report to the Premier (who was also Foreign Minister), and himself had preserved nothing in writing. But he well remembered the transaction: the initiative was Kühlmann's, and what Germany was to receive was a share in Moroccan public works and frontier rectifications in the French Congo; but when Chérisey tried to discover whether Kühlmann was authorized to make such proposals, he was merely told 'that they had the approval of influential men'. Here, in short, is a Kühlmann intrigue, too clever to succeed, but now furbished up into a historical transaction.

Kühlmann magnifies the colonial negotiations which he carried on in London into 'a great, constructive policy', fraught with far-reaching possibilities, and misinterprets (ill-advised) British attempts at meeting the Germans in a friendly manner. Could anyone have seriously expected a contingent agreement about Central Africa to extinguish Germany's naval ambitions or Britain's interest in the balance of power on the Continent? Elsewhere Kühlmann admits that war may have been rendered 'scarcely avoidable' by the problem of Austria-Hungary's future,[26] and that Britain was bound to join in immediately, lest she be 'confronted in a few weeks by a victorious Germany in occupation of the entire Channel coast'.[27] No wonder then if in July-August 1914 Kühlmann's spurious achievements proved piffle before the wind.

Kühlmann, in his account of the London negotiations, tries to make out that, while Arthur Nicolson and Crowe adhered to the Entente, Grey and Tyrrell were veering toward Germany and working with him behind the backs of the other two. But there is evidence of the distrust which Grey felt of Kühlmann,[28] and Kühlmann's

[25] See *Documents Diplomatiques Français,* 2nd series, vol. viii, p. 90, note 2.

[26] *Thoughts on Germany*, p. 78.

[27] Ibid., p. 257.

[28] Mr. Alwyn Parker, who in 1912 on behalf of the Foreign Office negotiated with Kühlmann about the Baghdad Railway, wrote in *The Times Literary Supplement* of 7 October 1949: 'Nobody in the Foreign Office had any illusions

story of his close understanding and collaboration with Tyrrell seems about as accurate as of its inception in the Isle of Mull. Of Tyrrell I can speak from personal knowledge, having served under him in the Political Intelligence Department of the Foreign Office from April 1918 till May 1920; and I agree with the reviewer in *The Times Literary Supplement* that Kühlmann 'seems never to have understood either the limitations of Tyrrell's influence or the mental reservations that may well have lain behind Tyrrell's politeness': Tyrrell was neither 'the true director of British foreign policy', nor the man 'unreservedly to show his hand' to Kühlmann. Complex, versatile, talkative, but exceedingly secretive, he was amiable, and even yielding on the surface, but a stubborn fighter underneath. He avoided, if he could, personal collisions, and professed a preference for 'long-range artillery'; yet he disliked writing—active and restless, he shunned the drudgery of office drafts, and, cultivating the laziness which Talleyrand enjoined on diplomats, was selective even in his reading of office files.[29] He was a contrast to that austere, somewhat rigid, tireless worker Eyre Crowe, one of the greatest Civil Servants this country ever had; but they were on the closest terms and never would Crowe have shown so much friendship to a pro-German within the Foreign Office. Tyrrell's curious, occasionally even impish, ways gave rise to doubts among some people; in reality he was a loyal friend who fought the battles of his chiefs, colleagues, and subordinates, often with complete disregard for his own person. Because even after the Foreign Office files have been opened, it may be found difficult to ascertain Tyrrell's views or actions, it is now incumbent on those who worked with him to defend him from Kühlmann's encomiums.

As for the negotiations about the Portuguese colonies, these were not conducted by Tyrrell, then Principal Private Secretary to Grey (and as such not in charge of negotiations with foreign Governments independently of the relevant departments of the Foreign Office), but first by Harcourt and the Colonial Office, and next by Crowe for the Foreign Office. Further, after the agreement had been initialled on 20 October 1913, it remained unsigned because the British

about Kühlmann. Sir Edward Grey warned me to be careful, adding that he had rather a full measure of self-esteem and was very *débrouillard*, and not over-careful to bring his actions to the touchstone of the moral sense.'

[29] An administrative question concerning our department was once submitted to Tyrrell in a long minute on the jacket of its file. Tyrrell, uninterested in the subject, initialled the minute unread. It was returned to him with the remark: 'This matter requires your decision.' Reply: 'I agree, W.T.' The decision was then obtained orally, and the jacket of the file was changed.

Government insisted on publishing it together with the Anglo-Portuguese Treaty of 1899, while Berlin objected, discerning a contradiction between the two. 'If that apparent perfidy of England against her old ally Portugal could trouble anyone,' writes Kühlmann, 'it was the English, but it was hardly a concern of Germany'. Does Kühlmann fail, or does he refuse, to understand that publicity was to deprive the Anglo-German agreement of the very character which he meant to give it?

While Kühlmann boasts of having managed in the East (on the basis of 'self-determination') 'to carve out of the body politic of Russia' whatever territories were coveted by Germany, in the West he claims to have aimed at a peace 'without annexations', negotiated and not dictated; this, he says, he meant to attain through secret negotiations with London. The story of his official approaches is told, at some length, in Lloyd George's *War Memoirs*.[30] His good faith was always in doubt, but the approach being made (in Balfour's words) 'through the orthodox channel of a neutral Foreign Office' (Spain), H.M. Government were prepared to deal with the matter in a proper understanding with their major Allies. But Kühlmann's 'No, never!' with regard to Alsace-Lorraine in his Reichstag speech of 9 October 1917 put an end to it.

Now Kühlmann in his memoirs has a story about peace approaches in which Tyrrell is made to appear as his opposite number.

> Certain signs seemed to me to warrant the assumption that Sir William Tyrrell thought a moderate peace settlement in the British interest, presumably because he foresaw that a fight to the finish would produce an unsound French preponderance on the Continent.

And next:

> Through a neutral personality I had entered into communication with my old political friend Sir William Tyrrell, and informed him that I could discuss peace only on the basis of territorial integrity for Germany and Austria-Hungary. . . . Tyrrell replied he was ready to start from that basis.

Indeed, it requires a Kühlmann to imagine, and to try to make others believe, that anyone in the Foreign Office could have, off his own bat, engaged in peace talks—and Tyrrell, the friend of Grey and Asquith, had no personal connexion with Lloyd George.

> My immediate aim [Kühlmann goes on to say] was to meet an English statesman for an informal talk at some Dutch castle in order

[30] Vol. iv, pp. 2081–107.

> to ascertain what possibilities there were of peace. German and British delegates were about to meet at The Hague to discuss an exchange of prisoners-of-war. This seemed to me a good opportunity to establish at least a first contact.

With this in view, Kühlmann included in the German delegation Prince Hatzfeldt, son of a late German Ambassador to London, educated and subsequently resident in England. To this hint, claims Kühlmann,

> the British duly responded . . . and Lord Newton led their delegation. —Tyrrell must have taken special care in selecting it. At the end of the very first session, Hermann Hatzfeldt and Lord Newton remained behind. . . . Newton immediately started talking about a general peace, and Hatzfeldt, in accordance with his instructions, promptly entered into the subject.

And once more Kühlmann's story can be proved to be rubbish from beginning to end. Since February 1916 Newton had been in charge of the Prisoners-of-War Department of the Foreign Office, and as such had been chief British delegate to the Anglo-German conference on prisoners-of-war at The Hague in June 1917, and to the Anglo-Turkish conference at Berne in December 1917: there would have been no need to 'select' him for it, and anyhow this would not have been within Tyrrell's competence. But in view of a bitter Press campaign which had preceded the Conference of June 1918, Newton, for once, did not lead the British delegation. He writes in his diary under date of 31 May:[31]

> Sent for by Bonar Law, who told me that it had been decided to send Cave,[32] myself and Belfield[33] as delegates to The Hague. The agitation had been so great that the Government had determined to send a Cabinet Minister and, according to Bonar Law, Cave had proposed himself.

That Hatzfeldt would be on the German delegation the British only learnt at The Hague. Newton writes on 7 June:

> Vredenburch[34] says that the Germans are much exercised over Cave's appointment, and in order to be represented by a man of equal official rank have sent Prince Hermann Hatzfeldt, son of the former German Ambassador in London.

[31] See Lord Newton, *Retrospection* (1941), p. 256.
[32] Lord Cave, at that time Home Secretary.
[33] Major-General Belfield, Director of Prisoners-of-War Department, War Office.
[34] Jonkheer van Vredenburch, a Dutch diplomatist, was chairman of the conference.

And here is the story of the peace talks as they appear in Newton's diary:

> ... although the work of our delegation had been to some extent disappointing. I had during our stay made a discovery that was at once important and unexpected, for we had not been there long when it came to my knowledge that the Germans were acutely, almost passionately, anxious to enter upon peace negotiations. We had been directed to confine ourselves to our own immediate business, but if two parties are in constant close communication for about six weeks it is a practical certainty that each side will learn something about the plans and intentions of the other. The information came to me as a complete surprise, for there was no indication of a German collapse. ... The important fact was that the Germans obviously realized that they were going to lose the war, otherwise they would never have made any such approach. I determined to keep my information secret until I could convey it personally to the Prime Minister.

He did so on 25 July more than a fortnight after Kühlmann's dismissal. Tyrrell is never mentioned.

Nor is there any ground to suppose that Tyrrell favoured lenient peace terms for the Central Powers. At the Paris Peace Conference, Crowe and he were in agreement with the French about Poland's western frontier. It was Lloyd George, supported by Philip Kerr and Headlam-Morley, who reduced Poland's acquisitions in Posnania, set up the Free City of Danzig, and conceded a plebiscite in Upper Silesia: while Tyrrell, in protest against such modifications, withdrew from the post of British representative on the Polish Committee. Of these matters I can again speak from personal knowledge; and so I can of an earlier significant transaction, on the very eve of the Hague Conference. In May 1918 the Czechs asked the Western Powers to acknowledge the National Committee under Masaryk as a quasi-governmental representation. This was during the Ludendorff offensive, and even some, not averse to Czechoslovak independence, doubted whether it was the time to assume new and far-reaching commitments. I myself was of those who thought that if a new Austerlitz was imminent, we had better unroll our future map of Europe, a sign of hope to nations engulfed by the German flood. Tyrrell knew this, and on 17 May, late in the afternoon, came to my room, carrying a pack of files; said that Beneš was to see Balfour next morning; that there was disagreement concerning the line to be taken about the Czech request; and asked me to prepare from those files a short minute of our previous dealings with the Czechs, and a memorandum on further action. I do not know what use was made of my paper which urged recognition of the Czechoslovak National Committee; but this was officially extended to them on 11 June, and the mere fact that Tyrrell had the matter put into my hands—it was not usual for our Department to deal with current executive work—illustrates his own attitude towards the 'territorial integrity' of the Central Powers. In April 1918, Clemenceau said about Kühlmann's Austrian colleague: 'Count Czernin has lied.' The same can now be said of Herr von Kühlmann.

# X

# THE DOWNFALL OF THE HABSBURG MONARCHY

## A. THE POLITICAL STRUCTURE OF AUSTRIA-HUNGARY BEFORE THE WAR

1. *The Austrian 'Staatsidee'*. During the First World War 'the idea of the Austrian State' (*die österreichische Staatsidee*) was habitually appealed to by those who defended Austria-Hungary's existence. The concrete meaning of the term was never explained: it had none which its votaries would have cared to explain, and the Austrian State, to which it referred as conterminous with the Habsburg dominions, did not exist except in reminiscences of the past and pious hopes for the future. The Habsburg Monarchy consisted of two separate, sovereign States, Austria and Hungary, with Bosnia-Herzegovina held by them in common. Since 1867 Austria was that which remained of the amorphous mass of the Habsburg possessions, the 'home-farm' of the dynasty, after national States had arisen in Germany, Italy, and in certain aspects also in Hungary; for nearly fifty years (until 1916) this residuum, which in proportion to its size displayed more frontier and less coherence than any other State in Europe, went officially by the colourless designation of 'the Kingdoms and Provinces represented in the Reichsrat'. The name of Austria, currently given to them, was kept in reserve in the hope that some day it might once more cover all the dominions of the Habsburgs, *des Hauses Oesterreich*. The Austria of 1867 was regarded by the Habsburgs as but a phase in the history of their dynastic power, their *Hausmacht*; for them there was nothing final about it, indeed they shunned finality—every piece of driftwood carried to their shore was to them a promising sprig which might yet grow into a crown. Their outlying western possessions were gone,

their age-long dreams of dominion over Germany and Italy were dead; their face was now to the east. Through Galicia and Dalmatia, Austria's fantastically shaped body, enveloping the massive block of Hungary, stretched out its arms towards Poland, the Ukraine, Rumania, and Serbia, which all found their place in the war-dreams and schemings of the Habsburg dynasty. The Habsburgs were the one dynasty which had never linked up its fate with that of any single nation; they had a capital and a territorial base but no nationality; they developed schemes territorially coherent though devoid of all national idea. Their instincts were purely proprietary, the one meaning of an Austrian State to them was that they possessed it; to the outside world, that it existed. For the few, and mostly interested, exponents of an Austrian State, its continued existence was an aim in itself; and this was the core of the alleged Austrian *Staatsidee*. But it was by no means this exceedingly frail basis which sustained Austria-Hungary's continued existence.

2. *The Partnership of the Germans, Magyars, and Poles.* There was more shape and sense in the remaining Habsburg dominions than appeared on the surface and more than the Habsburg Idea recognized; there was less justice to the subject nationalities than the dynasty could have admitted. Although inhabited by eight, and, counting sub-divisions, even by eleven peoples, the territory of the Habsburg Monarchy was completely covered by the historic, imperialist claims of three nationalities—the claim of the Magyars to the lands of the Crown of St. Stephen, of the Germans to Western Austria,[1] and of the Poles to Galicia; each claim was tenaciously asserted, though, unless statistical forgeries were committed and unless the Jews were included, none of the three nationalities formed a majority in the territory it claimed. If conceded dominion, the master-nations were ready to defend every inch of the Monarchy against the national claims of its neighbours, the co-racials of the subject nationalities—the Southern Tyrol and Trieste against Italy, the Illyrian provinces against Serbia, East Galicia against Russia, Translyvania against Rumania; whereas the subject nationalities, if conceded national self-government, would naturally have bethought themselves next of national reunion. The Germans and Poles in Austria, and the Magyars in Hungary, in their own interest, not

[1] 'Western Austria' is here meant to denote the western hereditary provinces which had been under the Habsburgs since 1526, had been included in the Holy Roman Empire and then in the Germanic Confederation of 1815, and lay within the orbit of German settlement, influence, and ambitions. It excludes the outlying provinces in the east and south-east, acquisitions of the late eighteenth century: Galicia, the Bukovina, and Dalmatia.

from any attachment to the dynasty, had to become the 'State-preserving elements' (*die staatserhaltenden Elemente*).

In turn the Habsburgs, for reasons of internal as well as of international policy, had no choice but to base their rule on the supremacy of the Magyars in Hungary, and of the Germans and Poles in Austria. This had its roots in history and was opposed to the national principle—like the Habsburg Monarchy. It rested on past empire and on consequent social superiority, and was therefore conservative, as was the Monarchy which lived by survival alone. The upper classes were Magyar throughout Hungary, Polish throughout Galicia; in Western Austria even in 1914 they still remained predominantly German. The choice between nationalities implied therefore a choice between classes—a medieval, clerical dynasty does not lead social revolutions, nor impose the rule of peasants on their landlords. Lastly, the German-Magyar combination alone could supply the Habsburgs with a suitable foreign alliance to safeguard their possessions against a coalition of the neighbouring States, each of which saw national territory of its own included in their Monarchy. The Germans within Austria were sufficiently strong to permeate the State and thus to accept dominion in lieu of complete national reunion; Germany alone seemed sufficiently powerful to preserve Austria-Hungary's existence and sufficiently concerned in it to attempt doing so; and lastly, Germany had no interests conflicting with those of Austria-Hungary in the Adriatic and the Balkans, which now became the main sphere of Habsburg ambitions. Hence the German alliance. The logical result of that alliance upon the internal affairs of the Habsburg Monarchy was once more the predominance of the Magyars in Hungary and of the Germans (with their indispensable associates, the Poles) in Austria. No one had chosen his partners, no deeper sympathy bound either the Poles or the Magyars to the Germans—in fact, when necessary, they could plead strong dislike of one another—and few statesmen except Bismarck, Julius Andrássy the elder, and Stephen Tisza seem to have understood and accepted all the implications of the system. It had been imposed on the contracting parties by the inherent necessities of their political situation and by the logic of events. Its intricacies no human mind could have thought out, nor any human skill readjusted; and its inherent force was so great that it survived to the very end, till October 1918.

In 1848, when the national and constitutional movement among the gentry and bourgeoisie found expression in revolt against the non-national, proprietary character of the Monarchy, the dynasty appealed to the subject peasant-races, the Czecho-Slovaks, the Yugoslavs, Ruthenes,[2] and Rumans, for help against their masters, the Germans, Magyars, and Poles. In 1867 the Habsburgs surrendered their late supporters to their late opponents. Reconciled to the most powerful and most articulate of their subjects, they proposed to resume the struggle against their hereditary enemy, Prussia. A German-Magyar veto prevented them from doing so in 1870. In 1879 the alliance with Prussia-Germany was concluded. The ideas of separation from Germany and of reform within the Habsburg Monarchy, which arose once more in the later stages of the War and waxed under threat of defeat, were froth and bubble, and the last desperate attempts of October 1918 bore no more resemblance to action based on a political system than mad antics do to the movement of swimming. The political developments of Austria-Hungary obeyed the necessities of its internal structure; illusions there were of dynastic power to shape them—in reality these developments were pre-determined as the movements of the stars, and subject to iron laws.

It had not been within the power of the Habsburgs and their centralist followers to refuse the claims of the Germans, Magyars, and Poles; as far as Austria was concerned, it had been within their power, and to their interest, to prevent the complete establishment of the system. Its full logical development would have left the Habsburgs stripped of all authority, without a 'home-farm', with an exceedingly limited base for dynastic schemings, with very little scope for an independent foreign policy, bound hand and foot to the three dominant nationalities. They would have changed into shadowy suzerains of excessively powerful subjects, the real masters of their possessions; in short, the Habsburgs would have been reduced to the position of constitutional monarchs in three States, each based on the artificially secured rule of a dominant minority. It was in opposition to the complete establishment of a system of which the principle had to be admitted if the Habsburg Monarchy was to be held together, that the interest of the dynasty coincided with that of the submerged nationalities. Cautiously, and as far as Hungary was concerned in a purely Platonic fashion, the Habsburgs sympathized with the outraged national rights of races whom they

[2] The Little Russians in the late Austro-Hungarian territories were known by the name of 'Ruthenes', though identical in language and race with the Little Russians of Southern Russia. Those among them who claimed to form a nation distinct from the Great Russians, to avoid all resemblance, adopted the name of 'Ukrainians'. Thus they have come to be known by three interchangeable names.

themselves, in their own dynastic interest, had surrendered to the master-nations. This was the outstanding peculiarity of the Habsburg system, the only concrete meaning of the so-called Austrian *Staatsidee.*

3. *The Magyar System.* In 1867 Hungary had crystallized once more into the imperialist domain of the Magyars and was, in its constitution, completely separated from the remaining Habsburg heritage, the Austrian Hereditary Provinces. The frontier drawn between Austria and Hungary cut across the lands *minorum gentium*, of 'the minor nations', the Czecho-Slovaks, the Yugoslavs, the Ruthenes, and the Rumans, whose national territories were thus partitioned even within the borders of the Habsburg possessions, an obvious fact which during the War was only too often overlooked or deliberately left out of count when internal reform and national autonomy within the Habsburg Monarchy were discussed. By forming Croatia into a separate, though absolutely dependent, State, the Magyars had secured for themselves a majority in Hungary proper, and by means of a narrow class franchise in a country where the upper classes were Magyar or Magyarized, they had given an almost exclusively Magyar character to their Parliament. This was an artificially constructed and delicately balanced system which did not admit of any radical changes within Hungary nor of a material extension of its borders; strongly conscious of this fact, Stephen Tisza was a bitter opponent of democratic reform at home and of any appreciable increase of territory at the expense of Serbia or Rumania. Hungary was not to be used or manipulated in the Habsburg interest; it was neither to be enlarged nor reduced. There were no Magyars outside Hungary's frontiers, and within they were to be dominant. They held the most convenient strategic frontiers, the Carpathian arc and the Transylvanian mountain-bastion, and had access to the sea. Hungary was complete.

The Magyars would have gladly seen the Germans and Poles attain the same position in Western Austria and in Galicia, which they themselves held in Hungary. It was not to their interest that in Austria the subject races should remain in immediate touch with the dynasty, and enjoy more favourable treatment than in Hungary, nor that the dynastic power of the Habsburgs should survive anywhere, and threaten with the help of the subject races once more to include or engulf the Magyar domain in the amorphous mass of the Habsburg possessions. In September 1866 Count Julius Andrássy the elder emphatically declared to the Austrian Minister Hübner that the Magyars 'could not suffer a federalist system to be established in

Austria, a probable centre for future attacks against Hungary'. Had full self-government been conceded within Austria such a system would have affected the nationalities oppressed in Hungary; the Magyars would have had to break off all connexion with Austria and the Habsburgs—for every surviving link and all reminiscences of a common past would have kept suggesting to the subject races of Hungary that through a reunion in a dynastic Habsburg State lay the road to national self-government. But as changes in the Austrian constitution required a two-thirds majority, and such a majority could not have been obtained in the Reichsrat against the German vote, federalist devolution could have been introduced by means of a dynastic *coup d'état* alone. In the Agreement of 1867 the Magyars therefore stipulated that the connexion between the two States was to continue only so long as both were governed in a constitutional manner. They thus reserved for themselves the power of vetoing any unconstitutional act even with regard to exclusively Austrian affairs —but they naturally never protested when the Austrian constitution was infringed to the disadvantage of the subject races.

The Magyars desired Austria to be centralized, and its centralism to bear a distinct German character. But with Galicia as an integral part of Austria, the Austrian State was ill poised. It would therefore have been to the interest of the Austrian Germans, as well as of the Polish and the Magyar oligarchs, had a separate constitutional status been conceded to Galicia. The exclusion of the Galician members from the Austrian Reichsrat would have given a decisive majority to the Germans over the Czechs, Yugoslavs, and Italians, while the Poles would have been left to deal with the Ruthenes in the Galician Diet, where, by means of electoral devices, they had secured for themselves a majority almost as good as that of the Magyars in the Hungarian Parliament. As long as within Austria no single nationality had a decisive, permanent superiority over its opponents, the Habsburgs were able to preserve their dynastic power, without the strictly constitutional Magyar system of government being reproproduced against them. Although they never seriously questioned the predominance of the Germans and Poles over the subject races, they used the contending nationalities as checks on each other. They could do so the more easily as they invariably had the support of the German clericals and of the Poles. Nationality was not the dominant, or at least not the exclusive, political instinct and interest of the German clericals, while the Poles had to think of the wider, international aspects of the Polish question and could not consider a settlement within the narrow frontiers of Galicia, which formed one province only of Poland, as anything but temporary. Neither for the German clericals nor for the Poles was there finality in the frontiers of Austria, as there was for the Magyars in those of Hungary, and neither therefore felt the same overwhelming interest in the complete and definite establishment of the triple Magyar-German-Polish scheme.

4. *Austrian Centralism and German Nationalism.* In the central, purely German districts of Austria national feeling had never completely divested itself of an Austrian imprint; it oscillated between the German national idea on the one hand and a peculiar Austrian sentiment on the other. In the Czech provinces of Bohemia, Moravia, and Silesia, bordering on Saxony and Prussia, the German minority developed an uncompromising nationalism, neither softened nor clouded by religious sentiment; so also, to some extent, in the southern Slovene borderlands. But in the centre, especially in Vienna, the population felt too closely associated with the Habsburgs in their power, and its profits and glory, to adopt the purely German point of view. The phantoms of the medieval Roman Empire, of the non-national world-idea centring in Imperial Vienna, surrounded the throne of the Habsburgs—*ils vivaient de l'ombre d'une ombre* ... For the devout peasantry of the Alpine provinces and for the Vienna petty middle class, Roman Catholicism was a further link with the dynasty, and even with the clericals of other nations, Czech, Slovene, or Italian. The intransigent German nationalists turned their backs upon Hungary and Galicia in order to concentrate on the Czech and Slovene provinces, in which they were directly concerned through their German minorities. The Great-Austrians could not be indifferent to any part of the Habsburg dominions, their old inheritance, and upheld the conception of the *Gesammtmonarchie* (a State embracing them all) with even more fervour than the dynasty itself. But while German nationalism and Austrian imperialism were clearly distinct in theory and in the minds of their most extreme exponents, they blended in the middle ranges, and most Austrian Germans were something of the one and something of the other. Austrian imperialism with Vienna for centre was German in its essence, and the Germans were in Austria the most important centripetal force.

The idea of the *Gesammtmonarchie* was a direct negation of the Magyar scheme. 'As long as a Magyar is left alive he will not allow his nation to be forced under such a superior State organization,' declared Count Tisza on 1 January 1916. The centralist Austrian 'patriotism' was agreeable to the Magyars, but only if enclosed within the frontiers of the western half of the Monarchy, i.e. while directed against Czech and Yugoslav national ambitions. 'I consider this feeling to be as sacred as our own patriotism,' Tisza went on to say in his exposition of the Magyar creed. 'I sympathize with it and value it, provided it does not turn against the independence of the Hungarian nation. . . . It is in our own interest to strengthen over there the centripetal as against the centrifugal forces. . . . Before now the Magyar nation has tried to fulfil its mission, to promote and strengthen the centripetal forces in Austria. . . . And if in the past it did not achieve full success, this was because Austrian patriotism had not been able to divest itself of the old tendencies in favour of a Monarchy including all the Habsburg dominions. . . .' Tisza spoke of an Austrian patriotism; he meant it. The Magyars wanted Austria, but not too much of it. They wanted it to be German, but not too German. It was to be sufficiently German to prevent the nationalities which were kept under in Hungary from forming national States across Hungary's border, but not so German as to lead to a fusion of Austria with Germany. The weaker Austrian partner would then have been replaced by an overwhelmingly, indeed dangerously, superior German neighbour, and the Magyar system in international politics, a marvellous machine which through a multitude of wheels and levers made one of the smallest nations in Europe into a Great Power, would have broken down. 'A proper centralization of Austria will secure the State against excessive Germanism (*Deutschtümelei*) on the part of the Germans by their being mixed up with the Slavs, while the Slavs will be prevented by the Germans from following out a centrifugal policy,' explained the elder Andrássy to the Emperor Francis Joseph I in July 1866. The aim of German nationalism was Great-Germany—comprising all territories of the former Germanic Confederation—even *Mittel-Europa*; the logical expression of 'Austrian' patriotism was Great-Austria—*die Gesammtmonarchie*. The Magyars wanted neither. For them, and them alone, the Dual Monarchy, as they had constructed it in 1867, was final.

The Austrian federalist schemes of 1860–73 were based on the historic provinces into which Austria was divided. There were seventeen of these, differing widely in size and population—e.g. Galicia had 22,000 square miles and, in 1910, 8,000,000 inhabitants, Salzburg 2,000 square miles and 200,000 inhabitants. Only some of the small German mountain provinces were nationally homogeneous. All the rest had their national minorities and their national problems. Whereas in the Austrian Reichsrat and government the Germans were practically dominant, there were Slav majorities and German minorities in Bohemia, Moravia, and Carniola; on the Adriatic coast there were pactically no Germans. Complete centralization in the Austrian Reichsrat alone could save the Germans in the Slav provinces from becoming minorities subject to non-German rule, and to achieve this was for the German Nationalists the purpose of Austria's existence. But again the particular interests of the German clericals produced divergences within the German camp. To the clericals, who were strongly entrenched in several of the Alpine Diets, provincial autonomy safeguarded their interests against a possible or actual anti-clerical majority in the Vienna Parliament. This was a further obstacle to German centralism in Austria.

5. *The Poles and the Habsburgs.* The Austrian Poles were neither federalists nor centralists, merely Habsburgites. They had been federalists at times, but half-heartedly; they did not really wish for an increase in the power and independence of the pro-Russian Czechs and Yugoslavs. They could not be centralists as long as Galicia remained an Austrian province. For themselves they demanded from Austria national liberty and dominion over the Ruthenes of East Galicia; on every other point they were prepared to compromise. They were willing to co-operate with the dynasty because they counted on Habsburg support in the reconstruction of Poland. While Russia in partitioning Poland had aimed at re-establishing her own national unity (White Russia and the Western Ukraine) and Prussia at consolidating her eastern frontier (West Prussia and Posnania), Austria had merely demanded her pound of flesh as counterpoise to the acquisitions of her neighbours. The same reasons which had moved the other two Powers to partition Poland maintained their opposition to its reconstruction; the Habsburgs were prepared to give up their pound of flesh provided they could get the entire man. Hostility to Prussia and Russia, and the common Roman Catholic religion, were bonds between the Poles and the Habsburgs, even before the agreement on the basis of Galician autonomy was reached; that agreement was the logical outcome of a community of interests. The idea of an 'Austro-Polish solution' can be traced back to 1794, 1809, and 1830; after 1848, and still more after 1867, the belief in 'Austria's historic mission' with regard to Poland became a fundamental article of the Polish creed in Galicia. Reluctantly the Poles accepted even the German alliance as necessary for safeguarding Austria and of course also their dominion over the Little Russian territory of East Galicia against Russia. Their anti-Russian and generally anti-Slav policy continued to bind them

to the Habsburgs and Magyars. It was not an accident that M. de Biliński, one of the chief leaders of the Galician Poles and Minister for Bosnia-Herzegovina in 1914, was one of the main authors of the ultimatum to Serbia—which fact did not prevent him in 1919 from attaining Cabinet rank in the reconstituted Poland.

6. *The Yugoslav Problem.* One stone in the structure of the Habsburg Monarchy was very loose—Bosnia-Herzegovina, acquired in 1878 for dynastic reasons, not coveted then either by the Austrian Germans or the Magyars. Yugoslav throughout in nationality, though partly Moslem in religion, and surrounded by Yugoslav territory—by Croatia, a nominally self-governing kingdom under the Hungarian Crown, by Dalmatia, an Austrian province nowhere bordering on Austria, and by the independent Yugoslav kingdoms of Serbia and Montenegro—Bosnia-Herzegovina had no political connexion with any of them but remained under the joint Austro-Hungarian government, which itself was not a government but a contractual formation based on the Agreement of 1867. The Austrian Prime Minister, Baron Hussarek, in his speech of 1 October 1918, described Bosnia-Herzegovina as *ein staatsrechtlich undefinierbares Neutrum.*[3] The dynasty would have willingly accepted a union of all Yugoslav territory provided it was effected under their sceptre. The Austrian Germans would not allow the Slovene territories, their sea-coast, to be detached from Western Austria, but would probably have agreed to a Serbo-Croat State or at least to a great Croatia—consisting of Croatia, Dalmatia, and Bosnia-Herzegovina. But as such a union of Yugoslav territories would have changed the balance within Hungary and the Habsburg Monarchy to the disadvantage of the Magyars, these naturally objected, and there was no way of fitting the Yugoslav stones into the structure of the Habsburg Monarchy. For various reasons the other national problems of the Habsburg Monarchy were internationally more or less dormant during the years preceding the outbreak of the War. The unsolved Yugoslav question opened up the problem of Austria-Hungary's existence and brought on the War.

The War in which Russia and Germany opposed each other unrolled the Polish Question which could not have been reopened in any other way, and the Polish Question raised all the other problems of Austria-Hungary's inner structure. Austria-Hungary, as it existed from 1867 till 1914, the creation of Magyar statesmanship, fully and finally satisfied none but the Magyars; on everybody else,

[3] 'A nondescript creation, which cannot be defined in terms of political science.'

not excluding even the dynasty, the Austrian centralists, and the German Nationalists, it imposed sacrifices and renunciations, offering them merely half-solutions and a *modus vivendi*. The War and the possibility, nay the certainty, of change unhinged at one blow the delicate system of compromises and balances, and liberated wildly divergent desires and forces. 'Great' Austria, 'Great' Germany, a reunited Poland threatened to destroy the balance and nature of the Dual System; the national ambitions of the subject races threatened to destroy the very existence of the Habsburg Monarchy and the 'integrity of Hungary'. Whichever side was to prove victorious, the Austria-Hungary of pre-War days was dead, and everything was once more unsettled.

## B. AUSTRIA-HUNGARY IN THE WAR

7. *The Austrian Solution of the Polish Question*. On the outbreak of war the Galician Poles declared for a union of Galicia and Russian Poland under the Habsburgs as a third component part of the Monarchy; this, the so-called 'Austrian Solution of the Polish Question', was the first suggestion for a recasting of the Habsburg Monarchy. The Habsburgs would have welcomed it as implying new acquisitions, the German Nationalists as crystallizing their domain in Western Austria, most of the Magyars as a consummation of the triple German-Magyar-Polish scheme. Tisza resisted. Alone in his generation he had a perfect understanding of Austria-Hungary's political mechanism. Under the Dual System the virile Magyar oligarchs had realized independence, i.e. predominance over an internally divided and paralysed Austria. Could they be certain of maintaining it in a 'triangle'? 'A political structure of the Monarchy which would make it possible for Hungary to be out-voted on essential problems of State, and therefore subject to an alien will, would nullify our achievements,' wrote Count Tisza to Count Czernin on 22 February 1917. Similarly Germany was loath to accept a union of Austrian and Russian Poland, which, leaving Prussian Poland the only unredeemed Polish territory, would have given an anti-German front to the Polish State, the new partner in the Habsburg Monarchy. Tisza's scheme was to join Russian Poland to Austria externally as a self-governing kingdom, while Galicia remained an integral part of the Austrian Empire; the German scheme was to form it into a nominally independent kingdom under Germany. Both were clearly unacceptable to Austria; among the

Austrian Poles either solution would have produced a desire for union with the new Poland, which, if unsatisfied, would have made them join forces with the Slav opposition in the Reichsrat, creating there a permanent majority in opposition to the Austrian State. A complete deadlock was thus reached over the Polish Question.

8. *The Habsburg Monarchy and Mittel-Europa.* The deadlock delayed Austria's internal reconstruction; building operations could not begin on undefined ground, although the plans were complete. A political consolidation had been effected between the Austrian Germans who were primarily Austrians and those who were primarily Germans. Axiomatic truths about Austria-Hungary, hitherto obscured by surface contradictions, were revealed in practice. Germany in her own interest safeguarded the existence of the Habsburg Monarchy: the fight for it was a German national war. But the races opposed to German-Magyar rule became the enemies of the Habsburg Monarchy. Experience had taught them that cultural liberties without national independence meant the right to develop nationality coupled with the duty to ignore it in wars brought about by the dominant races. The logic of events forced on the subject races a program of complete independence, tantamount to the break-up of the Habsburg Monarchy. The Austrian imperialists who, non-national as they were in their ideas, would have preferred to build on a wider rather than an exclusively German basis, were in their turn forced into an attitude and policy towards the subject races hardly differing from that of the German Nationalists.

On the other hand, the War proved Austria-Hungary's value to Germany. The Habsburg Monarchy, which to short-sighted Pan-Germans (not to Bismarck) had seemed a cumbersome survival impeding the road to a reunion of the entire German nation, proved to be the most valuable asset for *Mittel-Europa* and the German World-Empire. Even extreme Pan-Germans in Austria became converted to the Habsburg Monarchy. There was now a platform common to all the Austrian Germans—Austria was to be maintained, reconstructed on a German basis, and firmly fitted into the Germanic system; her policy was to be subordinated to that of Central Europe, and the entire Habsburg inheritance was to be taken over and secured by the strength of the reunited German nation. Through *Mittel-Europa* the Austrian Germans returned both to the Pan-German and to the Great-Austrian idea, now reconciled with each other. They beheld themselves once more an integral part of the German nation, and as part of it resumed an imperialism too wide for them in their previous isolation.

The Polish program of a union of Austrian and Russian Poland threatened to change the balance within the Habsburg Monarchy; the German program of Central European Union, to destroy its independence. Either would have marked the end of Austria-Hungary, the Dual Monarchy within the frontiers of 1867. The structural concept of Austria-Hungary was broken down by the races dominant in Austria three years before defeat, and the action of the subject races razed the building and obliterated its foundations.

Naturally the Habsburgs did not relish the idea of being permanently reduced to a dependent position within the Central European Union. Nor was Tisza prepared to admit a union infringing Hungary's sovereignty and independence. The domain of the Magyars in Hungary was to remain intact; Austria was to remain common yet neutral ground between Germany and the Magyars. If a Central European *bloc* was to be formed this too was to rest on a dual basis. The European and trans-European West might pass under German leadership, but the 'Turanian' East—Bulgaria, Turkey, etc.—was to pass under that of the Magyars. *Mittel-Europa*, like Austria, was to stop at the western frontier of Hungary; this was the Magyar conception of it. The 9,000,000 Magyars were to stand back to back with the 80,000,000 Germans, not to obey them. Tisza was a bold, silent man. He worked for aims which possibly a sense of proportion did not allow him to avow.

9. *Schemes for Reconstruction in 1915*. In the summer of 1915 the armies of the Central Powers had occupied Russian Poland. A declaration of policy seemed urgently needed. Count Julius Andrássy, a bitter personal and political enemy of Tisza, opened a campaign in favour of the 'Austrian solution'. Towards the end of the year, when the tide of *Mittel-Europa* propaganda rose rapidly, Andrássy linked up the two ideas in one scheme of compromise all round. The Habsburgs were to waive their dynastic pride by accepting a subordinate place in *Mittel-Europa*, and in exchange receive the Polish Crown. The Poles were to be conceded this, the widest measure of national reunion compatible with the German Alliance. The Austrian Germans were to attain dominion in Austria and German reunion in *Mittel-Europa*. In the complete discomfiture of the subject races of Western Austria and Galicia and in the establishment of the Central European *bloc* as the dominant Power in Europe, the Magyars were to find full safeguards for the integrity of Hungary and against any effective revival of Slav schemes from within or without the Monarchy. Tisza maintained a cold refusal. When on Easter Sunday, 23 April 1916, Andrássy once more de-

veloped his pet scheme in the Vienna *Neue Freie Presse* and in the *Frankfurter Zeitung*, Tisza's paper, the *Budapesti Hirlap*, published two articles, one declaring Magyar *désintéressement* in the Polish Question ('If we started discussing the Polish Question we should only be talking about other people's possessions and interfering with other people's business'), the other bitterly protesting against German economic activities in Hungary, though the closest economic union was to have been the essence of the Central European scheme.

10. *Rifts in the Monarchy.* Serbia was not to be annexed because the Magyars did not want any more Yugoslav territory; Rumania could not be placated because the Magyars would not cede an inch of Transylvanian territory; the Austrian-Polish scheme was to be dropped, because the Magyars—through Tisza—insisted on preserving the Dual System; complete Central European Union was not to be, because the Magyars refused to submit to any superior political organization. The Habsburg Monarchy was not to be remodelled, enlarged, or even saved if a sacrifice were required of Hungary's integrity or sovereignty. And this list of prohibitions was enforced by a Premier who had neither his country's foreign policy nor its army under his direct control,[4] since the Ministers for Foreign Affairs and War and the Supreme Army Command were common to both States of the Monarchy and had their offices and headquarters in Austria, not in Hungary. The Austrian patriots at the Vienna Court and in the army bitterly resented the 'Magyar egoism' and fretted at its dictation. The Magyars, on the other hand, now fully realized the dangers which in case of victory would arise from their troops being mixed up with those of Austria under a command hostile to the separatist Magyar doctrines about Hungary's sovereignty and independence. But if Austria, owing to the wretched ineptitude of her rulers, were to break up or be permanently subordinated to Germany, the Magyars did not want Hungary to be involved in her fate. Lifelong champions of the Agreement of 1867, such as Tisza and Wekerle, became converted to the demand for a separate Hungarian army. 'The great task of completing the structure of the Hungarian National State' mentioned in the Royal Rescript of 6 May 1918, covered among others a promise of a Hungarian national army to be established after the War. Even on the Magyar side rifts appeared in the structure of 1867.

[4] During the war, however, Tisza established a certain control over Austria-Hungary's foreign policy; all wires and despatches received had to be communicated to him immediately, and he demanded that no important notes should be sent off until he had had time to give his opinion on them (cf. Czernin's *In the World War*, pp. 128–9 and 134).

The Polish understanding with Austria was with the dynasty and the German Nationalists rather than with the Austrian centralists, the high Vienna bureaucracy, and Supreme Army Command. The *ex-officio* partners of the Habsburgs were jealous of any Habsburg territories not subject also to their authority. When in the War the Supreme Army Command obtained exceptionally wide powers the Austrian Poles suddenly beheld the face of the centralists which they had not seen since 1867. The dynasty solicited Polish support for the Austrian Solution, but Polish volunteers from Russia, invalided while fighting in the Austrian Polish Legions, were interned as alien enemies by the Austro-Hungarian Higher Command. Austrian-German governors were appointed to Galicia, the Galician railways were militarized and Germanized, and, to the joy of the subject Ruthenes, who were nearly as numerous in Galicia as the Poles, the established Polish character of the Galician administration was ignored. Everything was done to teach the Poles that Austrian generals and bureaucrats had no use for unwritten conventions. Sometimes it almost looked as if they took their revenge for having been so long excluded from Galicia. On the high level of international politics the Austro-Polish leaders continued to spin their intrigues with the Vienna Court, but the feeling which all the Polish parties of Galicia had evinced for the Austrian cause at their meeting at Cracow on 16 August 1914 was vanishing fast. This was true even of the unpolitical popular masses. In 1914 a stream of refugees poured into Vienna from the Galician theatre of war; they were treated as burdensome, undesirable aliens. In 1915 most of Galicia was recovered by Austria-Hungary, but the Vienna Government refused to spend money on its reconstruction. There was none of the warm sentiment which the Germans displayed towards the war-stricken districts of East Prussia. Austria and Galicia were strangers to each other, and this was brought home to every one by the War. Yet another rift was opening in the structure of Austria-Hungary.

Before the War a very large part of Austria's food supply was derived from Hungary; for years the industrial population of Western Austria had paid inflated prices because of the high protective duties on food established for the benefit of Magyar landowners. When the food shortage arose during the War, Hungary closed the frontier against Austria, supplying but ridiculously small quantities of food to her starving population. 'We can forgive the hunger blockade instituted by our enemies, never that by the Magyars,' declared a leader of the Austrian-German Socialists at the conclusion of the War. It taught the German-Austrian enthusiasts of the Habsburg Monarchy to ponder over the hyphen in Austria-Hungary. 'Economic partnership did in practice mean the starvation of Austria,' wrote the Vienna *Arbeiter-Zeitung* on 17 October 1918, the day after the Magyars had declared Hungary's separation from Austria. '...We part from them with a light heart.'

The three dominant races of the Habsburg Monarchy, the Magyars in Hungary, and the Germans and Poles in Austria, while unable to develop a common program for the future, were losing the instincts of a common political existence within the Habsburg Monarchy. Even in their unpolitical masses everyday experience sapped the sense of community in the Monarchy, while whatever had remained of a feeling of citizenship in the subject races, the Czecho-Slovaks, Yugoslavs, Ruthenes, Italians, and Rumans, was completely eradicated by mass executions, imprisonments, internments, petty persecutions, constant chicanery—in short, by a régime which made them look upon the Habsburg rule as a hostile military occupation.

11. *1916.* A year of political exuberance had followed in Austria on the collapse of Russia and Serbia in 1915. It closed with the Lutsk disaster, a repetition of the initial defeats in Galicia and Serbia which Austria-Hungary's rulers had too easily forgotten in the noise of victories gained for them by the Germans. No positive results had been reached in the discussions concerning Poland, Austria's internal reconstruction, and Central European Union when they were cut short by General Brussiloff's offensive. Merely the difficulties of remodelling the Habsburg Monarchy in case of victory had been revealed. The Russian successes in 1916 having once more rendered Austria-Hungary absolutely dependent on Germany, the German scheme with regard to Poland was proclaimed on 5 November 1916 in the declaration of the two Emperors, setting up Russian Poland as a State separate from Germany and Austria alike. Austria-Hungary's rulers, humiliated in the field, war-weary to the last degree, with their ambitions disappointed even in the days of victory, with the economic resources of their countries exhausted, their military reserves utterly depleted, would have gladly accepted the *status quo ante bellum*. The Magyars had always deprecated any change in Austria-Hungary's frontiers, the Habsburgs and their followers wished for it no longer. Their Monarchy, saved by German arms, was to be preserved by disarmament and a new Holy Alliance. Once more they were converts to pacifism.

Still, a complete return to pre-War conditions was impossible, and at least a partial realization of the ideas of 1915 seemed necessary. Simultaneously with the proclamation of a Polish State in Russian Poland, very wide autonomy was promised to the Galician Poles, although it was obvious that an autonomous Galicia could not have existed alongside of the Polish kingdom, and that sooner or later the two would have been united either within or outside the framework of the Habsburg Monarchy. But unless Galicia was excluded, Austria could not be effectively Germanized. As, however, in the Austrian Reichsrat the Germans and Poles united had not the necessary two-thirds majority over the subject races, it was proposed to carry out the changes by means of unconstitutional Imperial edicts (*Oktroi*)—the Magyars would not have vetoed changes completing the triple German-Magyar-Polish scheme. But once more the discussions were cut short before any results had been attained. The Russian Revolution supervened in March 1917, with hopes for peace and fear of social upheaval. The Austrian Reichsrat, which had not been summoned since the outbreak of the War, had to be convened, the appearance at least of constitutional government had to be restored. The dominant races were promised that their wishes should be realized at some more convenient time, in some more convenient form.

12. *The Russian Revolution.* To many the Russian Revolution came like a current of fresh air through a stifling heavy atmosphere, like the promise of a new, better world. Europe was turning in a vicious circle, and a struggle was dragging on which by then every one wished had never broken out. But peace without victory could not be concluded by those who thought in categories of nationality; genuine controversies are settled, not solved in their own terms. Decisions are imposed, but the real solution comes with change in modes of thinking and indifference to previous issues. The non-national Habsburgs became pacifists in a war of nationality, which they themselves had provoked in order to defeat nationality. The popular revolt against war assumed the form of social upheaval, cutting across the lines of purely nationalist ideology. Social revolution, at a Peace Conference dominated by the fear of it, might have saved the Habsburg Monarchy by diverting attention to new lines of cleavage. But further war under revolutionary conditions was bound to destroy it. 'The responsibility for continuing the War is much greater for a sovereign whose country is united by the ties of dynasty alone, than for the ruler of a country where the people itself fights for a national cause,' wrote Count Czernin in his memorandum of 12 April 1917. With the dynasty, its inheritance was bound to disappear.

The fear of social revolution in Europe in 1917 sprang from an intellectual illusion. The book-reading world knew the Socialist doctrine to be non-national, and forgot that this was not true of those who professed it, least of all of the Socialist intelligentsia. Whatever divergences there were in social interests, all alike had been educated in nationalist ideologies. Therefore the danger or chance of proletarian revolution stood, *ceteris paribus*, in an inverted ratio to the diffusion of education. Revolutions after defeats were proletarian despair let loose by nationalist exasperation. But while the War lasted nationalist zeal neutralized social antagonisms, and it is immaterial whether this was because of national sentiment even in the lower classes or because of their inability to act without a strong lead from members of the intelligentsia. In oppressed or endangered nations the Socialist intellectuals proved the most uncompromising of nationalists. They cultivated nationality with a radicalism peculiar to their nature and ideas. Their nationalism was based on the living popular masses, not on theory; this did not render it less deadly in nationally mixed territories or where nationality hopelessly conflicted with geography. In Austria-Hungary the rise of socialism, stimulated by the Russian Revolution, produced in all races a movement which in a more than ever absolute manner insisted on complete national reunion and independence, irrespective of historic tradition, established States, existing frontiers, and most of all, independent of inherited dynasties or dynastic inheritances.

The less a nation shared the interests of the dynasty, the stronger was the repercussion produced on it by the Russian example. 'Your Majesty is acquainted with the secret reports of the Governors,' wrote Count Czernin in his memorandum of 12 April 1917. '... the Russian Revolution works more strongly on our Slavs than on the Germans in Germany.' When after more than three years the Austrian Reichsrat reassembled on 30 May 1917, the representatives of the subject races came forward with programs revolutionary in substance, although in form they still acknowledged the dynasty. The Czechs greeted the Russian Revolution 'with boundless admiration and enthusiasm', declared 'solemnly before the whole world the Czech people's will to freedom and independence', demanded the reshaping of the Monarchy into 'a federal State of free national States with equal rights', and, as a logical sequence, the joining-up of the Czechs and Slovaks in a single unit. The leader of the Yugoslavs similarly demanded 'the union of all territories of the Monarchy inhabited by Slovenes, Croats, and Serbs in an independent State organism, free from the rule of any foreign nation.' The

Ruthenes passionately protested against East Galicia being kept in constitutional union with Polish territories or forced into it still further, demanded self-government for the Little Russian territories of the Monarchy, and hinted at their fundamental unity with the Russian Ukraine. The foundations of Austria-Hungary's structure, which 'created ruling and oppressed peoples', were openly assailed.

13. *The Attitude of the Poles.* By May 1917 the attitude of the Poles towards Austria had lost its precision. Their dominant position in Galicia had suffered diminution in the war, the Habsburgs had proved unable in face of German opposition to realize their Polish schemes, and the fear of Russia among the Poles disappeared to a very large extent when, on 30 March 1917, revolutionary Russia acknowledged Poland's independence and renounced all claims to ethnically Polish territory. It was now from the Central Powers in occupation of Polish territory that Poland's independence and reunion had to be extracted. Still the consequent change of front among the Poles was by no means complete. The 'conciliatories', those who always favoured compromise with whatever Power was dominant in Poland, could not disregard the possibility of the Central Powers remaining supreme; the fear of revolution spreading from the east replaced with many the previous fear of Russia—against social revolution the Central Powers were the bulwark in Eastern Europe; lastly, few Poles would have been satisfied with national independence within ethnically just frontiers—they aspired to conquests in White Russian and Little Russian land, in the vast territories beyond Poland's eastern ethnic border, where the Polish land-owning nobility ruled over many millions of non-Polish peasants. Polish designs on such a socially conservative basis, could best have been realized in conjunction with the Central Powers. The weakening of Russia seemed to offer an incomparable opportunity for Polish imperialist expansion.

Under the influence of the Russian Revolution the more radical elements among the Galician Poles adopted a sharper attitude towards Austria. On 28 May 1917 a resolution was voted at the Cracow conference of the representatives of Austrian Poland demanding a reunited and independent Poland with free access to the sea. The Polish Socialists were moving towards opposition to the Austrian Government. But in Parliament practically all the Polish members belonged to one single Club. The cautious and conservative in it insisted on continuing to negotiate with the Austrian Government, and tried by means of compromise and agreement to regain for the Poles their previous position in the Galician administration, to secure their dominion over the Ruthenes of East Galicia, to obtain concessions in late Russian Poland, and to gain an extension of frontiers at Russia's expense. But the response of the Central Powers to their advances was perfunctory. The Polish Club in the Austrian Reichsrat, embarrassed by continuous rebuffs and under pressure from the Left, occasionally passed into opposition to the government, only to return to its side when able to point to any concessions, however problematical. 'If at present our representatives have passed into opposition, this is chiefly because the administration of Galicia has been entrusted to alien hands . . .' wrote the correspondent of the *Kurjer Poznanski*, the chief organ of the National Democrats in Posnania, on 24 July 1917. 'But it is said that a return to the previous condition is imminent. Then willy-nilly the Polish Club will have to resume its previous attitude towards the Austrian Government; for power at home it will have to pay by supplying the government with the necessary number of votes in Parliament.' 'Exactly as half a century ago', wrote the Vienna *Neue Freie Presse* on 8 March 1918, after the most serious conflict between the Poles and the Government,[5] 'the Poles have refused to make common cause with the Czechs and to share in political wickedness.' The balance within the Polish Club itself and its leadership had lost steadiness; but every change in its attitude meant on a division a turn-over of about 150 in a House of 500 members. Neither satisfied nor irreconcilable, the Poles became the uncertain quantity in Austrian politics.

14. *Bolshevism and Austria-Hungary.* Russia under Kerensky moved within accepted State traditions, respecting their limitations. Bolshevism broke through the framework of the past, established the victory of a mass movement over an inherited organization, and in international relations poclaimed the unlimited right of every nation to determine its own fate. The Austro-Hungarian Government in sublime naivety allowed, even encouraged, the press to describe the break-up of the Russian Empire, the dissolution of its armies, and the disappearance of authority. Finally at Brest-Litovsk it appeared wise in its own eyes when it argued with the Bolsheviks on their own principle of self-determination, but forgot that force alone could not permanently exclude it from the territories of the Habsburg Monarchy. In Austria the subject races and the starving, suffering masses eagerly watched how a great and strong empire was trodden to dust by 'the feet of the poor and the steps of the needy', the picture of an army in dissolution became vivid to the rank and file of the Austrian

[5] On the subject of Kholm, see *infra* § 17.

troops, the idea that a new era had opened up irresistibly imposed itself on the minds of men. 'The Peace' (of Brest-Litovsk), wrote the Vienna Socialist *Arbeiter-Zeitung* on 2 March 1918, 'promises independent statehood to the Finns, Esths, Letts, Lithuanians, Poles, and Ukranians. Even the German Nationalists in their mental blindness cannot seriously believe that it will be possible to refuse statehood to the Czechs, when it is conceded to nations far inferior to them in wealth, culture, and power.' Hitherto the German Socialists in Austria had stood by the program of cultural autonomy for the different nationalities; educational matters were to have been handed over to voluntary organizations resembling churches, yet endowed with considerable governing powers. Under the influence of the Bolshevik Revolution they advanced beyond their previous program. 'In the great world-league of free nations . . .' wrote the *Arbeiter-Zeitung* in the article quoted above, 'there is no room for the old Austria; if Austria is to exist at all, it must change into a union of free nations.' 'No fully developed, self-conscious nation can renounce its right to a State of its own.' 'To every nation its State with its own government and its own Parliament; all nations united in the Empire for the common administration of the joint economic body—on this basis alone a constitution is possible which the nations would voluntarily accept and which would put an end to conflicts of nationality.'

15. *The Impossibility of reconstructing Austria-Hungary.* Two difficulties were silently passed over in the program. One was the problem of Dualism, the other the problem of territorial delimitation in the Czech provinces. 'All nations united in the Empire . . .' —did 'Empire' stand for Austria plus Hungary? If so, the Magyar State in Hungary had first to be destroyed, and to effect this was not within the power of Austria, but of the hostile Allied and Associated Powers alone. Meantime the Czechs and Slovenes refused to enter into any negotiations on constitutional reform if this was to be circumscribed within the Austrian half of the Monarchy. The German Socialist leader, Dr. Renner, subsequently first Chancellor of the German-Austrian Republic, preached nationalism to the Germans in the Vienna Parliament. They should not remain satisfied with the nondescript Austrian State, he declared in a speech on 25 February 1918, but should 'as a nation demand national unity and national self-determination within the framework of a federal State based on nationality. . . .' And he added: 'It is unthinkable that the Czechs should enclose German territory or the Germans Czech territory within their respective States.' But the German

mountain fringe cannot be separated from the Czech plain. Statehood attained by such a carving-out of territory as could never form an independent State would indeed have been a Danaan gift for the Czechs. It would have been preferable for them to remain amorphous in the anonymous Austrian State than to have the German Borderlands of Eger and Reichenberg, of Trautenau and Troppau, formed into a German State. Yet obviously, whatever the hitherto dominant Austrian Germans could do, they could not voluntarily allow three million Germans inhabiting the Czech provinces to be reduced to the position of a national minority within a Czech State. The hostile Allied and Associated Powers alone could do so. On the two rocks of the Dualist system and of German Bohemia every attempt at reforming Austria-Hungary from within was bound to founder, however sincerely undertaken.

But, in fact, no such attempt was honestly made. The constitutional reform, which the Austrian Prime Minister, Dr. von Seidler, outlined on 7 March 1918, aimed at destroying the possible foundations of national States within Austrian territory. He professed the doctrine of cultural autonomy which the Socialists had put up in 1899 and abandoned as insufficient in 1918. 'We, in our time,' he declared, 'must see to it that the conflicts of nationality should find their solution within the framework of the State', i.e. of the one, undivided Austrian State. He acted in understanding with the German parties and consequently in their interests. 'He wants a settlement in Bohemia and an understanding with the Yugoslavs in the Alps, in every province apart . . .' was the comment of the *Neue Freie Presse* on 8 March. 'That which is a policy of peace between the nationalities in Bohemia, would be a policy of war between the nationalities in Styria. . . .' Put into plainer language, this meant that the measures which suited Austria and the Germans in Bohemia, where the Germans were in a minority, did not suit them in Styria, where they were in a majority; that the separation of the German from the Czech parts of Bohemia would have destroyed the foundations of the Czech State, but the separation of the Slovene from the German districts of Styria and Carinthia would have led to the formation of a Slovene State and its ultimate inclusion in Yugoslavia. A significant passage in the speech acknowledged the existence of a Yugoslav problem. The idea which was at the back of Seidler's mind was more clearly explained in his speech of 3 May 1918. Bosnia and Dalmatia were to be joined up with Croatia into a 'Great-Croatian' State. But 'the Austrian provinces which lie on the road to the Adriatic and are closely connected with the German-speaking provinces could not be included in this State'. The Austrian Government seems still always to have counted on the old Croat sentiment which they hoped to revive by creating a State in which the Roman Catholic Croats would have had a very marked preponderance over the Greek Orthodox Serbs. But even if the setting-up of such a State might have scuttled the idea of a united Yugoslavia, which by 1918 seemed more than doubtful, the Magyars naturally failed to see why they were to hand over to it provinces which lay on their road to the Adriatic, and why they were to agree to the setting-up of a State which, if it had successfully grown into a Habsburg dependency, would have changed the balance within the Monarchy to the disadvantage of the Magyars. That is why the scheme could never be realized.

On 2 April 1918, Count Czernin, the Austro-Hungarian Minister for Foreign Affairs, in a public speech bitterly attacked the Czechs for demanding Czecho-Slovak union and independence and for sympathizing with the Czecho-Slovak Legions which fought on the Allied side. 'The wretched and miserable Masaryk is not the only one of his kind. There are also Masaryks within the borders of the Monarchy.' Czernin's speech marked a return to the anti-Slav militancy of 1915 and 1916. In April 1917 Czernin himself had called for a suspension of anti-Slav action in view of the efforts which were then to be made to obtain peace with Russia. A year later, after Brest-Litovsk, he gave the signal for resuming the old course.

16. *The Clemenceau Disclosures and the Austrian Germans.* Czernin's speech led to unexpected results. It provoked Clemenceau's revelations concerning the secret peace negotiations which in 1917 the Emperor Charles had conducted behind the backs both of his own Foreign Minister and of Germany.[6] The speech resulted in Czernin's resignation (15 April); and the publication of the Emperor's letter exasperated the German Nationalists and turned them against the Habsburgs, a fact which was to weigh heavily in the decisive days of October 1918. They had gone far to renounce their own distinct German nationalism and had forgone German national reunion in favour of the anonymous Austrian State, trusting that in fact they would remain in exclusive control of that State. And now, during a war which was to have led to the consolidation of German

[6] For Count Czernin's speech of 2 April 1918 *v.* G. L. Dickinson, *Peace Proposals and War Aims* (1919), pp. 174–5; and for the Emperor's letters, etc., *v.* pp. 30–41. For details of a proposed negotiation with Austria *v.* documents in *L'Opinion*, 10, 24, 31 July 1920, which also published Prince Sixte's account. The accuracy of the latter was formally denied by President Poincaré, cf. G. Manteyer, *The Austrian Peace Offer.*

*Mittel-Europa*, the Habsburgs, who had so often paid lip-service to the German idea and the German alliance, were found conducting a purely dynastic policy of their own. The attempt was childish, it disregarded the most elementary facts of the situation, consequently was utterly futile, yet was made; and was a prelude to an equally absurd attempt in the last days of October 1918, and supplied the background to this. It was with cold eyes of estrangement that the German Nationalists henceforth watched the fate of the Habsburg dynasty.

Meantime the incident supplied the Austrian Germans with matter for blackmail. They could force the Government to hasten the 'German course' in Austria. At this price they refrained from raising the question of the Emperor's letters in the Vienna Parliament. On 3 May, in a speech delivered at a conference of the Parliamentary leaders, Dr. von Seidler attacked the Czechs and Yugoslavs, more fully developing the program outlined on 7 March. On 6 May Dr. Zolger, a Slovene who had a seat in his Cabinet, had to resign. On 19 May an Imperial Rescript was published separating the predominantly German from the predominantly Czech districts in Bohemia. The Czechs were thus brought up against the alternative of winning independence or of seeing their natural boundaries obliterated. The Austrian Government by its continuous tergiversations and its short-sighted palliatives estranged even the dominant nationalities, and exasperated those which were anyhow in permanent opposition to it.

17. *Kholm and East Galicia.* In the peace treaty concluded with the Ukrainian puppet Government at Brest-Litovsk on 9 February 1918, the entire district of Kholm, even its purely Polish west, was ceded to the Ukraine. Such a violation of Polish territory in the east, where the Poles counted on annexing tens of thousands of square miles of non-Polish territory, drove the Poles frantic. The Polish outcry made the Austro-Hungarian Government reopen negotiations with the Ukrainians, who, on 3 March, agreed to a rectification of the frontier. In compensation, however, a secret promise seems to have been given to them that the Ruthene part of Galicia would be withdrawn from Polish dominion and, together with the Ruthene parts of the Bukovina, formed into an autonomous province. This the Poles discovered in the first days of June, and again threatened to pass into an intransigent opposition. Consequently the notorious Magyar diplomat, Count Forgách, the author of the Friedjung forgeries, and one of the men who had drafted the ultimatum to Serbia in July 1914, was sent to Kiev to explain

to the Ukrainian Government that in view of their having failed to carry out the food clauses of the Treaty, the promises made to them had lapsed. Nevertheless the Poles remained bitter at heart against Vienna, while the Ukrainians in turn felt exasperated. One by one the nationalities in Austria saw themselves menaced by the activities of the Habsburgs and the governmental clique, and saw promises given and broken with equal recklessness.

18. *Poland and Central Europe.* Peace having been concluded with Russia, the time seemed to have come to settle the future of the territories ceded by her to the Central Powers. The problem of Poland and Lithuania, and indirectly of Central European Union, came up once more. Germany, no less than the Austrian Germans, hoped to blackmail the Habsburgs over the letters of the Emperor Charles. They forgot to reckon with the Magyars, who could not be moved to concessions by embarrassments of the dynasty. On 12 May the Emperor Charles, to expiate his indiscretions, went on a pilgrimage to German Headquarters, accepted in principle a union of his States with Germany, and received full absolution. The concrete application of the principle was to be worked out by the competent statesmen. But disagreements immediately arose as to what exactly had been agreed upon. Count Burian, the Austro-Hungarian Minister for Foreign Affairs, maintained that the conclusion of closer union between the Central Powers was not possible while Austria-Hungary's future frontiers and internal structure were uncertain, i.e. so long as the Polish question remained unsettled. The Germans replied that they were uncertain what concessions to make in that matter while ignorant of what Austria-Hungary's future relations to Germany would be. Burian asserted the essential and close connexion between the problems of the Austro-Polish Solution and of Central European Union, Germany insisted on Central European Union being a distinct problem and the Polish Question part of the general East European settlement. A complete deadlock was reached.

By 1918 the Magyars had acquired an interest of their own in the Polish Question. They had accepted the Andrássy plan of connecting the Austro-Polish scheme with *Mittel-Europa*, but on one condition. The new Poland was to be joined to Austria, but in turn Austria was to hand over Dalmatia and Bosnia to Hungary; not to Croatia, but unconditionally to the Magyars, who would thus acquire undivided control of the Serbo-Croat problem. The deadlock in the Polish negotiations with Germany was linked to a deadlock within Austria-Hungary.

19. *The Decay of Austria.* Meantime the Austrian State was

visibly dying. The financial position was becoming untenable. The Austrian National Debt had risen to 70 milliard crowns; Austria lived by printing money. The circulation of paper money had risen from 2 milliards before the War to 11 by the end of 1916 and to 27 by 1 October 1918. The population was starving. Stores and resources were exhausted. The army was far gone in decomposition. The towns were full of deserters; in country districts they conducted systematic brigandage. Austria still held together merely because there was no enemy near enough to give it the shattering blow.

20. *Last Attempts at Settlement and Reconstruction.* When the turn of the tide came on the Western Front in July 1918, and from day to day the situation became more threatening to the Central Powers, another effort was made to settle outstanding problems. Ludendorff's plan to create a Lithuanian and a Ukrainian State under German tutelage had broken down over the conflict between the socially conservative principles of Germany and the socially revolutionary interests of the Lithuanian and Ukrainian peasantries. A Polish settlement on a socially congenial, conservative basis was attempted. Prince Radziwill, the Polish Minister for Foreign Affairs, was summoned to German Headquarters on 10 August, and an extension of Polish frontiers in Lithuania and White Russia was offered in lieu of the Austrian Solution. The Polish delegates left German Headquarters on the 13th, and on the 14th the Austrian Emperor arrived, accompanied by Count Burian. The proposal to make Archduke Charles Stephen King of a Polish State built on the German plan seems to have been offered as a compensation to the Habsburgs. They refused, and it was agreed to let the Poles themselves decide between the rival schemes. 'A plan has been agreed upon', declared Burian in an interview on 19 August, 'which will considerably expedite matters.... The Poles are to be invited to participate in the Austrian-German negotiations.... They have the right freely to choose their own King....'

In September Tisza, apparently as *homo regius*, started out on a journey through Bosnia-Herzegovina. He was to ascertain how a settlement favourable to the Magyars could be reached in the Yugoslav provinces. The Magyars seem to have wished to tie up Bosnia and Dalmatia directly with Hungary, as Croatia was joined to her, but not to admit any direct connexion between the two Yugoslav units. The scheme was absurd in its complexity, and even humorous in the setting of September 1918. Every Yugoslav deputation received by Count Tisza, even that of the very moderate Bosnian Moslems, told him that Yugoslav unity was their aim. Tisza, to one of them, called the principle of self-determination 'an empty phrase', their memorandum 'silly nonsense', and in a fit of rage exclaimed: 'We may perish, but before we perish we shall have sufficient strength to crush all those who cherish such ambitions.' Still, not even between Austria and Hungary was there agreement as to the settlement of the Bosnian problem. The outstanding feature of Austria-Hungary's history in the War was the inability to remodel the system of 1867. It could be destroyed, and the Habsburg Monarchy with it, but it did not admit of development.

About the middle of August reports appeared in the clerical Austrian press alleging that a scheme of reform was being prepared for constructing four national States, a German, a Czech, a Yugoslav, and a Polish State, within Austria's framework. It was ascribed to Professor Lammasch and Dr. Redlich. On 28 August, an ambiguous official *communiqué*, while denying current reports, declared that the Government considered 'a revision of the constitution, preserving all the interests implied in the integrity of the State, one of its most important tasks'. But no one seemed worried by these rumours. The German-Austrian press was ironical; the Magyar papers declared that any such change in Austria's constitution would lead to a break with Hungary; the Czech leaders, however moderate, publicly denied having anything to do with the schemes. 'Negotiations are of no use, because our final aim cannot be reached by negotiations,' stated Stanek, President of the Czech Parliamentary Union, on 3 September. 'The time for negotiations is long past, and times are much too serious for any one to conduct valid negotiations with the Government . . . unless authorized by the Czech Parliamentary Union or the Czech National Committee.' 'In evil days we did not lose our heads', declared Klofać, another Czech leader, 'and threats could not break us. Nor shall we lose our heads now, and promises will not influence us. . . . The Czech question cannot be discussed with the Vienna Government which stands by the Dual System: under that system the Czech question cannot be solved any more than that of the Yugoslavs. The various proposals of the Vienna Government are therefore of no interest to us.' As if to prove finally the futility of such discussions, Baron von Hussarek declared on 11 September that there were two limits to constitutional reform in Austria—'respect for the rights and constitution of Hungary, and the determination to preserve a united Austrian State'.

The old difficulties and the deadlock reasserted themselves. True reform within Austria-Hungary was impossible.

### C. THE COLLAPSE

21. *The Twilight of the Gods.* In the summer of 1918, by acknowledging Czecho-Slovakia as an independent, co-belligerent nation, the Allied and Associated Powers completed the program of the root and branch destruction of the Habsburg Monarchy, previous treaties or engagements having assigned the Italian, Yugoslav, and Ruman parts of Austria-Hungary to the three neighbouring States and recognized the principle of Polish reunion and independence. Peace negotiations with Austria-Hungary would have been illogical when the destruction of the Habsburg Monarchy and of its two component States was the purpose in view. Hence, in the autumn of 1918, the ardent desire of their Governments to enter into immediate negotiations, and so to obtain an implicit recognition of their right to speak for the populations of the Habsburg Monarchy and to continue a supernational existence. The growing panic in military circles supplied the background to these attempts. In a speech delivered on 9 September, Count Burian complained of the intention of the Allies to destroy the Habsburg Monarchy; in the Note of 15 September, which proposed informal peace conversations, he quoted from old speeches of Allied statesmen to show that it was not their intention to destroy it: he shut his eyes to a threat which he could not face any longer. President Wilson referred the Austro-Hungarian Government to the principles which he had previously laid down as basis for negotiations. Burian replied on the 20th that Austria-Hungary's offer remained open. Then followed Bulgaria's military collapse. On 26 September she sued for an armistice, and on the 29th accepted terms practically equivalent to unconditional surrender. Every one felt that this was the beginning of a general *déroute*, and that the end was near at hand. No enemy army had as yet reached the frontiers of the Habsburg Monarchy, and extensive territories beyond its borders remained under its military occupation. Still, within a month the Habsburg Monarchy and its political framework were to disappear, destroyed not by an extraneous force but by the logic of hitherto repressed ideas. And the men who at the beginning of October were rulers, or were deemed rulers, of a great and ancient Empire, at its close were but a group of individuals with no definable political standing or connexions. They left the empty stage escorted by the echoes of desertion.

The October days of 1918 in Austria will for ever remain remarkable for their mass psychology and as an example of how ideas, talked about yet unthinkable on one day, acquire life on the next, while other ideas, which had seemed solid fact, pass out of reality. Austria-Hungary disappeared when it vanished from the consciousness of those concerned. The War had broken the habits and the approach of defeat disbodied the ideas which made up its political and social structure. The language changed; for the first time men drew conclusions from old familiar facts; the pace at which they did so, quickened daily; it became catastrophical. Diplomatic notes, speeches in the Vienna and Budapest Parliaments, declarations and manifestoes published at Prague, Zagreb, Cracow, or Lvov, were no longer mere moves in a political game. The masses listened to the march of events, the leaders watched the movements of the inarticulate masses. Elemental forces seemed to work through men and to control them, uncontrolled by them. The solid political foundations of inherited everyday existence vanished, and in the enormous void ideas seemed to move, free from hindrance, obeying their own laws.

22. *Hussarek's Speech of 1 October 1918.* The Austrian Parliament reassembled on 1 October 1918. The Prime Minister, Baron von Hussarek, opened with an elaborate speech, whose phrasing would have won him a prize in a school competition—the last 'Noodle's Oration' of the Austrian bureaucracy. 'At the [Balkan] front our troops stand shoulder to shoulder with German troops, and there, too, preserve magnificently and faithfully the firmly cemented alliance which in future also shall unshakeably resist all the tests of Fate. . . . The hour [for peace negotiations] must come. I look forward to it with calm and determination.'

(*a*) *Poland.* The problems discussed in July and August were dealt with as if it was in the power of Austria's rulers to shape their development. 'Poland is to become an independent factor in the political world of Europe. . . . The form of the Polish State must be freely determined by the Poles themselves. In Poland a strong current of opinion is known to favour establishing her independence in closer union with the Habsburg Monarchy, and no one can take it amiss if we, for our part, sympathize with the movement and try to meet it half-way. . . . We absolutely respect Poland's right to self-determination, and merely demand that others should respect it, even if it works out to our advantage.' Did he hope that the Poles would board a sinking ship, or was this a cheerful tune played to avert panic?

(*b*) *The Yugoslav Problem.* In Bosnia-Herzegovina Austria 'does not intend to renounce her rights or barter them away against hopes of territorial increase elsewhere.... The interests of its population and of the Monarchy are to be safeguarded. And now it clearly appears that the historical separation of Bosnia from Croatia and Dalmatia no longer answers the just desires of their inhabitants.' Here was the old dynastic Croat idea, directed against the Magyars: the Habsburg and the Magyar conceptions still opposed each other when the material foundations of both were crumbling fast. Nor had even the Austrian-German Nationalists freed themselves altogether of inherited Great-Austrian instincts. They, who implicitly acknowledged the Magyars as their closest associates and on 30 September decided to approach the Magyar leaders with a view to discussing 'the problems which concerned both States alike', on the very same day voted a resolution against ceding Dalmatia to Hungary; it could be ceded 'to Croatia alone, under very clearly defined conditions'.

(*c*) *National Autonomy in Austria.* 'Gentlemen, the iron march of the days in which Fate has placed us', continued the imperturbable Hussarek, 'compels us not to overlook the tasks of the future for the sorrows of the present day; having gained peace abroad, we shall have to go to work and set our house in order. Its structure has permanently valuable foundations, but it imperatively demands to be completed and renovated. We can no longer shut ourselves off from considering and solving the problem of autonomy for the different nationalities.... The fruitful principle of national autonomy can be applied still further, and this having been done systematically, a considerable improvement—nay, a complete *dénouement*—may be expected. The difficulty lies in its application.... The task will arise for the Government carefully to prepare and inaugurate this difficult work.'[7] What a sense of time! In October 1918 the Austrian Government proposed to prepare to face the task of careful preliminary work on initiating the difficult application of a 'fruitful principle' of internal reconstruction.

23. *The Attitude of the Parties.* (*a*) *The Austrian Germans.* 'How well this speech would have sounded ten years ago, and how useful it would have been!' replied the leader of the German-Austrian Socialists. 'Perhaps even four years, perhaps even a year ago. That it no longer appears the product of insight but of fear makes it now less or differently effective than was intended.' On the day on which Parliament met, the German-Austrian Socialists put forward their own proposals. All Italian territory was to be ceded to Italy, and the Poles and Ukrainians were to be left free to determine their own fate,

[7] 'Der Regierung *wird* die Aufgabe *erwachsen* diese grosse aber aussichtsreiche Arbeit *sorgfältig vorzubereiten und einzuleiten.*'

but Western Austria, the old German domain, was to be saved and preserved on a pseudo-national and pseudo-territorial basis. The members representing the nationalities in the Austrian Reichsrat were to form themselves into National Assemblies, draw up constitutions for their territories, and jointly consider what matters should remain common to them all: the German-Austrian Socialists had in mind the German Austrians themselves, the Czechs, and the Yugoslavs, though as yet the scheme was not explicitly limited to them. The Czechs and Austrian Yugoslavs were thus asked to accept the frontiers of Western Austria, to discuss their future apart from the Slovaks and the Yugoslavs of Hungary, Croatia, Bosnia-Herzegovina, and Serbia, while the deputies from the German fringes of the Czech provinces and even from their German enclaves were to enter the German-Austrian Assembly. This was chastened German nationalism, but still naively egoistic nationalism. The form had changed, the substance remained the same.

On 2 October rumours that the Austro-Hungarian Government would in a new Peace Note accept President Wilson's Fourteen Points, made the Pan-German deputies propose that, in such a case, the German members should immediately withdraw from the Austrian Parliament and form themselves into a German-Austrian National Assembly. The Czechs were to be forestalled with regard to German Bohemia; as for the Austrian State, it was no concern of the German Nationalists once it became incapable of serving their purpose. On 4 October, at a Conference of the three big German parties, the National Union, the Christian Socialists, and the Socialists, the scheme implied in the Socialist resolutions of 1 October was fully developed, and on the 5th the Socialist program was accepted by the other parties as basis for negotiations. They decided to recognize the right of the Latin and Slav nations to determine their fate and to form States of their own, but these were not to include ethnically German territory. All German territories of Austria were to form a German-Austrian State which would freely settle its relations to the other nationalities and to Germany. The Austrian Germans would enter into negotiations with the Czechs and Yugoslavs for transforming Austria into a league of free national commonwealths, but were this refused they would with all their strength oppose any attempt of the Austrian authorities or of foreign Powers to settle without their consent their fate or that of any part of their territory. Under the influence of the debate which followed on Hussarek's speech, the Austrian Germans had advanced a considerable distance in five days. The ballast of by now irrelevant inherited conceptions was thrown overboard. The Habsburg Monarchy, Austria-Hungary, the Austrian State itself, had disappeared from their consciousness; in their mind Western Austria remained the only reality. They would talk to the Czechs because of the German minorities comprised in their provinces, and to the Slovenes whose territory intervened between them and the sea. They would talk to their kinsmen in Germany. They passed over the Habsburgs in silence. Bosnia-Herzegovina and, it seems, even Dalmatia were forgotten, Galicia and the Bukovina were written off, Hungary was not mentioned, the Austrian authorities were treated as extraneous, almost alien, to the Austrian Germans. The final break had come in the consciousness of the old champions of the Habsburg Monarchy, even the Christian Socialists had to accept it. *Sauve qui peut*—and from that moment the Austrian Germans were Austrian Germans and nothing more.

(*b*) *The Czechs and Yugoslavs.* The Austro-Hungarian Government tried to inaugurate a Peace Conference in order to reassert the existence of the Monarchy and of the Dualist Constitution, and thereby implicitly to deny that of a Czecho-Slovak and of a Yugoslav nation. The Czechs and Yugoslavs in the Austrian Parliament answered Hussarek's speech of 1 October by demanding that in the peace negotiations they should be directly represented and heard, declared that they would not allow the Austro-Hungarian Government to speak for them, nor would they discuss their future with the Austrian Government, but would settle it in conjunction with the Allied and Associated Powers. They could consider no solution within the frontiers of Austria alone. 'Should the Austrian Government decide under duress to form Bohemia, Moravia, and Silesia into a Czech State to the exclusion of the Hungarian Slovaks', stated the leader of the Czechs, 'they would see therein but an attempt to break up their national unity....' They flaunted a defiant disloyalty. 'Not a drop of blood has been voluntarily shed by the Czechs on the side of the Central Powers.' The Czecho-Slovak Legions fighting in conjunction with the Allies have been called a rabble, but it is with them that the Austrian Government will have to discuss the future of the Czecho-Slovak nation, 'and that is why we will not discuss it with you here.' 'The Yugoslavs present their humble thanks for any schemes of autonomy', declared their spokesman in the Austrian Reichsrat. 'Baron von Hussarek comes too late. Through all Yugoslav lands the cry resounds: complete freedom or death! No trickery can any longer separate the Slovenes from the Croats and Serbs....'

In the first days of October the Czechs and Yugoslavs considered whether they should not withdraw from the Austrian Reichsrat, and thus definitely break with the Austrian State. But they were uncertain what line and procedure the Allies would adopt towards Austria-Hungary, and hesitated to make irrevocable pronouncements. They remained in the Austrian Reichsrat which offered them the best public tribune within the Habsburg Monarchy, while consolidating their national organizations in their own as yet provincial centres. On 5 and 6 October a conference was held at Zagreb of all the Yugoslav parties in the Austrian, Hungarian, Croatian, and Bosnian legislatures, and a National Council was elected to conduct Yugoslav policy.

(*c*) *The Poles.* In the debate following on Hussarek's speech, the President of the Polish Club spoke in softer tones than other Slav leaders, partly from habit and partly with the wish to coax the Austrian Government into not spoiling the Polish game in East Galicia. He was appreciative of the way in which the Prime Minister acknowledged the right of the Poles to determine their own fate, admitted that there was a movement in favour of establishing Polish independence in conjunction with the Habsburg Monarchy, explained that it was based on the past relations of the Poles to Austria, on the part played by the Polish Club in the Austrian Reichsrat, and on the battles fought in common with Austria by the Polish Legions, but at the same time claimed for the Poles a place among the suffering nationalities of Austria. He finished by demanding the complete reunion of Poland, including Silesia, with access to the sea, and direct representation at the Peace Conference for all Poles. The whole of Galicia was assumed to be Poland's due, although in East Galicia they formed only about one-fifth of the population.

(*d*) *The Ruthenes.* The Ruthene members entered a passionate protest against being subjected to Polish rule. 'We shall fight and die rather than let ourselves be annexed to Poland.'

24. *Austria-Hungary accepts President Wilson's Fourteen Points and awaits a Reply.* On 4 October[8] the Austro-Hungarian Government, in conjunction with Germany and Turkey, offered to enter into peace negotiations on the basis of President Wilson's Fourteen Points of 8 January 1918, of the four principles laid down in his speech of 11 February, and of his speech of 27 September. Point 10 had stipulated that 'the peoples of Austria-Hungary, whose place among the nations we wish to see safeguarded and assured, should

[8] The Note was transmitted by the Swedish Minister at Washington on 7 October.

be accorded the freest opportunity of autonomous development'. Austria-Hungary accepted it without inquiring into its precise meaning. Henceforth nothing could be done in Austria until Washington had spoken. 'Austria has a Prime Minister who resides at Washington,' wrote the *Neue Freie Presse* on 9 October. 'His name is Woodrow Wilson, and his executive officer in Vienna is Baron von Hussarek.' Changes in the Austrian Government, new declarations or offers, schemes for the future, might all prove equally futile. 'We might do too much or we might do too little.... The Prime Minister is Woodrow Wilson at Washington,' it repeated on the 12th. 'He knows what policy he proposes to prescribe for Austria....' And day after day the Vienna press impatiently complained: 'Still no answer from America.' In the weeks of supreme crisis the Austrian Government became completely paralysed. It waited for an answer, or rather for a verdict. It had to wait a long time. In the process of waiting it ceased to be a government.

On 8 October Baron von Hussarek read out the Peace Note of the 4th in the Austrian Reichsrat, admitting that it marked 'a modification of the political conceptions on which Austrian official policy had hitherto been based', and that the time had come for 'full-grown nations (*mündige Völker*) to determine their own future'. Austria abandoned all pretence of dominion or claim to it, she capitulated before an unknown future. 'She is going to play "King Lear",' was the comment of one of her votaries.

On 9 October President Wilson's answer to Germany was received; it declared that an evacuation of Allied territory must precede the conclusion of an armistice, and asked whether the Imperial Chancellor was 'speaking merely for the constituted authorities of the Empire who have so far conducted the war'. A Reuter wire of 8 October from Washington added: 'It is officially announced that no answer to the Austrian peace proposals is contemplated at present.' Dismay spread among the ruling circles of the Habsburg Monarchy. On 4 October Germany and Austria-Hungary had addressed the same offer to America. Germany alone received a reply. What was the meaning of the omission? Austro-Hungarian troops no less than those of Germany were in occupation of Allied territory. Was Austria-Hungary to heed an answer which ignored its existence? But how could she afford to ignore the Note? And what could the Austro-Hungarian Government have replied were it asked in turn whom it represented?

On 12 October the German Government in its reply to President Wilson's Note of the 8th specially mentioned Austria-Hungary as agreeing to the evacuation of Allied territory. President Wilson, in conclusion to his Note of the 14th, wherein he laid down that the military advisers of the Allied and Associated Powers would settle the terms of armistice, announced that a separate Note would be sent to the Austro-Hungarian Government. They had to wait.

25. *The Last Habsburg Bid.* In the meantime an attempt was made to form a government which could say whom it represented. Lammasch, the old pacifist professor who in August 1918 had talked about an internal 'rejuvenation' of Austria, was to succeed Hussarek, although the Austrian Germans were averse to him because they did not trust him to stand faithfully by Germany. On 10 October representatives of all the Austrian nationalities were summoned to audiences with the Emperor for the 12th and 13th; the scheme to be discussed was roughly known. The nationalities were to be given the right to constitute States of their own within the framework of Austria. The change was to be carried out by a Cabinet representing all the nationalities. The Poles alone were to be let out of the Ark (*en route* for Warsaw) in accordance with Point 13 of President Wilson,[9] and also in the hope that this Habsburg dove, might return with an olive leaf—increase of territory. The Czechs were the first to see the Emperor and flatly refused to enter the proposed Cabinet. They demanded that a Czech Government should be set up immediately at Prague, that it should take part in the Peace Conference, and that all Czech regiments should return to the Czech provinces, with the natural corollary that non-Czech troops should be withdrawn. They warned the Emperor that the Czech popular movement could no longer be repressed, and that, unless something decisive was done, the nationalities would act on their own. Tusar, one of the Czech delegation to the Emperor (and subsequently Prime Minister of the Czecho-Slovak Republic), published after the interview an article pointing out that the purpose of trying to form a Cabinet representing all the Austrian nationalities was to say to the world: 'In Austria everything is in perfect order. You need not trouble your heads about us!' 'We ourselves, and we alone, shall settle our future,' was Tusar's answer. 'We shall give ourselves the constitution we need. We shall determine our relations with neighbouring States, and we refuse to admit any interference from Vienna or Budapest. . . . A Czech State must arise with a Czech government

[9] *Point* 13: 'An independent Polish State should be erected which should include the territories inhabited by indisputably Polish populations, which should be assured a free and secure access to the sea, and whose political and economic independence and territorial integrity should be guaranteed by international covenant.'

at its head. Its representatives will appear at the Peace Conference. There the future organization of the world will be decided.' Before the Czechs negotiate with Vienna, Austrian officials must cease to rule in Bohemia.

The refusal of the Czechs, followed by that of other nationalities, killed the idea of the Coalition Cabinet. 'No *coup d'état* from above and no revolution from below', wrote the *Arbeiter-Zeitung* on 12 October, 'can produce a government trusted by all the nationalities to negotiate peace in their name, because many nationalities do not want Austria any longer, do not feel citizens of Austria any more, and deny the right of any Austrian Government whatsoever to conduct their affairs. This is a naked, brutal fact, which no clear-sighted person can deny. . . . We must reckon with the fact that Wilson will not invite the Austro-Hungarian Government to the peace negotiations, but only representatives of each of the nationalities of Austria-Hungary.' 'There can be no doubt', wrote the *Arbeiter-Zeitung* on 15 October, 'the dissolution of the State of mixed nationality into separate and independent nations is in progress; if not yet in law and fact, it already has occurred in the minds of men. . . . The nations exist, have long ago constituted themselves, their will to be free and independent is unshakeable. . . .'

What, in that case, was to become of German Austria? On 13 and 15 October, Otto Bauer, subsequently Minister for Foreign Affairs of the German-Austrian Republic, pointed out in the *Arbeiter-Zeitung* that there could not be one German Austria, but there would have to be three geographic fragments—Inner Austria (Vienna and the Alpine provinces), Northern Bohemia (the German fringe from Eger to Trautenau), and the Sudetenland[10] (a few frontier districts in Eastern Bohemia, Northern Moravia, and the western part of Austrian Silesia down to Troppau), which, unless united by remaining within an Austrian super-State, could preserve their connexion by union with the German Empire alone. An Austrian Federal State would necessarily have to retain very wide powers over economic matters, but it seemed highly doubtful whether any of the other nationalities would agree to such a surrender of governmental powers. 'Because the German Austrians as an industrial nation have a strong interest in maintaining the united economic territory, they suppose the same feelings in the others,' but in reality the non-German nationalities, being mostly agricultural, do not feel the same need. Therefore even for economic reasons German Austria

[10] The name of Sudetenland at that time was not as yet made to cover all predominantly German districts of the three Czech provinces.

would have to join Germany. The Austrian Germans were rapidly losing hope of being able to keep together Western Austria.

26. *Hungary and the Sinking Ship.* The Magyars carefully watched the disruption of Austria. They felt that the moment was fast approaching when Hungary would have to break off her connexion with Austria in order to escape being pooled with her in the bankrupt mass against which the creditor nations would enter claims. The Magyar Kingdom of Hungary was to masquerade as an oppressed nationality which now at last attained the freedom it had yearned for—why was it not to retain its direct hold on Slovakia, Transylvania, and the Banat as the Poles proposed to retain their hold on East Galicia? The Magyar Socialists, in a manifesto published on 7 October, offered cultural autonomy to the subject races in a Hungary 'which claims the right to determine her own fate.' 'Self-determination'—such as Count Czernin claimed for Austria-Hungary in the argument which he addressed to the Bolsheviks at Brest-Litovsk. Vienna was to be the scapegoat. And Germany, whom Apponyi and Andrássy, no less than Tisza and Wekerle, had but recently described as the natural, indispensable ally of Hungary,[11] was to be abandoned. On 10 October Tisza delivered a significant speech. Recent developments in Austria, he declared, had shaken the foundations of the Dual Monarchy, and should the expected changes occur, Hungary would have to reassert her complete independence. As to the German alliance, it had been necessary only as long as Hungary was threatened by Tsarist Russia. Even more explicit was Dr. Wekerle (who became Premier in August 1917 after Tisza had resigned in May), when, on 11 October, he addressed the Executive Committee of his party. 'A fundamental change has occurred in our relations with Austria. We are confronted by an accomplished fact. . . . It is a serious matter that Austria should have turned entirely towards federalism. Bohemia proposes to break off completely on a federalist basis and to form a separate State. . . . Austria has not the strength to withstand such attempts. . . . We no longer face the Austria with which we concluded our agreements in the past.' She cannot fulfil her obligations with regard to common defence or economic matters. Hungary must strike out her own line and guard her own interests; territorial integrity is her first concern.

[11] See, e.g., Andrássy's speech in the Hungarian Parliament, on 20 June 1918: 'The German Alliance I consider necessary, natural, and in accordance with the only sound policy. I am convinced that without it it is impossible to conduct a proper Hungarian policy, for the Germans are the only great race in whose interest it is that there should be a strong Hungary. It cannot be to the interest of Hungary to estrange this faithful ally. . . .'

Little was said about the dynasty, but both speeches implied that no immediate change was contemplated. The Magyars seem to have feared that by prematurely breaking with the dynasty they might give it a chance of securing more favourable conditions for Austria at the expense of Hungary, i.e. by an attempt at a genuine federalization of the entire Habsburg Monarchy, the Magyar domain included.

Negotiations were carried on for a new Magyar Coalition Cabinet. Different leaders were offered the Premiership but declined. Count Michael Karolyi advised the Emperor to summon a Cabinet consisting of Radicals and Socialists, and refused to co-operate with the representatives of the old system. On 14 October Wekerle formally resigned, but next day withdrew his resignation on condition that a special clause guaranteeing Hungary's territorial integrity was inserted in the coming Imperial Proclamation federalizing Austria. In the Hungarian Delegations,[12] Michael Karolyi demanded the immediate declaration of Hungary's complete independence and the abolition of all institutions common to Hungary and Austria. On Tisza's motion, however, the Delegations adjourned until an answer was received from President Wilson. They too had to wait.

27. *The Federalizing Manifesto of 16 October.* In spite of the refusal of the different Austrian nationalities to join a Reconstruction Cabinet, an attempt was made to do something which might look like realizing Point 10 of President Wilson, and might perhaps preserve Austria's existence.[13] An Imperial Manifesto, dated 16 October, proclaimed the federalization of Austria: it was countersigned by the same Hussarek who on 11 September had declared the Government's 'determination to preserve a united Austrian State', on 1 October had talked in very vague terms about national autonomy, and even on 8 October had refrained from explaining the nature and extent of the autonomy to be conceded. 'Now the reconstruction of the Fatherland on its natural and therefore most reliable foundations must be undertaken without delay,' read the Manifesto. 'The wishes of the Austrian nationalities are to be carefully harmonized and a beginning must be made to realize them. . . . Austria, in accordance with the will of her nationalities, is to become a federal State in which every nationality within its own territory

[12] The Delegations were Committees of the Austrian and Hungarian Parliaments set up to deal with affairs which the two States had in common.

[13] *Point* 10: 'The peoples of Austria-Hungary, whose place among the nations we wish to see safeguarded and assured, should be accorded the freest opportunity of autonomous development.'

forms its own commonwealth. This is not to prejudice in any way the union of the Polish territories of Austria with the independent Polish State. The town of Trieste and its territory, in accordance with the wishes of its inhabitants, receives a special position. The reconstruction, which in no way infringes the integrity of the countries belonging to the Holy Crown of Hungary, is to secure independence to every single State, but also effectively to protect the common interests.... I call upon the nations.... to co-operate in the great task through National Councils consisting of the members who represent each nationality in the Reichsrat, and to secure the interests of the nations as against each other and in relation to my government....' The Emperor and his Government thus acknowledged themselves extraneous to the national States, but still tried to maintain themselves through the administrative machinery; not a word was said in the Manifesto of national governments, the indispensable, logical corollary to the new national States.

On the day before the Manifesto was published it was to have been read by the Prime Minister to the leaders of the different nationalities in Parliament. The Czechs refused to appear at the meeting, the Polish leaders were away at Warsaw, the Ukrainians, expecting a Polish attempt to declare East Galicia 'Polish territory', protested against the vagueness of the Manifesto, the Yugoslavs, who put in an appearance, declared their solidarity with the Czechs. On 16 October the Czechs and Yugoslavs made a common statement in the Delegations for Foreign Affairs. They 'irrevocably insisted that the Czecho-Slovak and Yugoslav questions being international problems could be satisfactorily solved at the general Peace Conference alone', and that 'previous to the publication of President Wilson's answer to the Austro-Hungarian peace offer all discussion of the proposals contained in the Imperial Manifesto was devoid of practical value...'.On 19 October the Czech National Committee in Prague and the Yugoslav National Council in Zagreb confirmed the declaration, once for all refusing any further discussions with Vienna or Budapest.

On the same day on which the Manifesto was signed (16 October), Wekerle declared in the Hungarian Parliament that in view of the federalization of Austria the connexion between the two States would in future be reduced to personal union, and Hungary would have to settle her political and economic problems on a completely independent basis. Within Hungary the nationalities were offered nothing beyond language rights; the unity and integrity of the Magyar State were to be preserved. Dr. A. Vaida-Voevod, subsequently Rumanian Prime Minister, replied by demanding complete and free self-determination for the Hungarian Rumans, and denied the claim of the Hungarian Parliament and Government to represent them. A similar declaration was made in the name of the Slovaks by their representative Father Juriga.

28. *Developments in Poland.* It had been necessary to leave out the Poles from the Imperial Manifesto of 16 October, because the thirteenth of President Wilson's Points, accepted on 4 October both by Germany and Austria-Hungary, stipulated that 'an independent Polish state should be erected which should include the territories inhabited by indisputably Polish populations. . . .' On 7 October the Polish Regency Council at Warsaw, formed in the autumn of 1916 from among the most conciliatory elements, drew the obvious conclusions from the Note of the Central Powers (and also from the speech of the new German Chancellor Prince Max of Baden, who on 5 October had declared in favour of freely elected Diets in the occupied territories in the East), and published a Manifesto to the Polish nation foreshadowing the formation of a representative National Government and the summoning of a Polish Diet. The Manifesto finished with the watchword of 'a free and re-united Poland'. On 15 October the Polish representatives in the Austrian Delegations declared in the name of all the Polish members of the Austrian Reichsrat that they henceforth considered themselves 'subjects and citizens of a free and re-united Polish State'. They called on the Austro-Hungarian Government to undertake the necessary steps for realizing the principles of President Wilson and for clearly defining the right of the Polish nation to participate in the general Peace Conference. On the same day the leaders of the Galician Poles were summoned by the Regency Council to Warsaw to take part in forming the new Polish Government.

Its formation met with peculiar difficulties. The National Democrats, who had the full support of the French Government, tried to proscribe their political opponents among the Conservatives and moderates, and to reduce the radical Left to a decorative place in a predominantly National Democrat Government. After long-drawn negotiations the Regency Council surrendered to the National Democrats, and on 19 October one of their leaders was entrusted with the formation of a new Cabinet, of which the list was accepted by the Regency Council on the 23rd. The Left refused any share in that Government, which thus came to consist exclusively of members and friends of the National Democrat party. M. Stanislas Glombinski, their leader in Galicia, became Minister for Foreign Affairs, and on 24 October despatched the following wire to the German Secretary of State, Dr. Solf, and the Austro-Hungarian Minister for Foreign Affairs, Count Burian: 'Assuming the office of Minister for Foreign Affairs, I desire to assure Your Excellency of my best intentions to maintain friendly relations between our neighbour States'—a peculiar performance on the part of a man and group which at that time claimed a monopoly in relations with the Entente.

29. *East Galicia.* On 28 October a conference of the Austrian-Polish representatives met at Cracow and elected a commission to wind up Galicia's relations with Austria. Representatives of the 3,200,000 Ruthenes do not seem to have been invited, nor of the National Jews—a majority among the 900,000 Galician Jews. Nevertheless the Polish Liquidation Committee set out to act for the entire country and, under the leadership of the National Democrats, resolved within five days to transfer its seat from Cracow to Lvov—a provocation to the Ruthenes.

The Ruthene members of the Austrian Reichsrat, at a meeting in Vienna on 10 October, had decided to summon a conference of representatives from all Ruthene territories of Austria-Hungary to Lvov for the 18th. Meantime the Imperial Manifesto was published on the 16th. Having met, the conference elected a Ukrainian National Council, to act as 'the Constituent Assembly of the part of the Ukrainian nation inhabiting territories of the Austro-Hungarian Monarchy. . . .' The Ukrainian Socialists pressed for immediate reunion with the Russian Ukraine and, when out-voted, left the Assembly; the moderate parties, obviously afraid of plunging into the chaos of the Russian Ukraine, preferred first to organize the government and administration of their own territories. 'The Ukrainian National Council has the right and duty, at a time which it will consider proper, to exercise the right of self-determination for the Ukrainian people and to decide with which State to unite the territories inhabited by Ukrainians.' Next day the National Council decided to form the Ukrainian territories of Austria-Hungary into a separate State, to invite the Polish and Jewish national minorities inhabiting these territories to send representatives to the Council, to prepare for summoning a Diet elected by universal suffrage on the proportional system, and to grant cultural autonomy and a share in the government to national minorities; lastly, to demand direct representation at the Peace Conference, denying to Count Burian the right to represent them.

By 2 November the Polish Liquidation Commission was to have met at Lvov, the capital of East Galicia. The Ukrainian

National Council forestalled them. In the early morning of 1 November Ukrainian troops, acting under orders from the Council, occupied the government buildings at Lvov, and the Council assumed the government of East Galicia. The Polish minority refused to accept the offers of the Ukrainians, and on the same day fighting commenced between them.

30. *President Wilson's Reply to Austria-Hungary.* President Wilson's answer to the Austro-Hungarian Note of 7 October was published on the 21st. The Note, dated 18 October, explained that the President could not entertain the suggestion of the Austro-Hungarian government 'because of certain events of the utmost importance which, occurring since the delivery of his Address of January 8th last, have necessarily altered the attitude and responsibility of the Government of the United States. . . .' Having recognized the Czecho-Slovaks as a belligerent nation and their National Council as 'a *de facto* belligerent government', and having 'also recognized in the fullest manner the justice of the nationalistic aspirations of the Jugo-Slavs for freedom', the President is 'no longer at liberty to accept a mere "autonomy" of these peoples as a basis of peace, but is obliged to insist that they, and not he, shall be the judges of what action on the part of the Austro-Hungarian Government will satisfy their aspirations and their conception of their rights and destiny as members of the family of nations.'

The verdict broke the last links in Austria-Hungary's structure. The Czecho-Slovaks and Yugoslavs were acknowledged as independent nations, the frontier between Austria and Hungary was obliterated, the two States on which the Austro-Hungarian Government based its existence were no more. Austria was reduced to its German, Hungary to its Magyar, territory. The complex structure raised on the historic imperialisms of the dominant races and on the Imperial traditions of the Habsburgs was shattered. The Austro-Hungarian Common Ministries, the nondescript, nationally anonymous Austrian Government, and even the national Magyar Government of Hungary, were of a world which had vanished overnight.

On 21 October, in a Manifesto dated the 18th, and signed by Professor Masaryk, Dr. Stefanik, and Dr. Beneš, the Czecho-Slovak National Council in Paris published a Declaration of Independence and constituted itself the Czecho-Slovak Provisional Government. It declared that 'federalization, and still more "autonomy" would mean nothing under a Habsburg', that the Czecho-Slovak nation refuses 'any longer to remain a part of Austria-Hungary in any form', and denied all Habsburg claims 'to rule in Czecho-Slovak land, which we here and now declare shall henceforth be a free and independent people and nation'.

The Czecho-Slovak and Yugoslav Councils in Prague and Zagreb which had already refused to negotiate with Vienna and Budapest previous to the general Peace Conference, could now gain nothing by discussing either the constitution or the exact frontiers of their States with the enemy Powers in the absence of the Allies. They demanded once more that alien troops should be withdrawn from their provinces, their own regiments allowed to return to their homelands, and the administration of Czecho-Slovak and Yugoslav territories handed over to their National Councils. In fact, the Czechs did not await permission. Many civil servants henceforth treated the National Council as their government; e.g. most of the railway employees in the Czech districts were Czechs, and these, ordered by their leaders, began to control food transports to Vienna. They instituted what the Germans described as a Czech blockade, a formidable weapon against a half-starved city. The central authorities were daily losing power over the non-German provinces.

31. *German Austria.* On 21 October, the day on which President Wilson's Note was published, the German members of the Austrian Reichsrat, following up the Imperial Manifesto of 16 October, met in the building of the Lower Austrian Diet. They could no longer shirk the question what their own relations should be to the old, non-national Austrian authorities, the legacy of a vanishing Empire. The resolutions as passed, and still more some of the speeches delivered in the German National Assembly, clearly went beyond the terms of reference drawn by the Manifesto. 'The German people in Austria,' began the unanimously adopted resolutions, 'will itself determine its future State organization, form an independent German-Austrian State, and by free agreement settle its relations to the other nationalities.' The Imperial Austrian Government, which had offered its guidance to the nationalities, was passed over in silence. Then the claim to all territory inhabited by Germans was reasserted, the German districts in the Czech provinces being specially mentioned. The summoning of a German-Austrian Constituent Assembly was foreshadowed, but not a word was said to safeguard the monarchical principle; in fact the Habsburgs were never mentioned. 'Until a National Constituent Assembly meets, the Provisional National Assembly claims the right to represent the German people of Austria at the peace negotiations, to carry on negotiations with the other nationalities for the transfer of the administration to the new national States and concerning the mutual relations to be

established between them . . .' Again the Austro-Hungarian and the Austrian Governments were passed over in silence. They appeared only in the resolution setting up an Executive Committee which, 'until the German-Austrian Government is formed, is to represent the Austrian Germans in relations with the Austro-Hungarian and the Austrian Governments, and with the other nationalities. . . .' All alike were treated as extraneous.

The Socialists, although they held only about one-fifth of the seats in the National Assembly, were clearly the driving force. They represented the organized labour masses, and had a moral ascendancy over the German Nationalists and the Habsburgite Clericals whose past policy had resulted in national collapse and humiliation. Victor Adler, the Socialist leader, in a speech delivered at the first meeting of the National Assembly, voiced the new spirit rising among the Austrian Germans. 'The German people in Austria will form its own democratic State . . . which is freely to decide how to settle its relations with the neighbouring nationalities and with the German Empire. It will form a free confederation with the neighbouring nationalities, if they wish it. Should they refuse or make conditions incompatible with the economic and national interests of the German people, the German-Austrian State, which by itself is an economically impossible formation, will be compelled as a separate State to enter the German Empire. We demand for the German-Austrian State full freedom to choose between these two possible connexions.' He went on to state that the Socialists in the Constituent Assembly would declare for a republic. Meantime the Assembly, disregarding the bankrupt Habsburg institutions, should form a German-Austrian Government. 'The other nationalities will be represented at the Peace Conference; nor can the German people leave its interests in the hands of a diplomacy alien to the people. The German-Austrian Government is immediately to get in touch with the Slav nations of Austria and enter into direct negotiations with President Wilson for an armistice and peace. Lastly, it is to take over the administration of German Austria.'

Adler's speech declared for German-Austrian independence and renounced the Habsburg connexion. The Christian Socialists and most of the German Nationalists did not as yet go the whole way, still it was half-heartedly that they demurred. The idea was set forth, and in these days of quick maturing was to be realized sooner than the Socialists themselves expected.

32. *The Austrian Reichsrat.* Quaint interludes were supplied in the second half of October by occasional sittings of the Austrian

Reichsrat, where men seemed to meet to register the degree reached in the decline of the State. The meetings were badly attended and the discussions were perfunctory and futile. The process of Austria's recasting was carried on in the national capitals, the centre was dead. On 22 October the Reichsrat was asked by Count Burian to appoint a Committee for Foreign Affairs which would assist the Austro-Hungarian representatives at the Peace Conference. The request was refused by all the nationalities. Oppositions in parliament are used to moving futile resolutions without hope to see them accepted or realized—it's part of the job. In October 1918 the governing circles in Vienna found themselves in opposition to reality.

33. *The Crisis in Hungary.* In a very different spirit did the Hungarian Parliament, representative of Magyar nationalism, watch the growing danger to their domain. They were sitting on 23 October when news was received that the 79th Croat Regiment had mutinied at Fiume. This followed on Yugoslav national demonstrations at Zagreb. A storm broke out in the House; the sitting was suspended; a Cabinet Council was called; meanwhile the opposition members met in the reception hall of Parliament. It was generally felt that a new line had to be struck both on foreign and internal policy and this could not possibly be done by the exponents of the old, now discredited, system. Wekerle himself felt it, and although sure of a majority in the House—only the day before Tisza's party had fused with his followers—he did not feel equal to shouldering the responsibility any longer. When the House reassembled in the evening, he announced the resignation of his Cabinet. 'I shall submit to His Majesty a proposal for summoning a new government which would include representatives of all the parties in this House and possibly of national forces outside' (under the narrow Hungarian class franchise the Socialists had no seats in Parliament). The Cabinet crisis which followed had necessarily a revolutionary tendency. Out of the class Parliament there could emerge no government very different from the one which had resigned; while no government answering the supposed needs of the moment and the popular demands of the capital (a disproportionately prominent element in revolutions) could have maintained itself in that Parliament. The parties of the Left, under the leadership of Count Michael Karolyi, decided to form a National Council, a popular quasi-Parliament as a base for a Revolutionary Government, should the oligarchs refuse to surrender; further, they demanded that the complete independence of Hungary be proclaimed, a Hungarian

Minister for Foreign Affairs appointed, the alliance with Germany denounced, and a separate peace concluded.

Immediately on the fall of Wekerle, Count Burian, another nominee of the Magyar oligarchy, resigned office. Count Julius Andrássy, who, though himself of the oligarchal group, had for personal reasons always been opposed to Tisza, was appointed Burian's successor. All his life he had dreamt of filling the place which his father had held 1871–9, and he had striven for it by hard work and intrigue. When at last he got hold of the wheel there was nothing to steer any more. 'From various quarters I am asked', he said in an interview with the *Neue Freie Presse* on 25 October, 'how a Common Minister for Foreign Affairs can be appointed when work on the separation of Austria and Hungary has begun. In this there is no contradiction. Until the Act of 1867 is changed, nothing but a Common Minister for Foreign Affairs is conceivable or possible.'

34. '*Das Liquidierungskabinett.*' On 23 October the Emperor went to Budapest. The 25th was spent in negotiations with Andrássy and Michael Karolyi. On the same day it was announced that Professor Lammasch was to become Austrian Prime Minister. Pacifists were to be given office in both States in a faint hope that they might succeed in administering artificial respiration to the corpses. During the Lisbon earthquake of 1755 a man hawked anti-earthquake pills, in October 1918 the Emperor Charles changed his ministers. On the 26th he returned to Vienna with Karolyi, and negotiations were continued with Andrássy and Lammasch. On 27 October Hussarek's resignation was officially accepted, and Lammasch took over most of his Cabinet; the only new man of mark was the Minister of Finance, Dr. J. Redlich—another old, deserving ambition realized in a Cabinet posthumous to the State. From the outset the new government was described as *ein Liquidierungskabinett*, liquidators of a bankrupt concern. They were to assist in the transfer of administration to the national governments, and try to preserve a place for the Habsburgs and a central government. But even for liquidation they were not wanted: the State was breaking up of itself.

On 24 October the Executive Committee of the German-Austrian National Assembly had notified the central authorities that they considered themselves to be the provisional government of the German-Austrian State; they had proposed that a joint Committee be formed by the different National Councils to carry on common affairs; and that the armistice should be concluded by them in common, but the peace negotiations conducted by each separately. The Austrian

Government was no longer deemed competent to deal even with the problems which from their nature were common to its successors. The remnant of a power which they no longer recognized, it had no mandate from any one.

The appointment of Michael Karolyi as Hungarian Premier did not materialize because of disagreements between him and Andrássy. Archduke Joseph was appointed *homo regius* to conduct at Budapest further negotiations for a new Premier and Cabinet.

35. *The Military Collapse*. New frontiers were rising between the Successor States of Austria-Hungary, and every frontier threatened to become a battle-front. In each State the people demanded a concentration of its troops to enforce its will and claims, and no thought was given to the military fronts of the late Habsburg Monarchy. The war-weary troops listened to news from home, and felt that the force or idea which had sent them to those fronts had irrevocably perished.

36. *Andrássy's Peace Offer*. On 27 October Andrássy despatched via Stockholm his answer to President Wilson's Note of 18 October. The Austro-Hungarian Government declared that 'as in the case of the preceding statements of the President it also adheres to his point of view, as laid down in his last note, regarding the rights of the peoples of Austria-Hungary, particularly those of the Czecho-Slovaks and the Yugoslavs'. It further declared its readiness 'without awaiting the result of other negotiations, to enter into pourparlers in regard to peace between Austria-Hungary and the States of the opposing side.' Thus they acknowledged the independence of the Czecho-Slovaks and Yugoslavs and offered to enter into negotiations independently of Germany who had been given about twenty-four hours' notice of the impending *démarche*.

On 28 October, the day after the Note had been sent to Washington by the usual intermediary of a neutral State, but also the day after the Allies had crossed the Piave, Andrássy despatched a wire direct to Mr. Lansing endorsing all the points of President Wilson, declaring that preparations had already been made to give the fullest scope to the self-determination of the peoples of Austria and of Hungary, and asking the American Government to bring about 'an immediate armistice on all the Austro-Hungarian fronts and to initiate peace negotiations'. The same Note was sent to the British, French, Italian, and Japanese Governments.

However much the Notes tried formally to assert the continued existence of the Habsburg Monarchy, by their contents they admitted the end of Austria-Hungary to have come. For them to agree with President Wilson's description of the Czecho-Slovaks as an independent nation at war with the German and Austro-Hungarian Empires was not devoid of involuntary humour. To offer negotiations apart from Germany was as undignified as it was futile. It was believed at the time, perhaps with reason, that this was done under pressure from Michael Karolyi who had always been an opponent of the alliance with Germany; but Julius Andrássy signed the Note, he who throughout the War had been one of the strongest advocates of *Mittel-Europa*—the son of the man who in 1879 had concluded with Bismarck the alliance between Austria-Hungary and Germany.

37. *Czecho-Slovak and Yugoslav Independence* (28–29 October 1918). In Czecho-Slovakia and Yugoslavia the reply of the Austro-Hungarian Government to President Wilson's Note of 18 October gave the signal for a final break with the Habsburg Monarchy. Not even German or Magyar troops, or whoever else might have previously been inclined to defend its existence, could any longer oppose the revolutionary action of the Czecho-Slovaks and Yugoslavs after the Emperor and his Government had officially before the entire world acknowledged the existence and independence of these States. In Prague the Executive Committee of the National Council met on 28 October, and after a short sitting went to the Governor's office to declare that they took over the administration of the country. The officials promised to obey their orders and put themselves completely at the service of the National Council. The same was done by the police, and at 8.30 p.m. the general commanding the troops surrendered his command to the National Council. At 9.30 p.m. the town was entered by the 28th Prague Regiment, which in 1915 had been disbanded because some of its companies had by previous arrangement crossed over to the Russians. Everywhere the crowds which gathered in the streets removed the Imperial Eagles and other emblems of the Habsburg Monarchy and of the Austrian State, and replaced them by national colours and emblems. Similar scenes occurred throughout the Czech and Yugoslav provinces. The movement was spontaneous and general. The meaning of the Austro-Hungarian answer to President Wilson's Note of 18 October was obvious, and so were the conclusions to be drawn from it. There was no need to work out the logical absurdities of the Austro-Hungarian Government acknowledging Czecho-Slovak and Yugoslav independence. They were felt and the psychological break with Austria was complete.

On 29 October the Croat Diet met and a resolution was carried that 'Dalmatia, Croatia and Slavonia with Fiume are . . . a State completely independent of Hungary and Austria and . . . join the common national and sovereign State of the Slovenes, Croats, and Serbs.' The Generals commanding the military forces in Croatia accepted the change, the Serb prisoners of war were released and enrolled in the National Guard, and the same day a new government for Croatia, Slavonia, and Dalmatia was formed. In the course of 30 October the arrangements for taking over the civil and military power in the Czecho-Slovak and Yugoslav territories by their national governments were completed, and the Czecho-Slovak Government notified the Austrian Prime Minister that Dr. Tusar had been appointed Czecho-Slovak diplomatic representative in Vienna. Czecho-Slovakia and Yugoslavia, in name as in fact, became independent States. The national leaders had to restrain rather than rouse the masses: these were revolutions, generally bloodless since no resistance was offered.

38. *Revolution in Budapest* (28–31 October 1918). On 28 October a National Council was formed in Budapest by the parties of the Left, and the idea was canvassed of proclaiming Michael Karolyi Prime Minister of Hungary. Fighting occurred in the streets. The excitement of the masses was growing. Soldiers and officers joined the mob. The police declared that they would no longer do political service. On 29 October Count Hadik, a mild oligarch of the Andrássy type, was appointed Premier and assumed office on the 30th. He invited the Socialist Executive to negotiate with him but was told to apply to the National Council as they would not act independently. Soldiers' Councils were formed at Budapest. In the night of 30 October a rumour spread from barrack to barrack that the general commanding Budapest had ordered the dissolution of these Councils and the arrest of their members. The troops decided to offer resistance. Officers and soldiers put themselves under the command of the National Council and occupied a number of important government buildings. On the 31st at 8 a.m. Archduke Joseph, the *homo regius*, received Michael Karolyi. The Archduke claimed to have asked a few hours earlier that Karolyi should be made Premier. In the course of the next hour Karolyi received by telephone his appointment from the Emperor. Once more an attempt was made by the vanishing Empire to reassert its existence by formally acknowledging accomplished facts. Still Karolyi's Government, arising from the self-appointed National Council of the Left and composed of none but its members, was clearly revolutionary in character, and the fact that Karolyi had taken the oath

to the King (Charles was King in Hungary) roused dissatisfaction among the republicans, who were gaining strength. On 2 November Karolyi announced in the National Council that, seeing the people's wish freely to settle the future constitution of Hungary, the Government had addressed a request to the King to absolve them from their oath of loyalty. 'We received the answer that the King absolved the Government of their oath.' Karolyi was a Magyar aristocrat, punctilious in matters of constitutional law even while leading a revolution, like the Whig lords of 1688. Archduke Joseph, on the other hand, preferred the part of Philippe-Égalité. 'Absolved from his oath' to his Monarch and cousin, he enthusiastically swore in his own name (from now onward plain Joseph Habsburg) and in that of his son a new oath to the Hungarian nation. Anything to keep afloat.

Count Stephen Tisza, the grim Calvinist who had ruled Hungary in the days of her strength and greatness, an iron ruler and devoted servant, a master mind entangled in the absurdities of Hungary's politics, lived long enough to see the coming end, but was spared the pain of watching the ill-fated work of the small, weak, muddle-headed men whom he had despised, insulted, and bullied all his life. On 31 October, at 6 p.m., soldiers forced their way into Tisza's house and entered the drawing-room where he was with his wife and his sister-in-law Countess Almassy. Tisza stepped forward to meet them, unflinching to the last. After a few words had been exchanged, he was shot dead. His last words were: 'I die. It had to be.'

39. *The End of the Austrian Reichsrat* (30 October 1918). The Lammasch Cabinet was to have met the Austrian Reichsrat on 30 October. The conference of party leaders which assembled previous to the sitting did not press for a regular meeting of the House. Austria was dead but the time had not yet come for the formal registration of the fact. The House met at 11 a.m. and, 'because of the existing conditions,' adjourned at 11.10 a.m., the date for its reassembly being fixed for 12 November. When its German members and some ten members of other nationality, mostly stray black sheep, met on that day, in view of 'the fact that Austria had ceased to exist' and 'the House had no further functions to perform', it adjourned 'without fixig a day for its next sitting'.

40. *Revolution in Vienna* (30–31 October). When the German-Austrian National Assembly met on 30 October the German-Austrian State had been formed by the action of its neighbours. Czecho-Slovakia, Yugoslavia, and Hungary were independent. But there remained an Austro-Hungarian Foreign Minister in Vienna

who offered, in whose name no one knew, to negotiate peace with the Allies apart from Germany. Even the Christian Socialists, previously ardent Habsburgites, had not the courage to defend the Note of 27 October. 'The nation to which the Minister for Foreign Affairs belongs', declared one of their leaders, 'has refused all further connexion with Austria, and it is therefore extraordinarily difficult for the [Austrian] Germans to accept any one of that nation for representative of their interests.' The spokesman of the Socialists openly atacked 'the dynasty and the Hungarian feudal magnates' who 'choose the present moment for deserting Germany and stabbing German democracy in the back'. 'These gentlemen come too late to acquire merit in bringing about peace. All they achieve is cold, shameful betrayal, the proverbial gratitude of the House of Austria. The Magyar feudal lords pose as lovers of freedom and decide in favour of personal union. No one sheds a tear for the Dualist system which had long outlived itself. As to personal union we do not care either for the union or for the personnel. . . . The dynasty plans to gain over the Czechs and Yugoslavs at the expense of the Germans. We shall never admit that even a shadow of a German national interest should be sacrificed to that of the dynasty. . . . The German Socialists consider that the nation cannot be guarded against such dynastic schemings except by German Austria constituting itself a republic. From this point of view we ask once more: in whose name has Count Andrássy sent his Note? He has nothing to declare or offer in the name of the German people.'

A provisional constitution was voted for German Austria, and the German-Austrian National Assembly declared that it alone and its organs were authorized to speak for the German-Austrian people in matters of foreign policy and to represent them at the peace negotiations. A proclamation was issued to the German people of Austria. 'The German-Austrian National Assembly has voted to-day the fundamental law of the new German-Austrian State. A Council of State will immediately appoint the first German-Austrian Government, which is to conduct peace negotiations and assume the administration of the German districts of Austria and the command of the German troops. . . .'

On the same day enormous crowds marched through the streets of Vienna raising cries for a German-Austrian Republic and singing socialist revolutionary songs and, here and there, also the *Wacht am Rhein*. Revolutionary excitement was growing throughout the country. The Socialist party was leading the way, the other parties, especially the German Nationalists, in view of the Emperor's offer to abandon Germany, had no heart to resist.

The first Government of German Austria was appointed by the Council of State on 31 October, without any reference to the Emperor.

41. *The Austrian 'Staatsidee' once more.* On 1 November the Hungarian Government ordered the Hungarian troops at all the fronts to lay down arms; on the 3rd the Austro-Hungarian Military Command signed an armistice which amounted to unconditional surrender. The Austro-Hungarian Army, the oldest and last bulwark of the Habsburg Monarchy, had ceased to exist. 'The End of the Military Monarchy' was the title of a leading article in the *Arbeiter-Zeitung* of 3 November, expressive of the frame of mind in which the Habsburg nationalities were at the close of the War.

> The armies melt away, all territory is given over to the enemy, he need not conquer any more, for there is no one for him to fight. The Hungarian Minister for War has ordered all Hungarian troops to lay down arms. The most important harbours have called in enemy fleets.... The Italians will not conclude an armistice except on terms such as have seldom marked the end of a war. This is the end of the war which Austria-Hungary had arrogantly provoked, and this is the end of the military Monarchy. A shameful end, this War and its conclusion, but truly worthy of her existence, the end she deserved. For all the wars which Austria-Hungary has conducted—and an infinite amount of blood has been shed by her rulers—were made only to maintain the dynastic power, to preserve its glory, to assert its importance. What business had Austria in Germany, or, still more, in Italy?... How did we get to Bosnia-Herzegovina? German Austria protested against its occupation, the Magyars did not want it, but it answered the needs of the dynastic power.... The dynasty needed compensation, a substitute for the 'subjects' whom it had lost in Germany and Italy.... For centuries it had impeded German unity; it had been an obstacle to the union of Italy; it had to obstruct the Serb national cause, for such was its vocation.... The end of the military Monarchy, be it shameful beyond expression, does not move our hearts.... An edifice of lies collapses, a system of dynastic power, which has been a plague to the world ever since it started on its infamous course, has reached its term in the world's history. All wrappings fall from the State Idea and here it stands in its nakedness... With what insolence has the legend about the loyalty of all the nationalities been drummed into the world throughout history, and especially during the War, and with what insolence was the world told that the nationalities were glad to belong to the Habsburgs. And now that the force is broken which had bound them all

—and it was nothing but force which bound them together—now that they can speak and act as they think and feel, their true feelings for Austria break forth like a flood : hatred against that Austria, joy to be rid of her. In the Czechs, Poles, Slovenes, Croats, Italians, not a shadow of grief can be found, not a trace of the feeling that a bond has broken which had existed for centuries, no emotion, no sadness, no woe, none of the sentiments which even prisoners feel on leaving gaol. And this state of things, which cannot be the growth of a day, but in its origins must reach back for years and tens of years, had been painted to the world as the happy and united Austria where all the nations prayed to God to bless whatever Emperor there was, finding their ecstatic happiness in having him for ruler. And for this lie of a State Idea, for a Monarchy which the nations fly like an evil, we have made the War, millions and millions have shed their blood, our present and our future have been sacrificed.

42. *The End of the Monarchy* (9–16 November). On 9 November the German Emperor and the Crown Prince resigned the thrones of Germany and Prussia. On the 11th the Emperor Charles renounced all share in the government of German Austria without, however, explicitly renouncing the Crown; he merely promised to submit to the verdict of the people whatever it might be. 'I do not want to be an obstacle to the free development of my peoples. I recognize beforehand the decision which German Austria will make as regards her future constitution. . . . I renounce all share in the business of the State. Simultaneously I relieve my Austrian Government of office.' So too, on 13 November, he renounced all share in the government of Hungary, recognizing beforehand any decision she might take as regards her constitution, though refusing to abdicate.

On 12 November the Council of State decreed German Austria 'a democratic Republic' and 'a component part of the German Republic'. On the 16th a Republic was proclaimed in Hungary. The last Successor States of the Habsburg Monarchy had renounced their Habsburg allegiance.

# XI

# BASIC FACTORS IN NINETEENTH-CENTURY EUROPEAN HISTORY

THE basic factors which I have in mind concern the political history of Europe in its international aspects during the period 1815–1919, the nineteenth century of European history. That century and its aftermath witnessed on the Continent the triumph of linguistic nationality, and of democracy in the sense of a levelling of classes rather than of constitutional growth; and it was foremost nationality and the struggles engendered by it that in Central and Eastern Europe defeated the movement toward self-government and liberty. 'The language chart is our Magna Charta,' was the slogan of nationalism on the European Continent; and a comparison of the political map of Europe in 1920, and still more in 1945, with that of 1815 shows that, by and large, the program has been realized, though hardly with the results its enthusiasts had anticipated: the operation was successful, but at what cost to the patient? I propose to examine the patterns that can be discerned in the seemingly confused historical process which recast the map of Europe on a linguistic basis. I refrain from inquiring into the sense of the envenomed struggles we have witnessed; for such inquiry would take us into inscrutable depths or into an airy void. Possibly there is no more sense in human history than in the changes of the seasons or the movements of the stars; or if sense there be, it escapes our perception. But the historian, when watching strands interlace and entwine and their patterns intersect, seeks for the logic of situations and the rhythm of events which invest them at least with a determinist meaning.

The political problems of the European Continent in the nineteenth century were posed by the French Revolution; and the basic change which it ushered in was the transition from dynastic to national sovereignty, and a progressive widening of the 'political nation' from the privileged orders to democracy, till the nation came to comprise, in theory at least, the entire people. The emphasis of dynastic sovereignty, quasi-proprietary in character, was on the territory of the State; the emphasis of national sovereignty was on the human community—which postulated that a true sense of community should weld the population into one people. From the principle of national sovereignty spring constitutional movements and national demands, claims to self-government and to self-determination. In appearance these had cognate aims, a delusion fostered by their having that common source, and a common opponent in autocracy based on dynastic heritage. In practice, however, there is an antithesis between self-government, which means constitutional development within an existing territorial framework, and self-determination for which there is no occasion unless that framework is called in question and territorial changes are demanded; and acute disputes concerning the territorial framework naturally retard, or even preclude, constitutional development.

In linguistically mixed regions delimitation is a thorny problem even where there is mere juxtaposition of national groups. But in Europe intermixture was as a rule the result of past conquests, political and cultural, which had reduced the original national group to a state of social inferiority. Conquests created Ulsters, and over further, wider regions spread the network of an 'ascendancy' primarily based on the landowning classes and the town population, alien to, or alienated from, the peasantry which retained its own language or religion, or both. Self-government meant, in the earlier stages, the rule of the big landowners and their retainers in the countryside, and of the upper middle-class and the intelligentsia in the towns; their language or religion determined the national character of the country (Grattan's Parliament, composed of Anglo-Irish Protestants, deemed itself representative of the Irish nation). Hence in the numerous Irelands scattered all over Europe turmoil and strife were bound to result from the rise of the lower classes, and especially of the peasantry, to political consciousness and action. National and religious conflicts interlocked with agrarian movements, envenoming each other: war was waged for both the national and the personal ownership of the land, and either side felt that it was fighting not for private interests only. An educated upper class, for centuries accustomed to consider the country its own, would not easily allow itself to be reduced to the position of alien interlopers, while peasants rooted in the land, as only they can be, fought the long-drawn battle with an obstinacy unsurpassed by any other class. Moreover the dominant minority invariably had the backing of its Ulster and of its homeland: even under democracy. With the progressive widening of the political nation, the unprivileged orders, one by one down the social scale, were taking over the quasi-proprietary claims of dynasties and feudal oligarchies to territorial dominance; they became ideological partners or heirs of their *quondam* rulers, and frequently their actual partners by being settled on the land or in government posts in the disputed territory. Peasant-settlers planted as a garrison to keep down the subject race, school-teachers sent to spread the language of the minority, and a host of petty officials, constituted a master-nation whose rule was much harder to bear, and more galling, than that of a dynasty or of a remote oligarchy. Consider the amount of disturbance which during the nineteenth century was caused in the political life of this country by an Ireland geographically isolated and not subjected to any further encroachments; and you can gauge the effect which two dozen Irelands were bound to have on the life of nineteenth-century Europe as borderlands between contending nations, especially while attempts continued to be made to complete conquest and conversion.

On the European Continent incomplete conquests fell into two patterns. The main stream of migrations, which had overrun Europe from East to West, was reversed about the eighth century: from West to East the French pressed against the Flemings and Germans, the Germans against the Lithuanians and Slavs, the Lithuanians and Poles against the Russians, and the Russians against the Finnish tribes, and ultimately also against the Mongols; each nation was yielding ground in the West, and gaining much more at the expense of its Eastern neighbours: in the East were wide spaces and a reduced capacity for resisting pressure. Similarly the Swedes spread across the Baltic, and the Italians across the Adriatic. The Flemish-Walloon problem in Belgium and the Franco-German problem in Alsace, the numerous problems of Germany's ragged Eastern border, Poland's problems both on her Western and on her Eastern flank, and the conflict between the Yugoslavs and the Italians, all originate in that great West to East shift on the linguistic map of Europe. The other pattern of conquests whose consequences were formative of nineteenth-century European history, goes back to the continued Asiatic incursions, of the Avars, Magyars, and Turks into South-Eastern Europe. The Germans met them at the gate of the Danube, between the Bohemian quadrilateral and the Alps: this is the origin of Austria whose core was the Ostmark round Vienna, with its flanking mountain bastions and its access to the Adriatic. Germans and Magyars in their head-on collision split off the Northern from the Southern Slavs and established their dominion over that middle zone; and next the subjection of the Southern Slavs and the Rumans was completed by the Turkish conquest of the Balkans.

And now compare the political map of Europe in 1815 with the nationality map which forms the approximate basis of the frontiers of 1920 and 1945. Practically all the territorial changes occurred in Central and East-Central Europe. In 1815, the Germans and the Italians, the two most numerous nations in that region, were disunited through dynastic fragmentation. Between them in the West and the Russians in the East, thirteen to nineteen smaller nations inhabit a belt stretching from Petsamo to Candia (their exact number depends on what linguistic divergences or historical differences are deemed to constitute a nation): in 1815 all these smaller nations were engulfed in the Habsburg and Ottoman Empires, in the Eastern fringe of Prussia, and the Western fringe of Russia. But if in that year anyone had attempted to draw a nationality map of Europe, he would have treated Finland as Swedish; the Baltic provinces, all East Prussia and Upper Silesia, and the Czech and Slovene provinces of Austria as German; Lithuania, Latgalia, White Russia, and the Western Ukraine as Polish; practically all Hungary as Magyar; the Austrian Littoral as Italian; and the Christian populations of Turkey possibly as Greek. Thus between the Gulf of Finland and the Turkish border there were only four nations that counted; and in 1848 an educated Englishman discoursing on the rights of nationality would probably be aware of four problems only and of four programs deserving his sympathy: those of German and Italian unification, of Hungary's independence, and of Poland's resurrection (presumably within the frontiers of 1772). As enemies of these programs he would indict the Habsburgs and the Tsar; and if later in the year he heard that ignorant peasantries were fighting on the side of autocracy against those enlightened nations and their eloquent leaders, this would fill him with regret and disgust.

The nationality problem naturally first came up for solution in terms of the master nations; and the main obstacle to three of their four programs was the Habsburg dynasty with its prescriptive rights and policy: of the Polish Question alone, the origin and gravamen lay outside their sphere. No deeper need or conflict had caused Austria's participation in the dismemberment of Poland—only the indiscriminate passion of the Habsburgs for extending their dynastic possessions; and this in time gave rise to schemes for a reconstitution of Poland under Habsburg dominion. Very different was the position of Prussia and Russia with regard to the Polish Question. Geographical consolidation was Prussia's primary purpose in the Partitions: in West Prussia (the 'Corridor' of the inter-war period) there was a conflict between the unity of the seaboard and that of the Vistula river-basin; and in Posnania Polish territory came within seventy miles of Berlin. The Russo-Polish conflict was over White Russia and the Western Ukraine, territories almost twice the size of ethnic Poland, in which the landowners were Roman Catholic and Polish (or Polonized) while the peasants belonged to the Eastern Churches and continued to speak Russian dialects: the Poles could claim those territories on grounds of nationality so long as peasant-serfs politically counted for little more than cattle; but the frontier attained by Russia in the Third Partition was in 1919 reproduced in the Curzon Line.

One may well ask how in 1795 the Russians came to draw for themselves a frontier correct in the terms of 1919; and the answer sounds even more paradoxical: because they did not think in terms of nationality, or of the political rights of nations as then constituted. They thought in terms of religion, the only ones in which peasant-serfs counted; and by and large religion and nationality coincided. Thus backward Tsarist Russia jumped the period of the master nations, but without being able to destroy the social and economic foundations of the Polish claims to mastery over the disputed provinces: she could not even emancipate the serfs, still less dispossess the big landowners for their benefit, while serfdom and latifundia were maintained in the rest of Russia; nor could the Poles, in 1848 the General Staff of the *sansculottes* of Europe, raise the peasant masses against the Tsarist régime, or they would have destroyed their own hold on those Eastern borderlands. That incongruity of claims and realities, coupled with the impossibility of adjusting them, gave a unique turn to the Polish Question at a time when elsewhere nationality problems were being solved in terms of the socially and culturally dominant nations.

I pass to the alignment of the European Great Powers and the interplay of their interests and policies. What were in 1815 the leading *dramatis personae* on the European stage? Great Britain and Russia, Powers flanking Europe, in it but never altogether of it, possessed of growing extra-European interests—the rising World Powers; France and Austria, European Great Powers, whose political ambits covered the entire Continent; and Prussia, the least among the Great Powers in size and resources, with limited regional interests and objectives.

Even in 1815 Great Britain and Russia were conscious of their separation from Europe. Next, England expanded into the Second British Empire, which now seems about to combine with the Western half of the First Empire into an as yet unnamed and ill-defined working community of English-speaking nations, centring on Washington rather than on London. A similar shift away from Europe has transferred Russia's capital from St. Petersburg to Moscow, a distance not to be measured in miles only, while the centre of gravity of Russia's population and production has been moving East, toward the Volga and the Urals. Between 1815 and 1914 the full weight of these two Powers was seldom felt in Europe, partly owing to the dispersal or poor organization of their forces, and partly because they seldom actively intervened in European conflicts except when the Ottoman Empire was in question, an Asiatic Power which in the Eastern Mediterranean held the key position between three continents; and then they were usually ranged on opposite sides. Similarly in the ideological struggle between constitutional systems and autocratic régimes they were opposed to each other. But three times in 150 years their forces were joined, first to defeat the French bid for dominion over Europe, and next the two German bids; and in these German Wars, the United States started by supporting, and finished by virtually replacing, Great Britain as the flanking Power in the West. Now the English-speaking nations and the U.S.S.R., engaged in a contest of global dimensions, can hardly be said to flank Europe any longer: they face each other in the very centre of Europe —indeed, what remains of Europe, of its history and its politics?

On the Continent the game of power politics, in whatever terms it was played, normally made a neighbour into an enemy, and therefore the neighbour's neighbour on the opposite flank into an ally. Hence the rule of odd and even numbers in international politics: if Germany was France's enemy, then Poland was France's ally, and consequently Russia the ally of Germany—numbers one and three against two and four; and even sharp ideological divisions between Germany and Russia could not prevent that rule from asserting itself in 1922 and 1939. Yet during the first half of the nineteenth century there was latent, or even open, hostility between France and Austria which had no common frontier, while for a century a frontier of more than 500 miles never gave rise to conflict between Prussia and Russia. The intervening numbers, Germany and Italy, whose pressure against France and Austria would have forced them to recognize their common interest, were latent; whereas Prussia and Russia were acutely conscious of their common interest in Poland, the suppressed intervening number—a frontier across territory whose population is alien and hostile to both neighbours is not apt to produce friction between them.

In 1814–15 the Habsburgs withdrew from Belgium and the Rhine, and deliberately divested themselves of responsibility for the defence of Germany; while Prussia, which before 1789 had been primarily an East European, Baltic Power, was entrusted with the 'Watch on the Rhine', and, stretching from Königsberg to the Saar, now covered the entire length of Germany. This redistribution of territory predetermined the ultimate exclusion of Austria from Germany, and Germany's ultimate inclusion in Prussia. But so long as Prussia made the 'Watch on the Rhine' her foremost duty, and *deutsche Treue* toward Austria her leading principle, she was internationally immobilized, and Germany neutralized; and the struggle between France and Austria was carried on across the power-vacuum of Italy. That struggle, begun when Habsburg possessions flanked France both in the East and the West but discontinued during the last thirty-three years of the *ancien régime*, when the Bourbons and the Habsburgs recognized that Great Britain, Prussia, and Russia had become their real rivals, was renewed by the French Revolution and Napoleon, and continued by their epigoni for half a century after 1815.

Austria's existence and Habsburg hegemony over Germany and Italy rested on the principle of dynastic property in States; the presence of the Habsburgs kept the two countries disunited; their disunion secured French primacy in Europe; here was a basis for Franco-Austrian co-operation. But the French flaunted the principle of national sovereignty at Austria: a fit weapon against the Habsburgs, but not an ideological basis for a continuance of French power politics. French statesmen and diplomats from Talleyrand to Thiers were pro-Austrian, but the current of popular feelings ran against Austria—till July 1866 when the cry of *revanche pour Sadova* resounded on the Paris boulevards: the intervening numbers had emerged. But soon the basis disappeared for a Franco-Austrian alliance. Between 1815 and 1894 France had no ally on the European Continent, and only one constant friend, the Poles, whose friendship was a liability rather than an asset for her; because the implied threat, though never real, tended to draw Russia closer toward Prussia.

The co-operation between the Courts of St. Petersburg and Berlin was based on a human affinity between them, on a common autocratic ideology, and on the common anti-Polish interest. Berlin, on the very fringe of German-speaking territory, and St. Petersburg built in Finnish land and given a German name by its Russian founder, stood close to the two ends of the Baltic fringe, territory conquered in the thirteenth and fourteenth centuries by the Teutonic Knights, and ruled until quite recently by their descendants, the Prussian Junkers and the Baltic Barons. These Lutheran Germans, makers and servants of the Tsarist régime, and a power under it, were alien to Slav and Greek-Orthodox Russia, and averse to Pan-Slavism or to constitutional developments which would have endangered their own position. They were anti-Polish and friendly to Prussia; elsewhere they worked the power politics of the Russian Empire, with little distinctive colouring of their own.

The European nationality problems raised in 1848 fell almost all within the ambit of the Habsburg Empire which would have suffered disruption had the programs of the four master nations been realized: Western Austria would have been included in a Greater Germany, and the Czechs and Slovenes engulfed in it; Lombardy and Venetia would have gone to Piedmont; Hungary would have achieved independence, and full dominion over its Slovaks, Yugoslavs, Rumans, and Ruthenes; over these the Poles would have achieved similar dominion in Galicia. The subject races therefore came out on the side of the dynasty against their social and economic rulers: in order to prevent that rule from being reinforced by political dominion. It was all a phantasmagoria. The Tsar and the King of Prussia still stood by the Habsburgs on grounds of dynastic solidarity; revolutionary forces, which alone could in Germany have cut through the dynastic tangle by proclaiming a Republic one and indivisible, were lacking; the Prussian-Polish conflict in Posnania soon put an end to anti-Russian velleities among the Germans; Piedmont and the Magyars were not a match for the Habsburg Monarchy supported by Russia and the subject races. The transformation, if it was to be, had to be attempted in a different manner.

The Crimean War lost Austria Russia's support; Napoleon III opened up the Italian problem; Bismarck by anti-Polish action in 1863 secured Russia's friendship. In 1859–67, the Habsburg problem was solved in accordance with the modified programs of the master races. The Habsburgs were expelled from Lesser Germany and Italy, but retained the German and Italian provinces which were part of their old hereditary dominions (*Erbländer*); Hungary achieved complete constitutional independence while remaining within the military and international framework of the Habsburg Monarchy; and the government of Galicia was handed over to the Poles. The Austrian Empire changed into the Dual Monarchy, rebuilt on a German-Magyar-Polish basis; and the subject races were delivered to their masters (more completely in Hungary than in Western Austria or Galicia).

In one way Francis-Joseph built better than he knew. To the Austrian Germans Western Austria was their heritage, to the Magyars all Hungary, and to the Poles Galicia, and each of these three nations was prepared to fight to the last for every square mile of what it considered its own, while the three heritages together covered the entire Monarchy. No such community of interest could have been found between the dynasty and the subject races. On the other hand, the Emperor's conscious calculations miscarried: he concluded the compromise with the Magyars in the hope of gaining their support for future action against Prussia. In 1870 the Austrian Germans were not willing to fight on the side of France against other Germans, while the Magyars did not wish for a victory which would have re-established the dynastic power of the Habsburgs and might have enabled them to go back on the Settlement of 1867. The logic of the situation defeated Francis-Joseph's schemings.

If the struggle for supremacy in Germany could not be resumed any more, a German-Austrian alliance was in the logic of the situation. Austria-Hungary was surrounded by neighbours each of whom saw populations of his own language within its borders. The Habsburg Monarchy reconstructed on a German-Magyar basis was a fit ally for Germany, while Germany alone had an interest in its survival, and could therefore accept an alliance in lieu of complete national reunion (in fact, Bismarck did not want the Austrian Germans in the Reich, which inclusion would have unfavourably affected the balance between the Catholic South and the Protestant North). For Germany Austria-Hungary was a more convenient ally than Russia, for in such an alliance Austria-Hungary as the weaker and more exposed of the two was dependent on Germany, whereas Germany would have been dependent on Russia. Moreover Germany had to count with the possibility that the Power whom she did not pick for ally, would become that of France; and as such Austria would have been more dangerous because of the appeal she could make to the Roman Catholic Germans—Bismarck dreaded a Roman Catholic league against the Second Reich. Still, Bismarck did not mean to tie Germany to Austria-Hungary, nor to cut the wire to St. Petersburg. But again the logic of the situation prevailed:

even if Bismarck's successors had been wise and strong men, it seems doubtful whether the consequences of an Austrian alliance could have been permanently avoided. In 1877 Bismarck, when asked by the Russians what his attitude would be in case of a Russian-Austrian war, replied that much as he would regret such a war he could see either side win or lose battles, but not suffer one of them to be knocked out as a Great Power. Obviously he feared Germany being left as an isolated intervening number between two Great Powers, France and Russia or France and Austria. There was no need for Russia to seek a German guarantee for her existence; there was for Austria. But once Germany had committed herself to upholding Austria-Hungary's existence, she was moving from the Baltic fringe into the Danube Valley and the Balkans; and how long could the common anti-Polish and reactionary interest preserve Russia's friendship for a Germany which crossed her path in the Balkans?

Here Russia continued her 'historic mission' of freeing the Greek-Orthodox populations. Of the dominant nations the Turks had the weakest social, economic, and administrative hold over their subject races; even so, the process of destroying the Ottoman Empire in Europe took a hundred years, from the rise of Serbia and the liberation of Greece, across the Russo-Turkish War of 1877–8, to the Balkan War of 1912. But in that process Russia suffered surprises and disappointments; she found Hellenes and Rumans where she had merely seen members of the Greek-Orthodox Church; and the Bulgars, however pro-Russian in sentiment, from hostility to the Serbs twice joined the Germans in accordance with the rule of odd and even numbers. By 1914 the Balkan nations were free, and the problem of the Greek-Orthodox Serbs and Rumans in the Habsburg Monarchy was now at stake. In 1867, at half-time between Vienna and Versailles, the Austrian Empire changed into the Dual Monarchy; at the close, the Dual Monarchy broke up into the Succession States. But the Russian Empire having collapsed a year earlier, its alien Western fringe, too, disintegrated into national States. The end of the First World War saw the middle zone of the small nations resettled on the basis of linguistic nationality.

In three regions only, socially and culturally dominant minorities retained, or even regained, superiority and possession. The Polish-Masurian fringe of East Prussia and about half of Polish Upper Silesia were left to the Germans on the strength of plebiscites which should never have been held: for there is a nationality *in posse* no less than a nationality *in esse*, and in these territories the process of national revival, universal in Europe, had not yet reached its natural term. On the Adriatic the Italians acquired territory with Yugoslav majorities. And the Poles managed, against the decision of the Allied and Associated Powers, to substitute the Riga for the Curzon Line. All these gains were wiped out by the Second World War. The process which formed the essence of European history since the French Revolution has now reached its term.

Looking back, converted though we cannot be to the *ancien régime*, to the 'system Metternich' or to Tsarism, we no longer exult over the age of nationality and democracy and its victories. All past social superiorities have been wiped out behind the Iron Curtain, and most of the cultural values which the educated classes had created. Anti-Socialist, clerical peasant communities may yet arise in States now satellites of Russia. But a reinstatement of the dispossessed upper and middle classes is impossible. And it is even more idle to think of a reconquest of territories once held on the basis of those vanished supremacies. Now territories in Europe can only be regained with 'vacant possession': that is, radically cleared of their present inhabitants. The process of transfers or exchanges of population was started in the Balkans and Asia Minor at the end of the First World War. It was applied by Hitler where it suited him to withdraw German, or expel non-German, populations; and it was planned on an infinitely greater scale by the Germans had they won the war. As they lost it, the process was carried through against them. Hence their wrath.

# XII

# THE GERMAN FINALE TO AN EPOCH IN HISTORY

HITLER and the Third Reich were the gruesome and incongruous consummation of an age which, as none other, believed in progress and felt assured that it was being achieved. The 150 years 1789–1939 were an era of confident hope and strenuous endeavour, of trust in the human mind and in the power of reason. The rights of man were to be secured in self-governing democracies, humanized by education and increasingly equalitarian; the rights of nations, in States recast on the principle of self-determination, national unity, and independence. On the European continent language rather than territorial tradition, the bond of the intellectuals rather than the heritage of rooted communities, became the basis of nationality; the age was formed by the intellectuals and the city populations, uprooted men in undiversified surroundings.

Nationalism became a disruptive force intertwining with social radicalism. When in Eastern and Central Europe the war of 1914–18 unleashed revolution, the moderate Socialists, heirs and exponents of the progressive creed, seemed to come into their own—only to succumb, mostly without resistance, to the modern dictators. Intellectuals, who had seen themselves as the rational leaders of mankind set free by their thought, were to find that the disintegration of spiritual values—their work to some extent—had released demoniac forces, beyond control by reason. There was even travesty of thought—*la trahison des clercs*. Hitler was the grotesque German finale to the epoch.

Territorially the Habsburg Monarchy and the Ottoman Empire were Europe's engrossing problems from 1815 to 1919. Once adversaries, next joined in destiny, they were forced back and finally disrupted by linguistic nationality. Bismarck thrust the Habsburgs from the Reich and propped them up on the Danube, to hold and manage for the Germans their doubtful assets—uncompleted conquests and jagged linguistic frontiers—in a Monarchy in which the Germans were predominant, yet not masters. On the European continent the nineteenth century saw a rapid growth of German supremacy, intellectual, political, military, and economic. Yet linguistic nationality, the foundation of Germany's unity and power, was imperilling her Austrian 'heritage'. Could her will arrest a European process? This was the initial question in 1914.

Germany in command of Europe would have been a menace to the Anglo-Saxon countries. Their intervention decided the issue. The Habsburg Monarchy was broken up; Germany and Russia lost their alien fringes; territories on the Continent were redistributed on the linguistic principle (greed and the intermixture of races permitting). The settlement favoured the weak—but who in future was to defend them against Germany, Russia, and Italy? The United States had withdrawn from Europe, the British Empire wished it could do the same, while France grew increasingly averse to fighting. The League of Nations was but a paper phantom, invoked by France to prevent change, and by Britain to effect it by negotiation. Germany and Russia were recovering strength: together they might in a measurable time have dominated Europe.

Then the German scene was transformed by the entry of Hitler: never before had a man so malignant attained such power, nor a nation shown so little revulsion from evil. Crude and hysterical, full of virulent hatreds and envy, he powerfully appealed to the Germans, and set about doing their work in Europe. He knew the war-weariness of his generation, and with gangster-like audacity traded on it: first he took risks, and then he practised blackmail. Each time he raised his stakes, and each time he won. Every man, says Machiavelli, has but one method, and when it suits the circumstances we speak of good luck. Hitler had shrewd skill but no wisdom; with him there was no appealing to reason or even to rational interests—which fact men like Chamberlain were slow to grasp. Nor was there in him a conscious control of his own moves; hence he appeared incalculable and chaotic.

Yet a study of pre-1914 Vienna and of the Bohemian Pan-Germans, by giving the background to Hitler's confused political thinking, might have supplied a clue to his actions. He remained an Austrian, and to the Austrian Germans, in contradistinction to the Prussians, Russia was the enemy and the Poles were acceptable partners. Vienna was not interested in the sea or in colonies. The

Bohemian Pan-Germans despised the Habsburgs and Austria, adored Prussia, and revelled in the glories of 1870. That Hitler would attempt the *Anschluss* was obvious. But to the Great-Germans of 1848 and the Pan-Germans of 1898 'German Austria' included the Czech and Slovene provinces, and it was unthinkable that Hitler should permanently renounce Prague. He set out to reconstruct a Greater Germany, next a *Mittel-Europa*—and then? He had none of the realist restraint of the Prussian Junker, but a truly German *Masslosigkeit*—lack of measure and balance.

At no time did Hitler treat Munich as the close of his conquests. On the way to Munich he explained to Mussolini the need of reducing Czechoslovakia which otherwise, in a war against France, would immobilize forty German divisions. At Munich Ribbentrop talked to Ciano of a Triple Alliance with Japan. Hitler, on his return from Munich, ordered plans to be prepared for Czechoslovakia's final liquidation. He was not interested in the trappings and tinsel of Munich: a fortnight later, in his Saarbrücken speech, he attacked England. He expected France to keep out of Eastern and Central Europe. He offered to accept Poland as a satellite into his system, limiting his demands to Danzig and an extra-territorial line of communications across the Corridor. His immediate purpose was not necessarily joint action against Russia; on the Schlieffen principle he might have first turned against the West. Had he pressed his demand for Danzig before entering Prague, one may well wonder what would have been the reaction of the 'men of Munich'.

Prague was a blunder; Hitler's method ceased to suit circumstances, and he did not understand England. After Prague he pressed his 'offer' on Poland with greatly sharpened insistence, still hoping that she would agree. Poland's refusal, followed by her acceptance of a British guarantee, made Hitler order plans to be prepared for an attack on Poland: as she would not cover his flank in a war against the West, she had to be liquidated first. The final dispositions were made on 23 May 1939, the day after the signing of the 'Pact of Steel' with Italy.

His aim was now to isolate Poland. The Western Powers were negotiating with the Soviet Union. Between 23 and 26 May a dispatch was drafted in Berlin with a frank offer to Russia; it was not sent. But two months later Hitler reverted to the idea. He expected the Ribbentrop-Molotov agreement of 23 August to deter the Western Powers from supporting Poland. The attack was ordered for the 26th, but revoked when the news of the signing of the Anglo-Polish agreement of 25 August reached Hitler.

The attitude of the British Government was conciliatory but firm. Attempts to stage a second Munich failed. The declaration of war on 3 September 1939 is one of the great turning-points of history, and should be remembered in awe and gratitude. At the last moment Britain, though fully conscious of the mortal danger she was facing and of her own weakness, called a halt to a process which had gone much too far, and which, had Hitler pulled off his trick once more, would have subjected all Europe, and perhaps ultimately the world, to Nazi Germany.

In the end it was the entry into the war of the two great extra-European Powers, the Soviet Union, attacked by Germany, and the United States, attacked by Japan, which decided the issue. And when their armies met on 25 April 1945 at Torgau, in the heart of Germany and the centre of the European Continent, the victory was won and the century of German preponderance in Europe had reached its term. So, too, had the supremacy of Europe in the world.